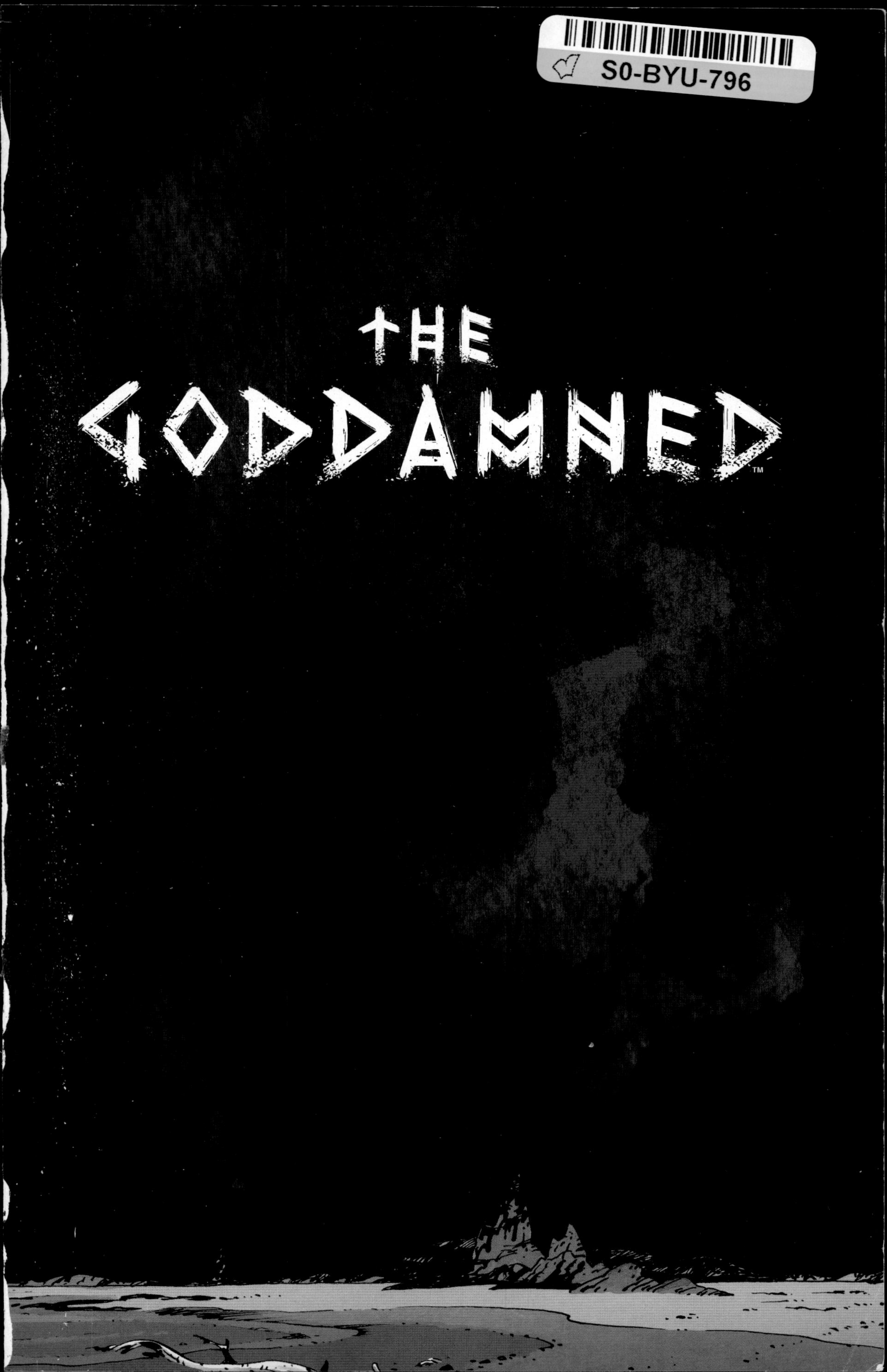
THE
GODDAMNED™

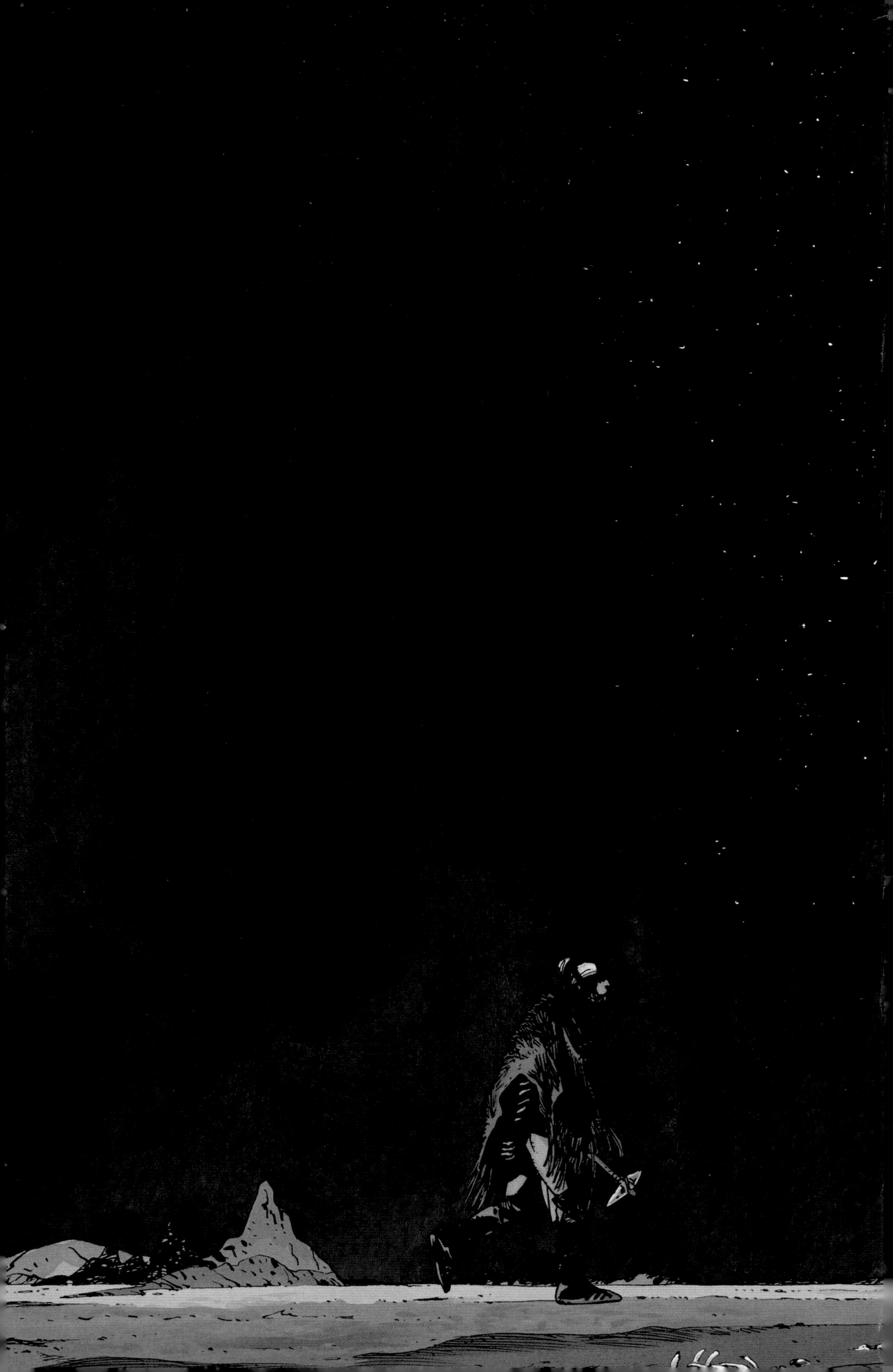

THE GODDAMNED™

Book One

BEFORE THE FLOOD

written by

Jason Aaron

illustrated by

R.M. Guéra

colors by **Giulia Brusco**

letters + design **Jared K. Fletcher**

editor **Sebastian Girner**

The Goddamned *created by* Aaron & Guéra

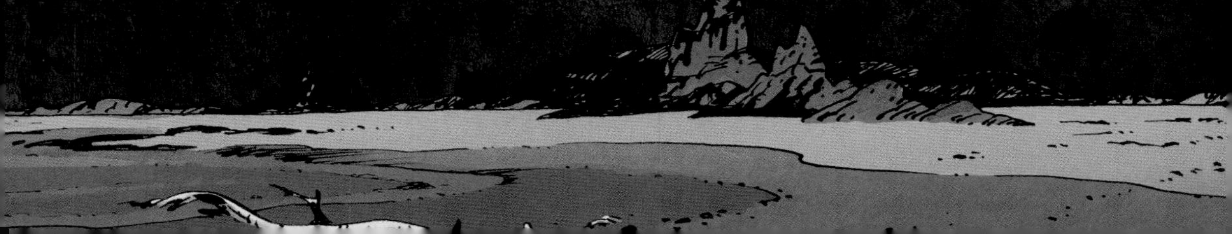

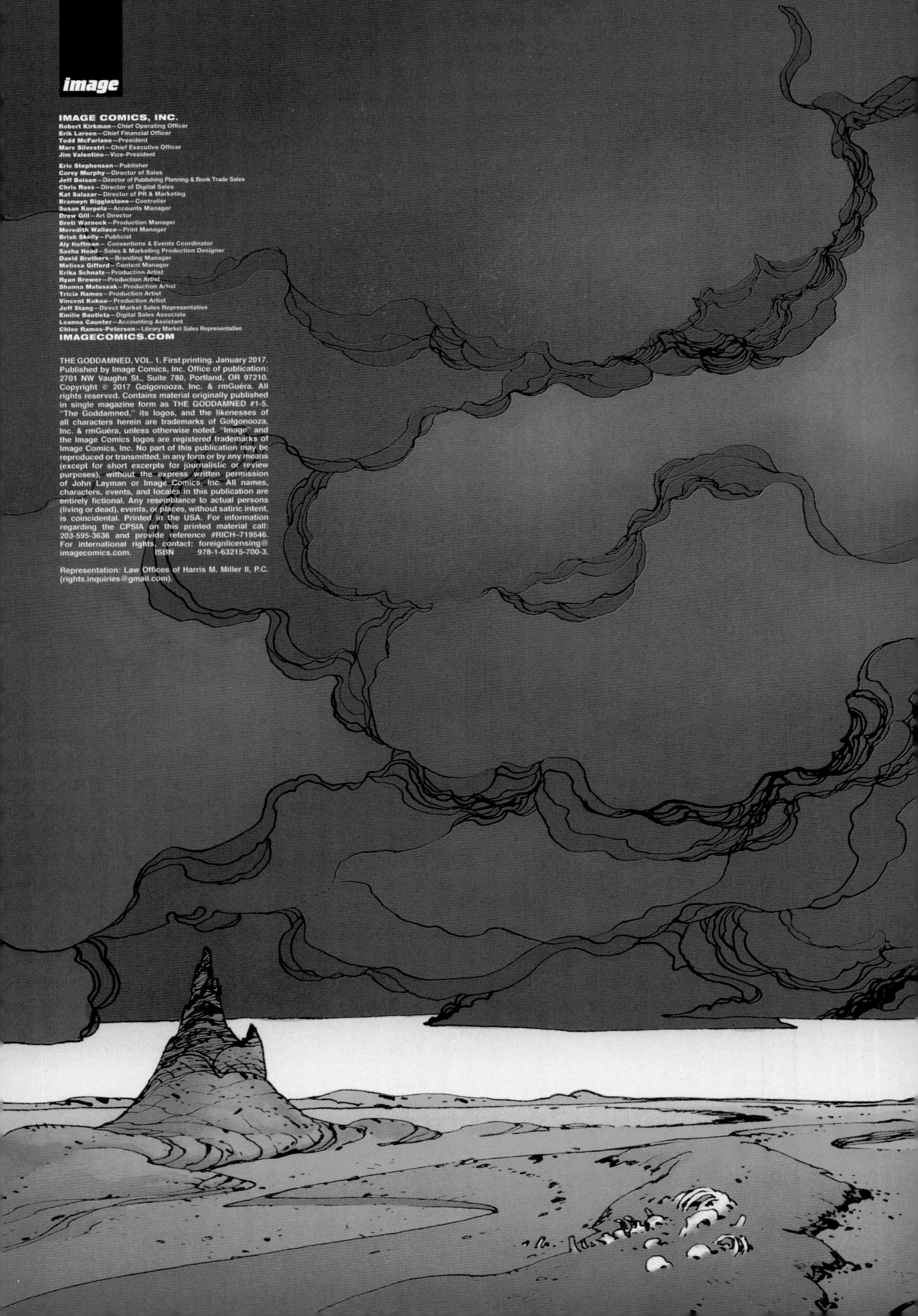

IMAGE COMICS, INC.
Robert Kirkman—Chief Operating Officer
Erik Larsen—Chief Financial Officer
Todd McFarlane—President
Marc Silvestri—Chief Executive Officer
Jim Valentino—Vice-President

Eric Stephenson—Publisher
Corey Murphy—Director of Sales
Jeff Boison—Director of Publishing Planning & Book Trade Sales
Chris Ross—Director of Digital Sales
Kat Salazar—Director of PR & Marketing
Branwyn Bigglestone—Controller
Susan Korpela—Accounts Manager
Drew Gill—Art Director
Brett Warnock—Production Manager
Meredith Wallace—Print Manager
Briah Skelly—Publicist
Aly Hoffman— Conventions & Events Coordinator
Sasha Head—Sales & Marketing Production Designer
David Brothers—Branding Manager
Melissa Gifford—Content Manager
Erika Schnatz—Production Artist
Ryan Brewer—Production Artist
Shanna Matuszak—Production Artist
Tricia Ramos—Production Artist
Vincent Kukua—Production Artist
Jeff Stang—Direct Market Sales Representative
Emilio Bautista—Digital Sales Associate
Leanna Caunter—Accounting Assistant
Chloe Ramos-Peterson—Library Market Sales Representative
IMAGECOMICS.COM

THE GODDAMNED, VOL. 1. First printing. January 2017. Published by Image Comics, Inc. Office of publication: 2701 NW Vaughn St., Suite 780, Portland, OR 97210.

ISBN 978-1-63215-700-3.

Representation: Law Offices of Harris M. Miller II, P.C. (rights.inquiries@gmail.com).

chapter one

The Mark of Cain

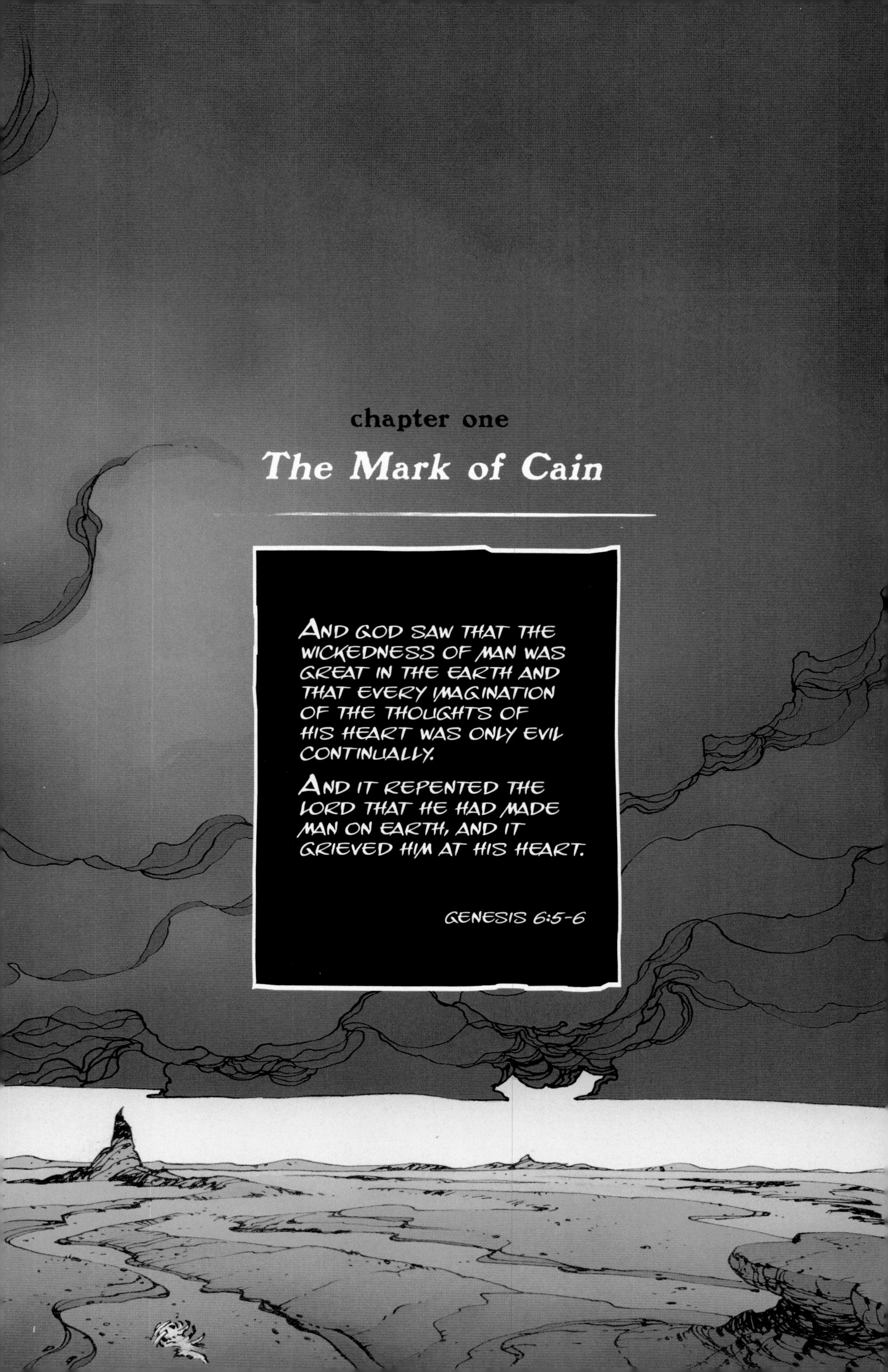
AND GOD SAW THAT THE WICKEDNESS OF MAN WAS GREAT IN THE EARTH AND THAT EVERY IMAGINATION OF THE THOUGHTS OF HIS HEART WAS ONLY EVIL CONTINUALLY.
AND IT REPENTED THE LORD THAT HE HAD MADE MAN ON EARTH, AND IT GRIEVED HIM AT HIS HEART.
GENESIS 6:5-6

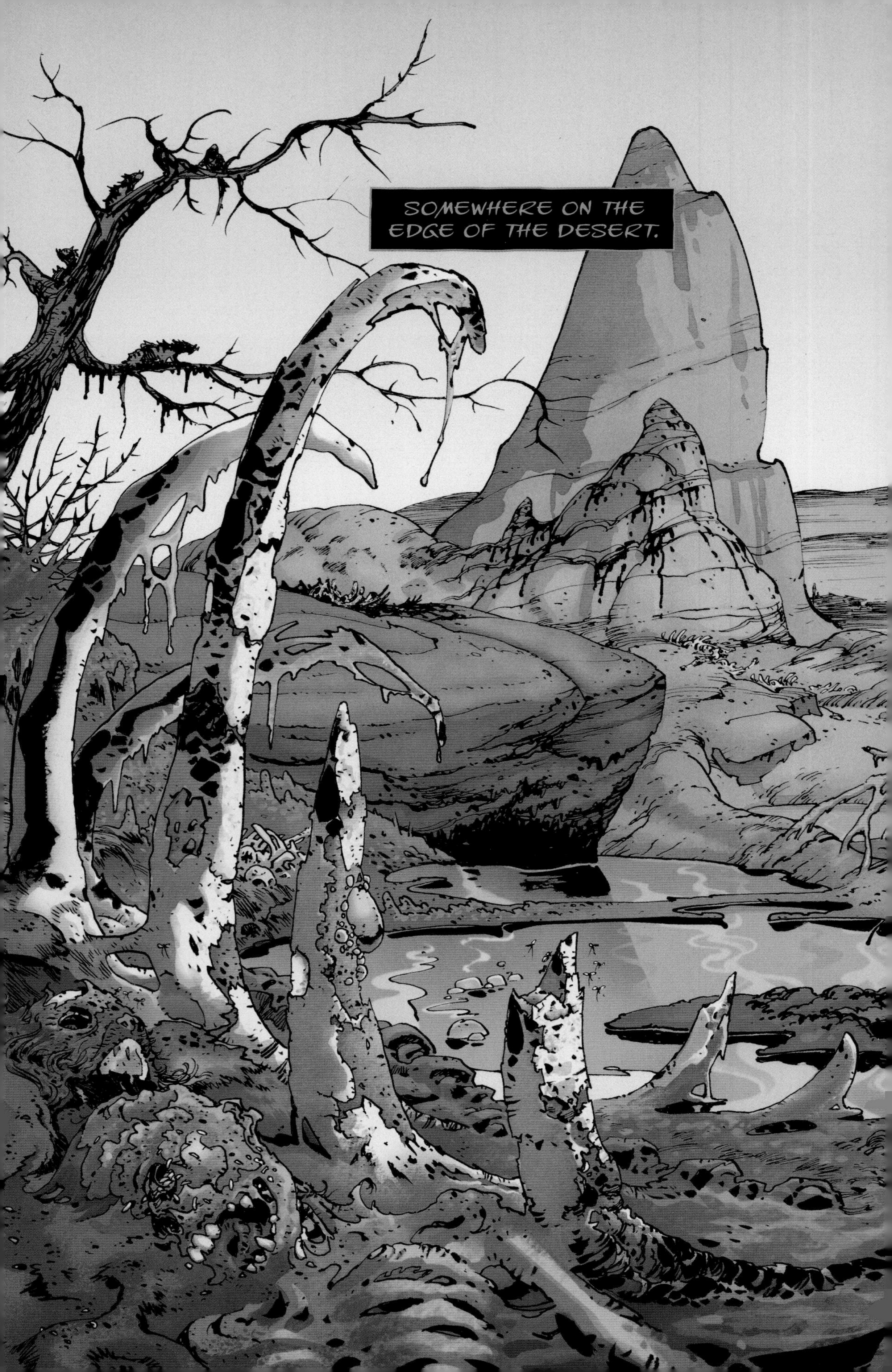
SOMEWHERE ON THE EDGE OF THE DESERT.

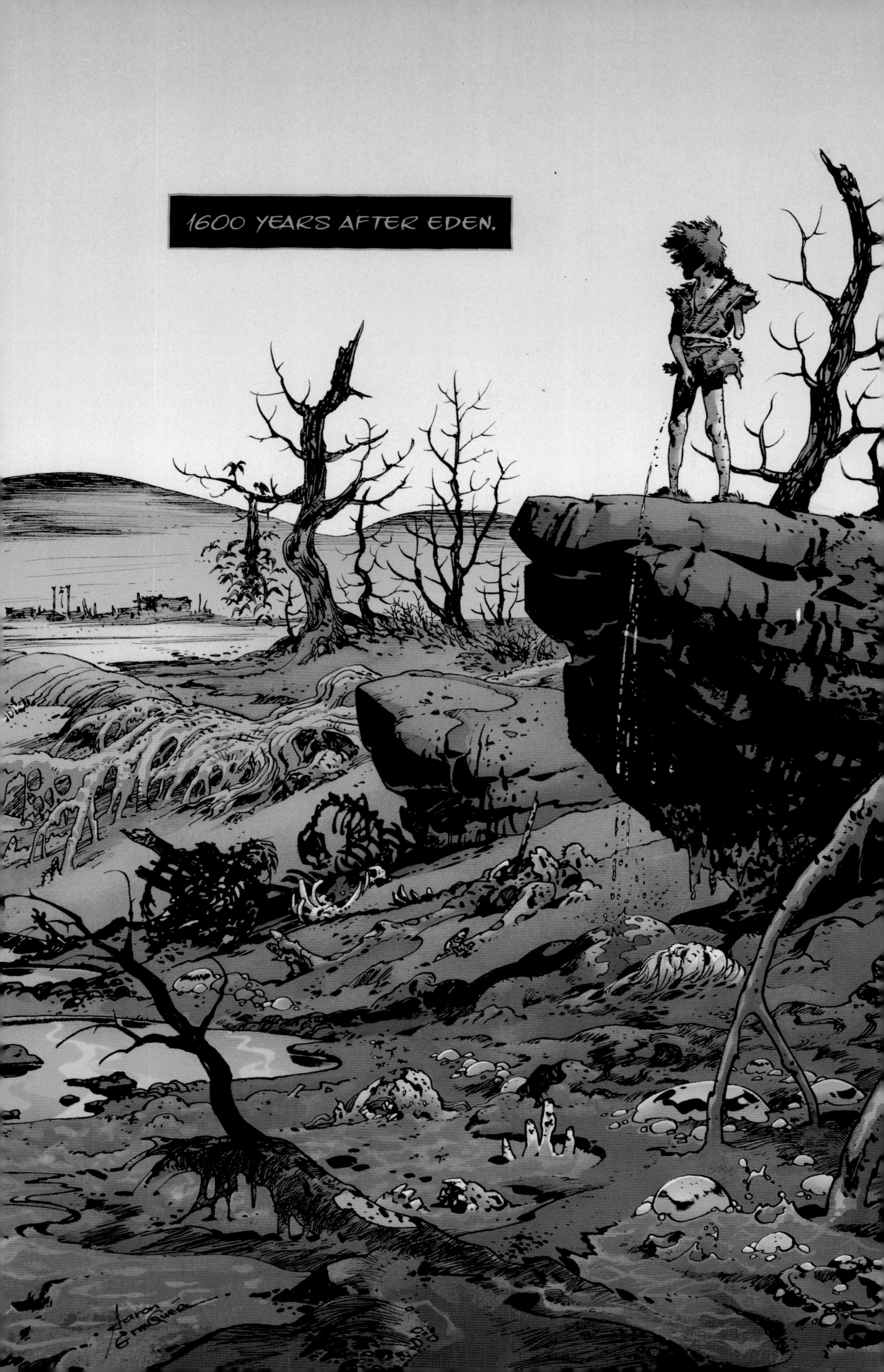
1600 YEARS AFTER EDEN.

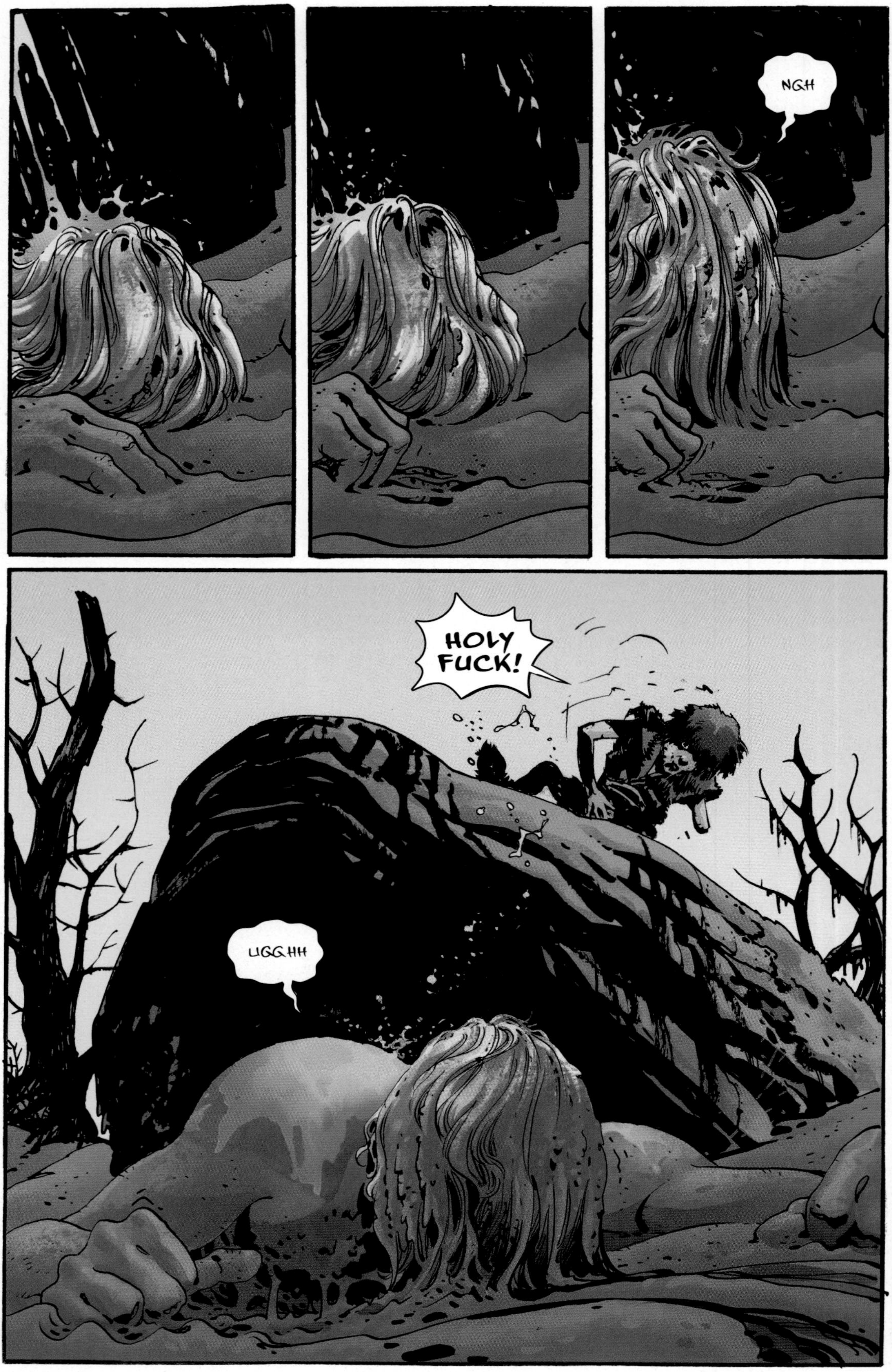
NGH
HOLY FUCK!
UGGHH

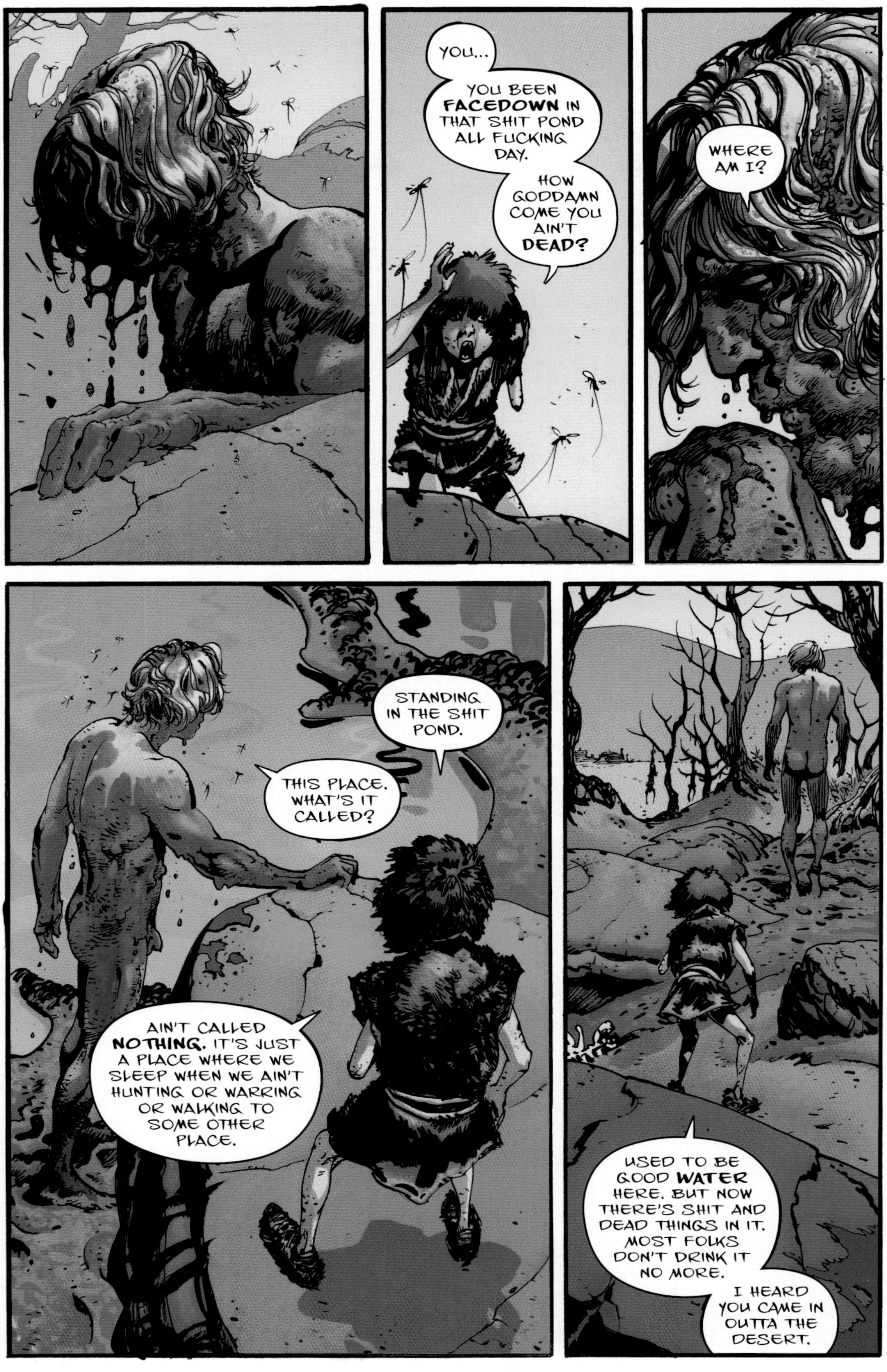
YOU...
YOU BEEN FACEDOWN IN THAT SHIT POND ALL FUCKING DAY.
HOW GODDAMN COME YOU AIN'T DEAD?
WHERE AM I?
THIS PLACE. WHAT'S IT CALLED?
STANDING IN THE SHIT POND.
AIN'T CALLED NOTHING. IT'S JUST A PLACE WHERE WE SLEEP WHEN WE AIN'T HUNTING OR WARRING OR WALKING TO SOME OTHER PLACE.
USED TO BE GOOD WATER HERE. BUT NOW THERE'S SHIT AND DEAD THINGS IN IT. MOST FOLKS DON'T DRINK IT NO MORE.
I HEARD YOU CAME IN OUTTA THE DESERT.

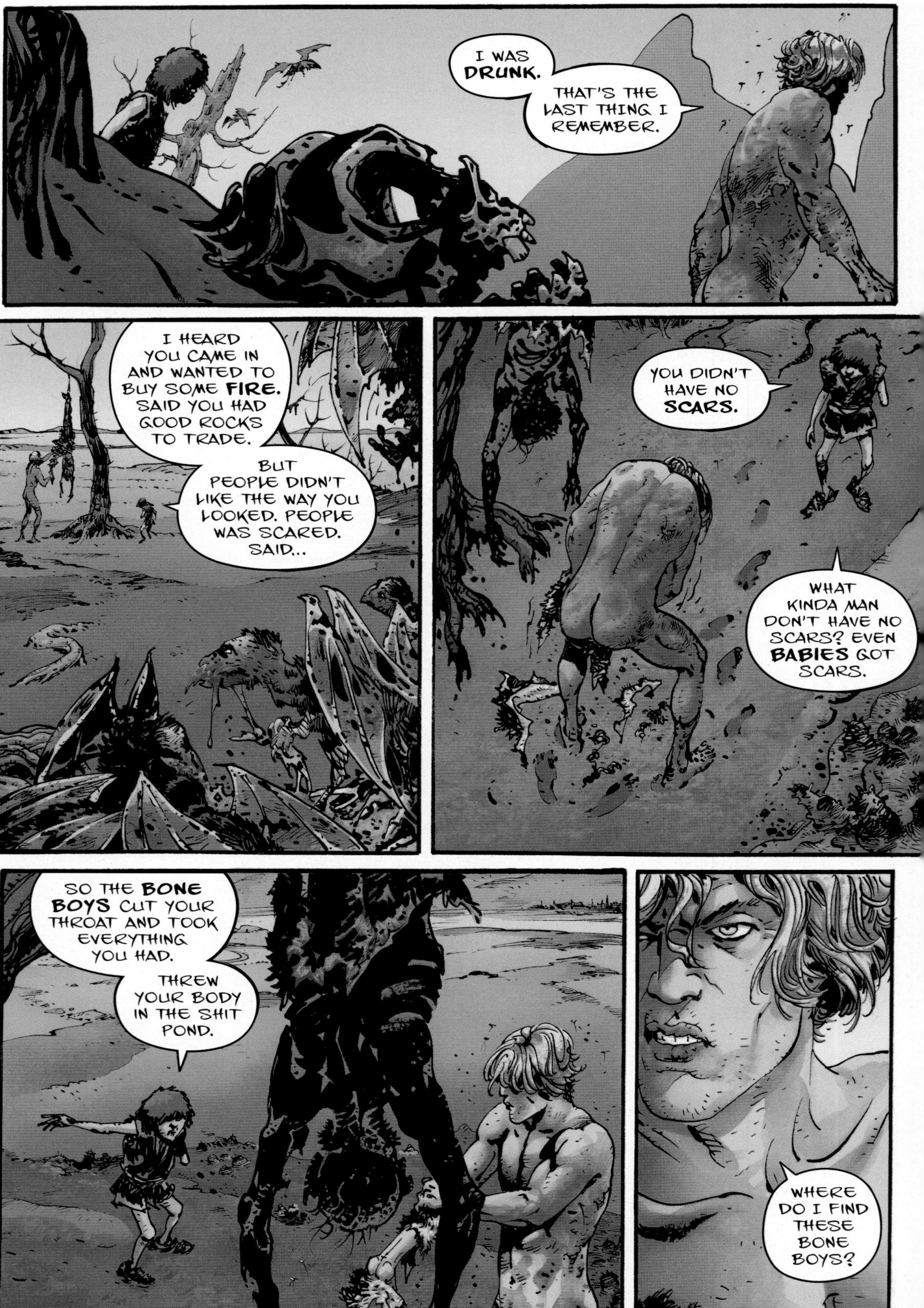
I WAS DRUNK.
THAT'S THE LAST THING I REMEMBER.
I HEARD YOU CAME IN AND WANTED TO BUY SOME FIRE. SAID YOU HAD GOOD ROCKS TO TRADE.
BUT PEOPLE DIDN'T LIKE THE WAY YOU LOOKED. PEOPLE WAS SCARED. SAID...
YOU DIDN'T HAVE NO SCARS.
WHAT KINDA MAN DON'T HAVE NO SCARS? EVEN BABIES GOT SCARS.
SO THE BONE BOYS CUT YOUR THROAT AND TOOK EVERYTHING YOU HAD.
THREW YOUR BODY IN THE SHIT POND.
WHERE DO I FIND THESE BONE BOYS?

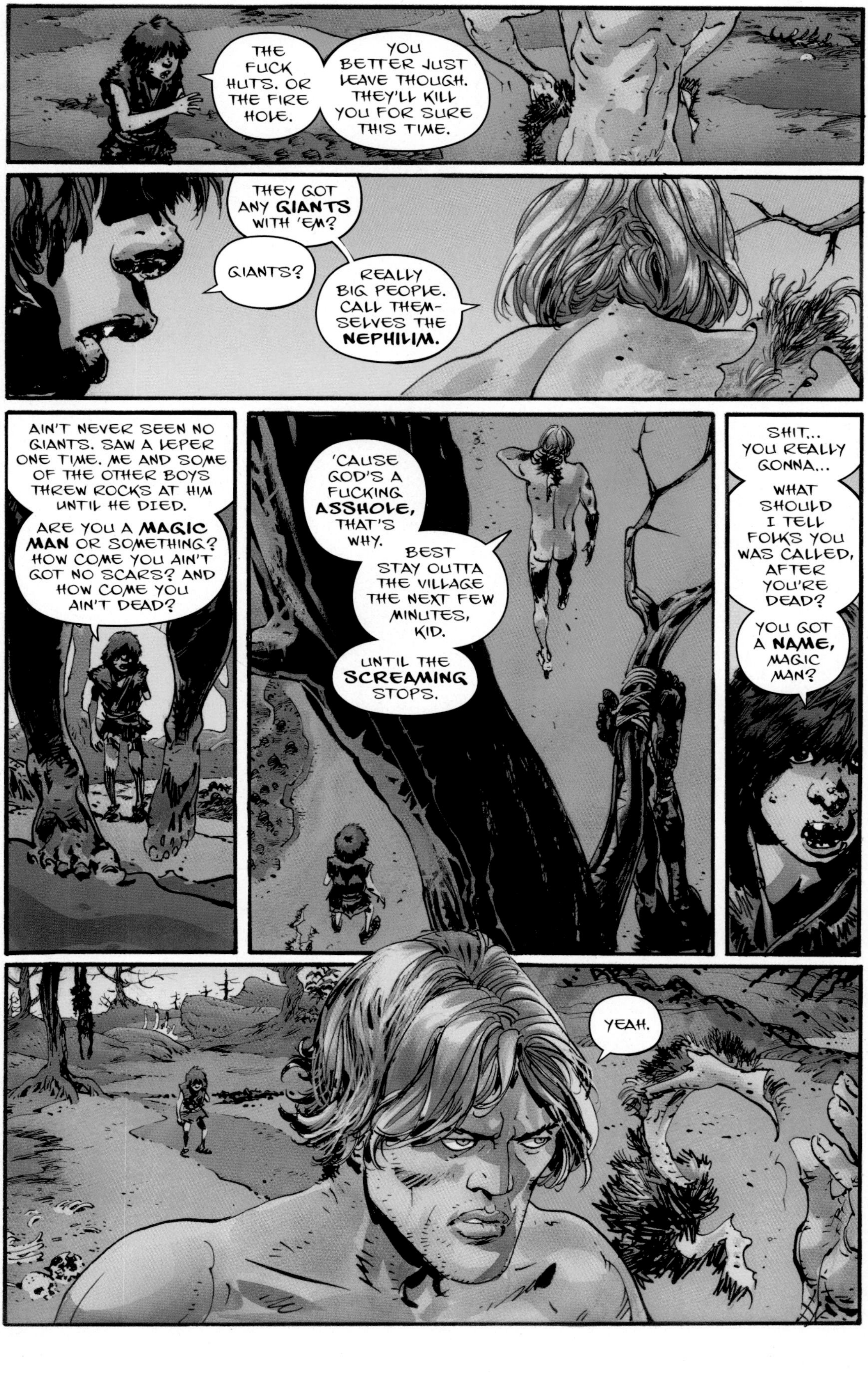
THE FUCK HUTS. OR THE FIRE HOLE.
YOU BETTER JUST LEAVE THOUGH. THEY'LL KILL YOU FOR SURE THIS TIME.
THEY GOT ANY **GIANTS** WITH 'EM?
GIANTS?
REALLY BIG PEOPLE. CALL THEM-SELVES THE **NEPHILIM.**
AIN'T NEVER SEEN NO GIANTS. SAW A LEPER ONE TIME. ME AND SOME OF THE OTHER BOYS THREW ROCKS AT HIM UNTIL HE DIED.
ARE YOU A **MAGIC MAN** OR SOMETHING? HOW COME YOU AIN'T GOT NO SCARS? AND HOW COME YOU AIN'T DEAD?
'CAUSE GOD'S A FUCKING **ASSHOLE,** THAT'S WHY.
BEST STAY OUTTA THE VILLAGE THE NEXT FEW MINUTES, KID.
UNTIL THE **SCREAMING** STOPS.
SHIT... YOU REALLY GONNA...
WHAT SHOULD I TELL FOLKS YOU WAS CALLED, AFTER YOU'RE DEAD?
YOU GOT A **NAME,** MAGIC MAN?
YEAH.

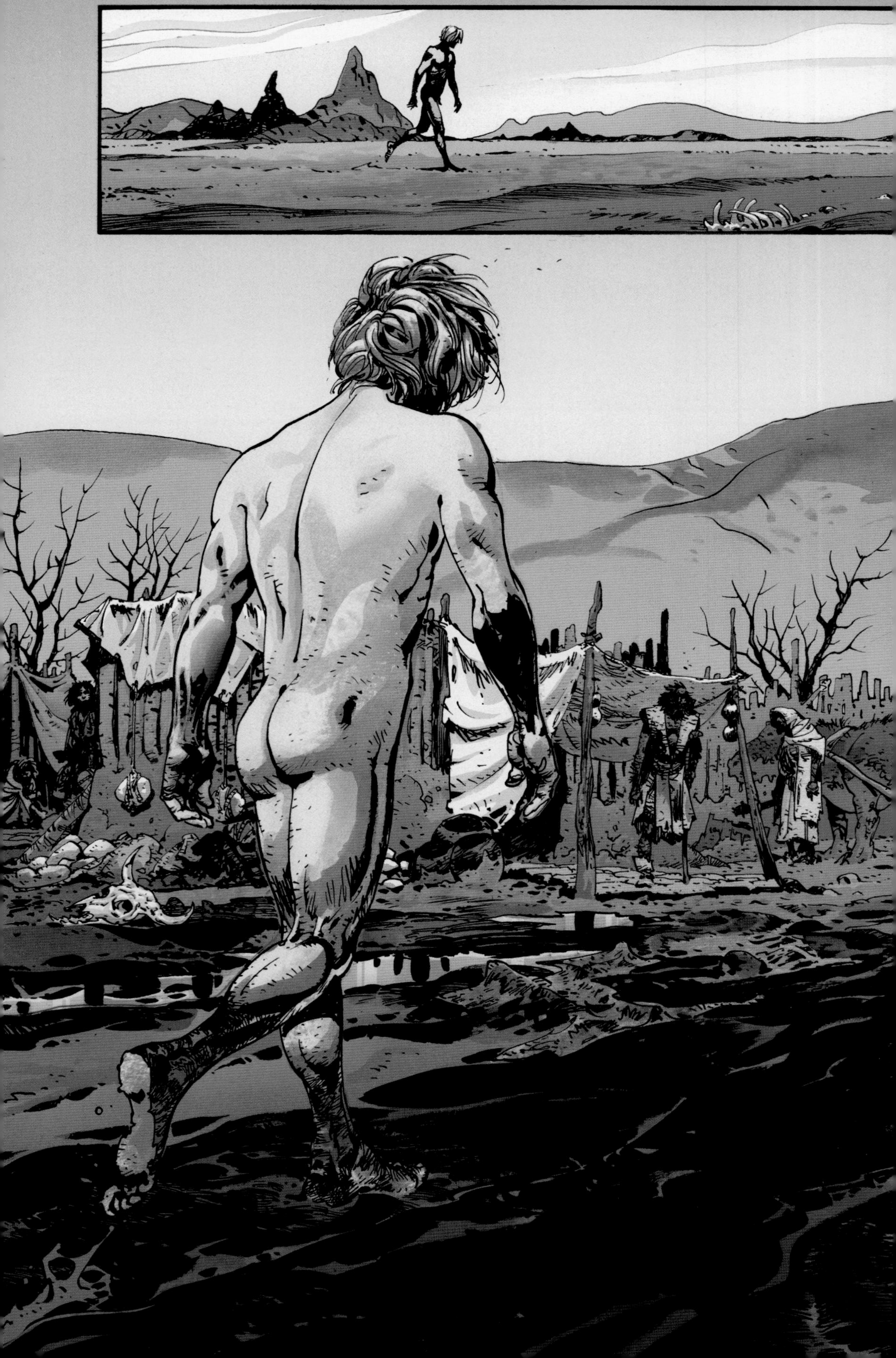

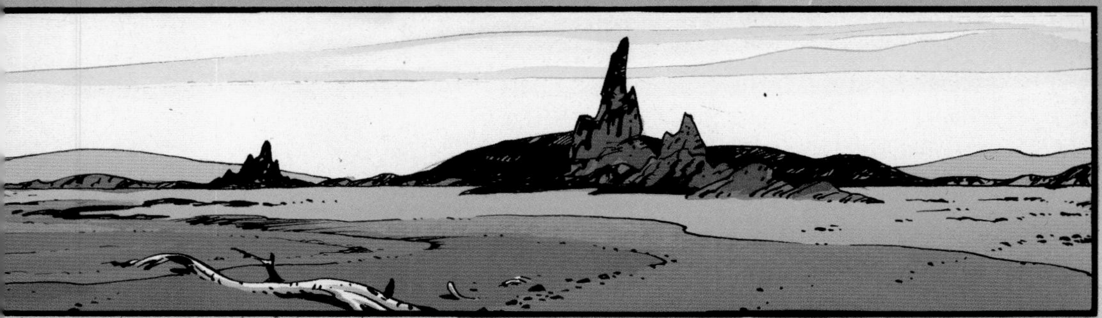

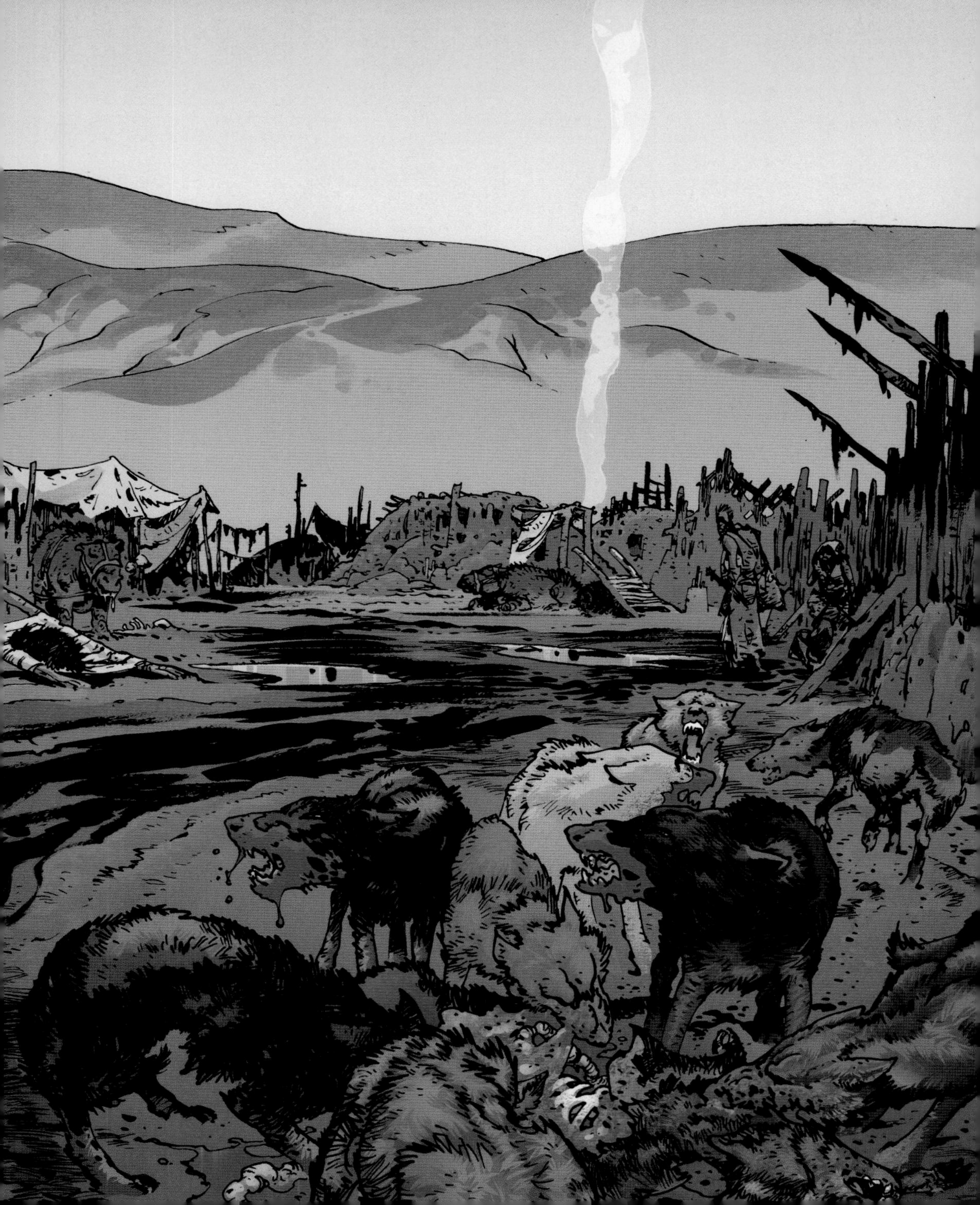

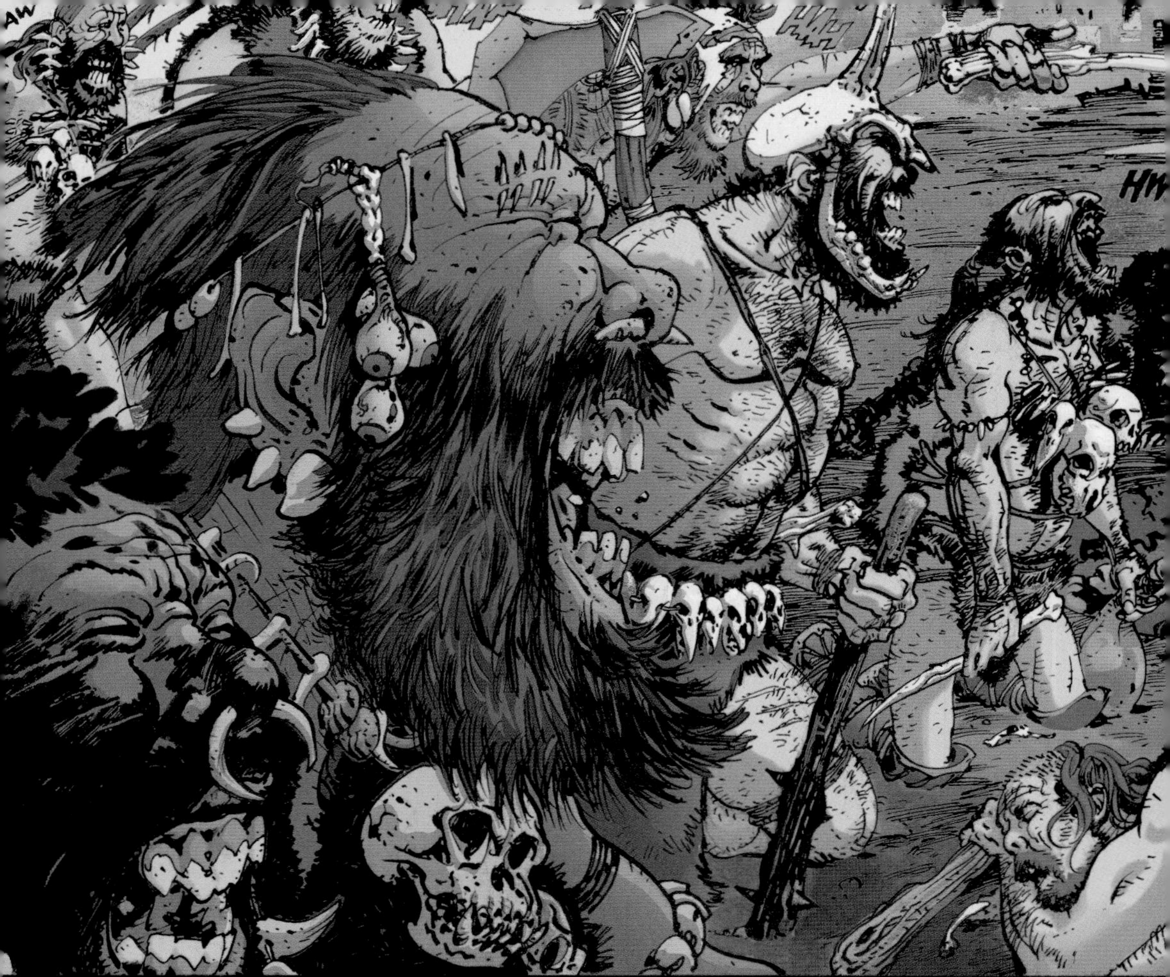

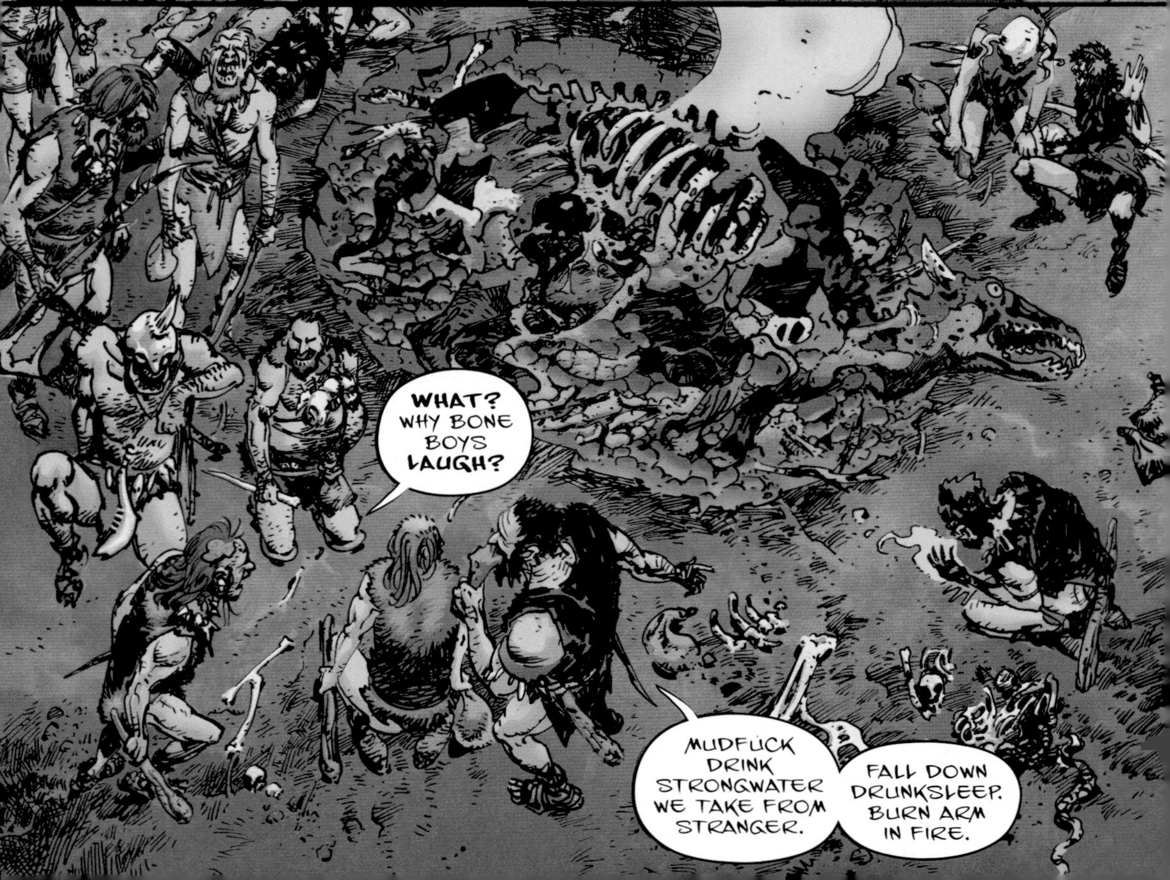
WHAT? WHY BONE BOYS LAUGH?
MUDFUCK DRINK STRONGWATER WE TAKE FROM STRANGER.
FALL DOWN DRUNKSLEEP. BURN ARM IN FIRE.

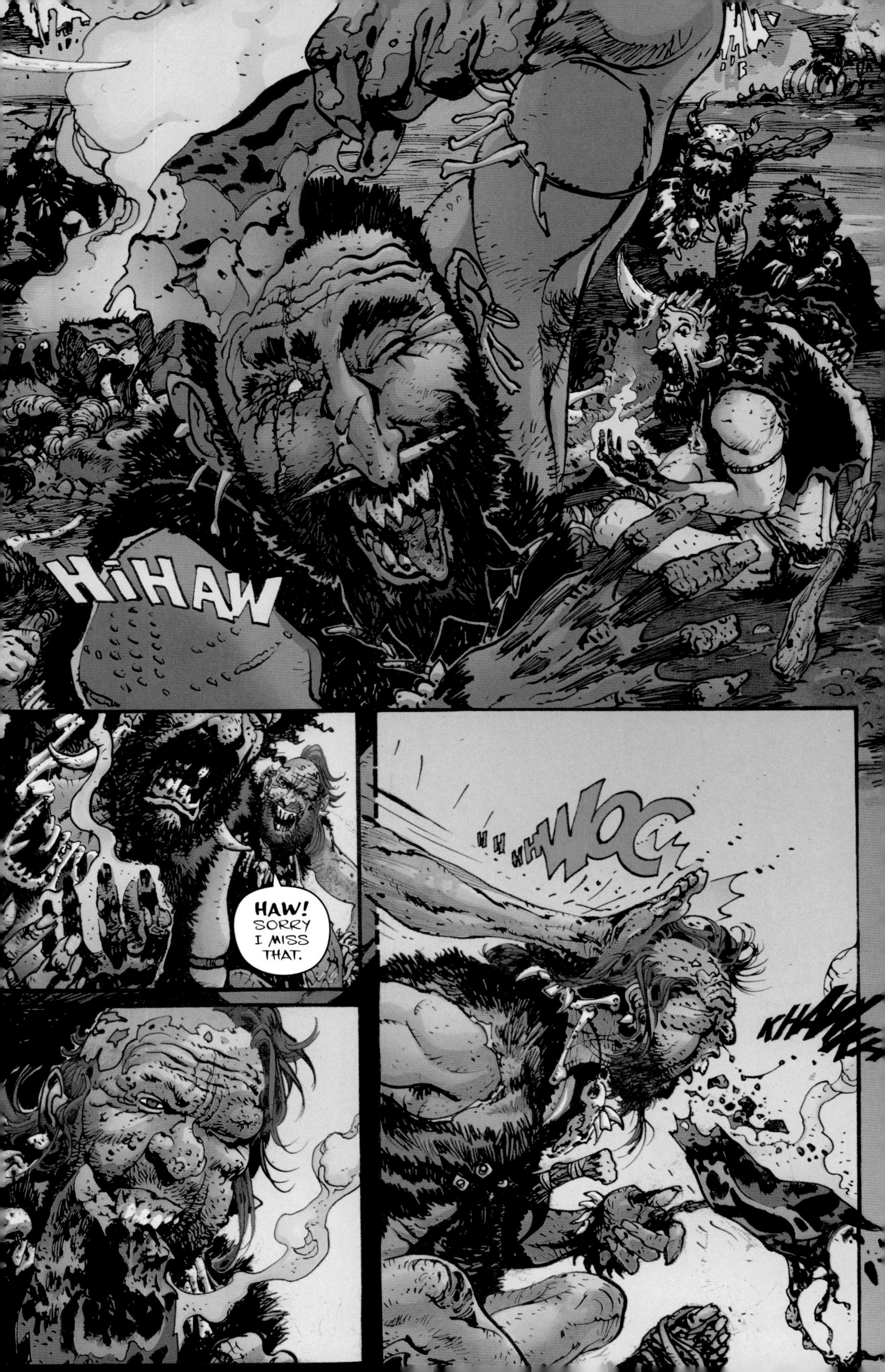
HIHAW
HAW! SORRY I MISS THAT.
WOC
KHANK

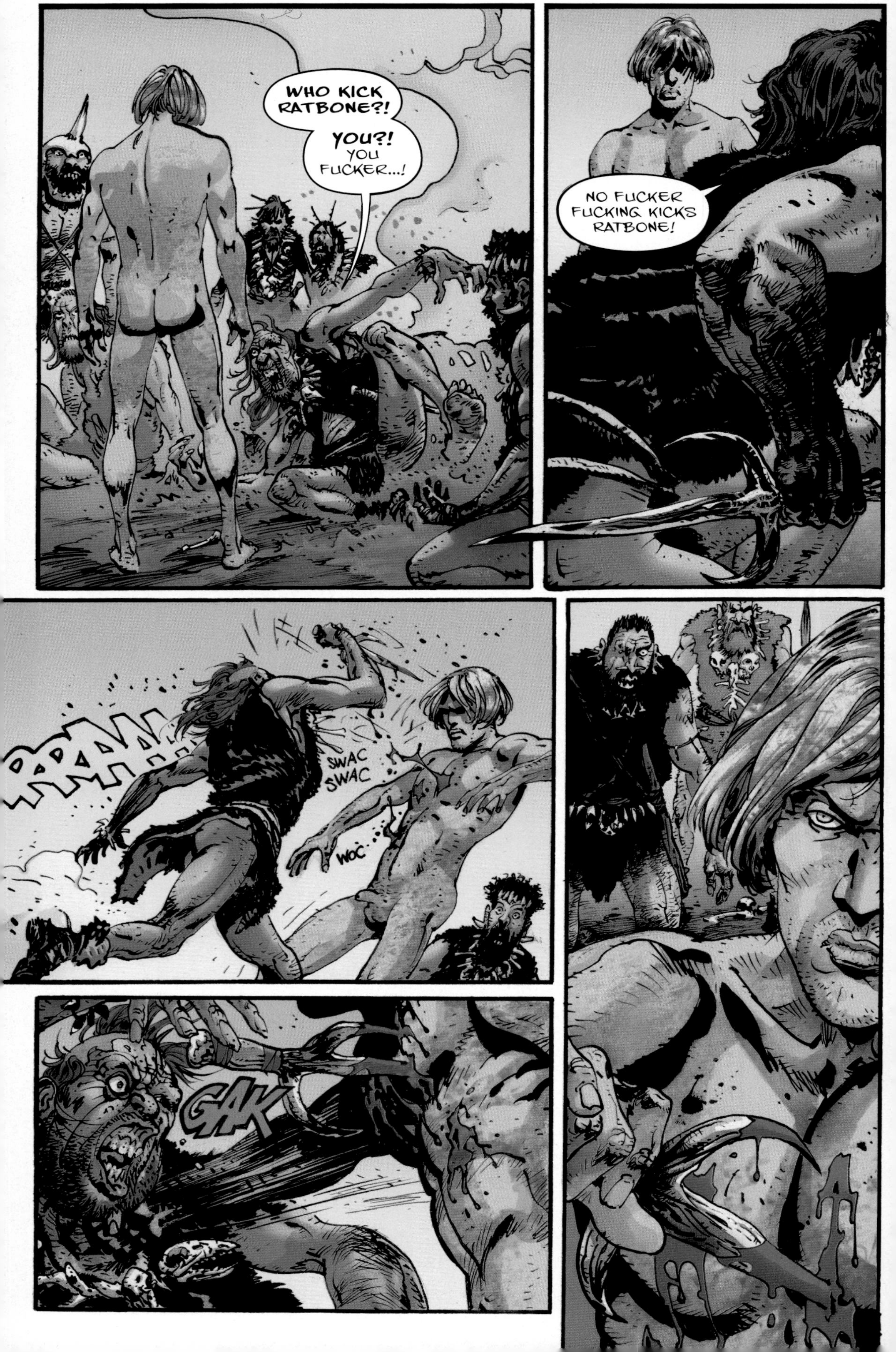
WHO KICK RATBONE?!
YOU?! YOU FUCKER...!
NO FUCKER FUCKING KICKS RATBONE!
SWAC SWAC
WOC
GAK

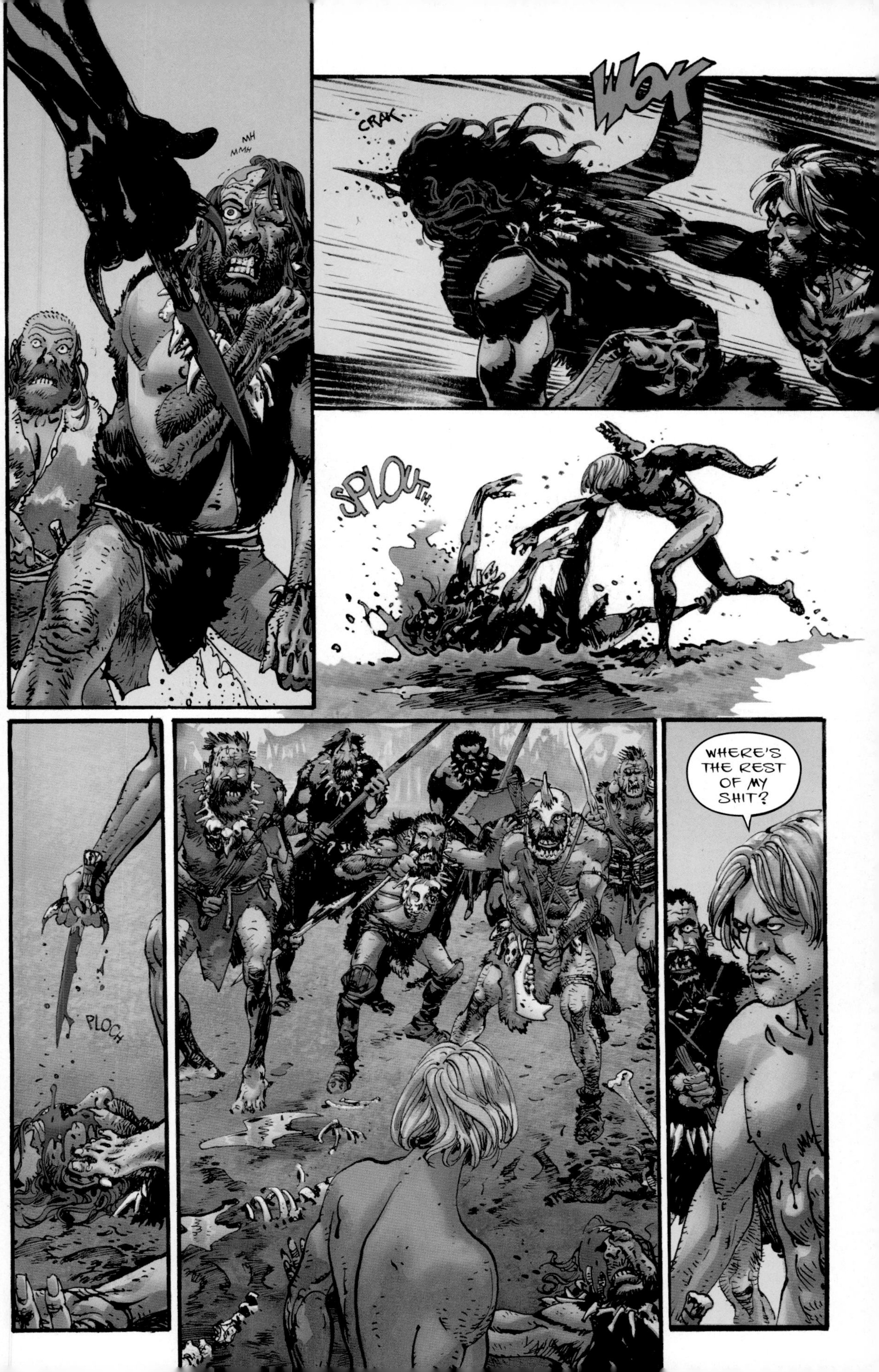
MH
MMH
WOK
CRAK
SPLOUTH
PLOCH
WHERE'S THE REST OF MY SHIT?

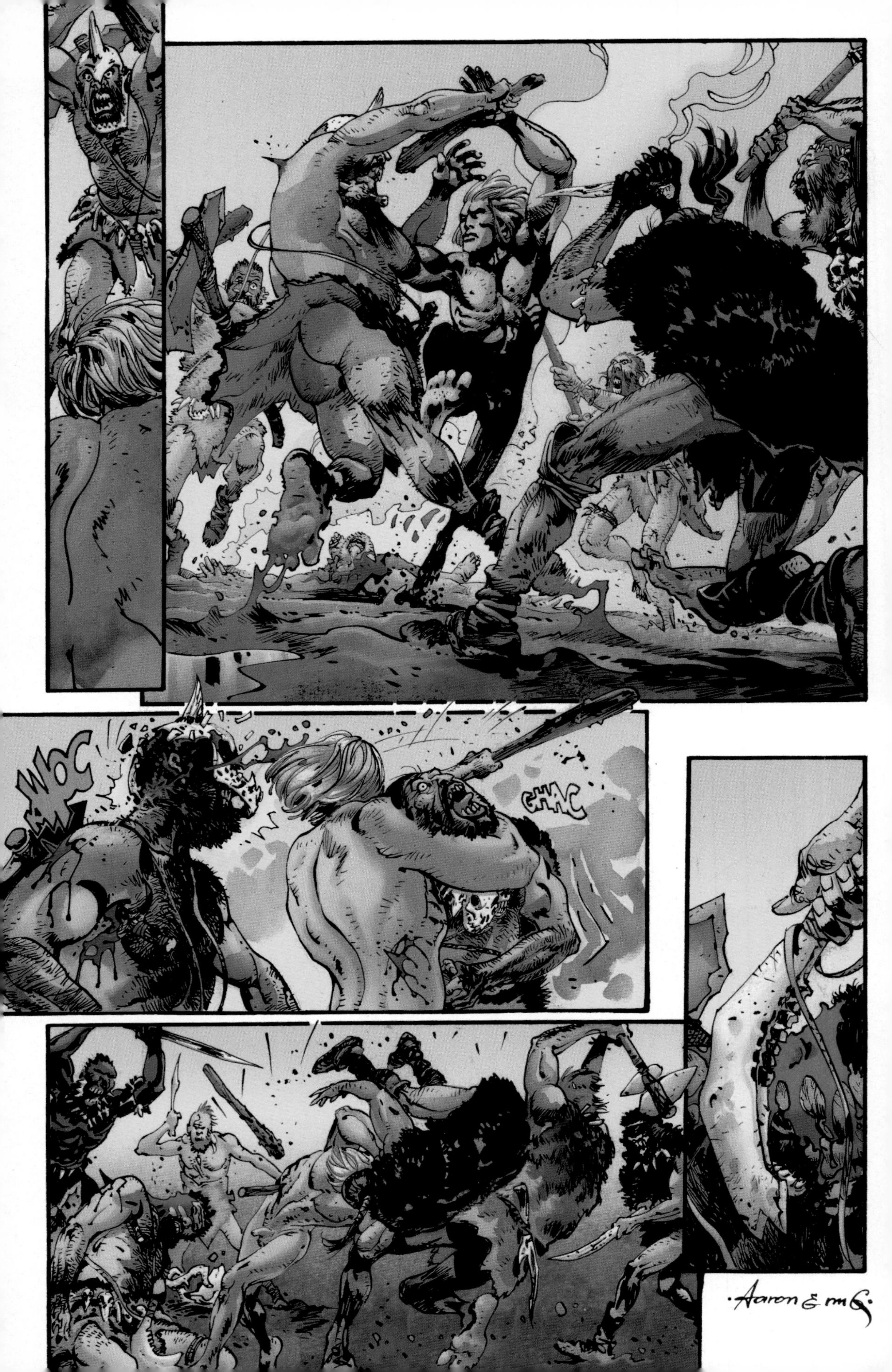
WOC
CHAC
Aaron & mG

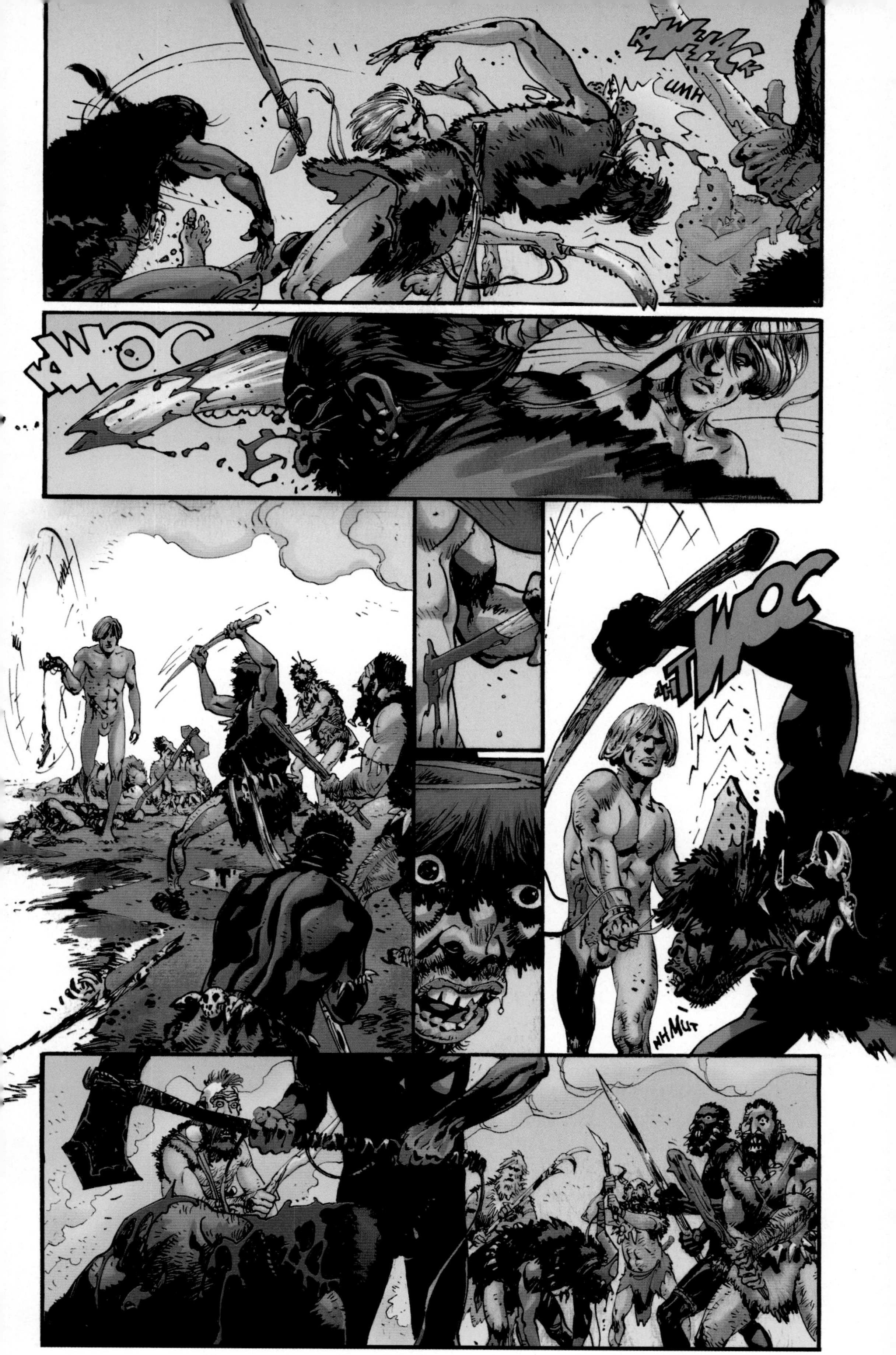
WHACK
UMH
WOC
TWOC
NHMUT

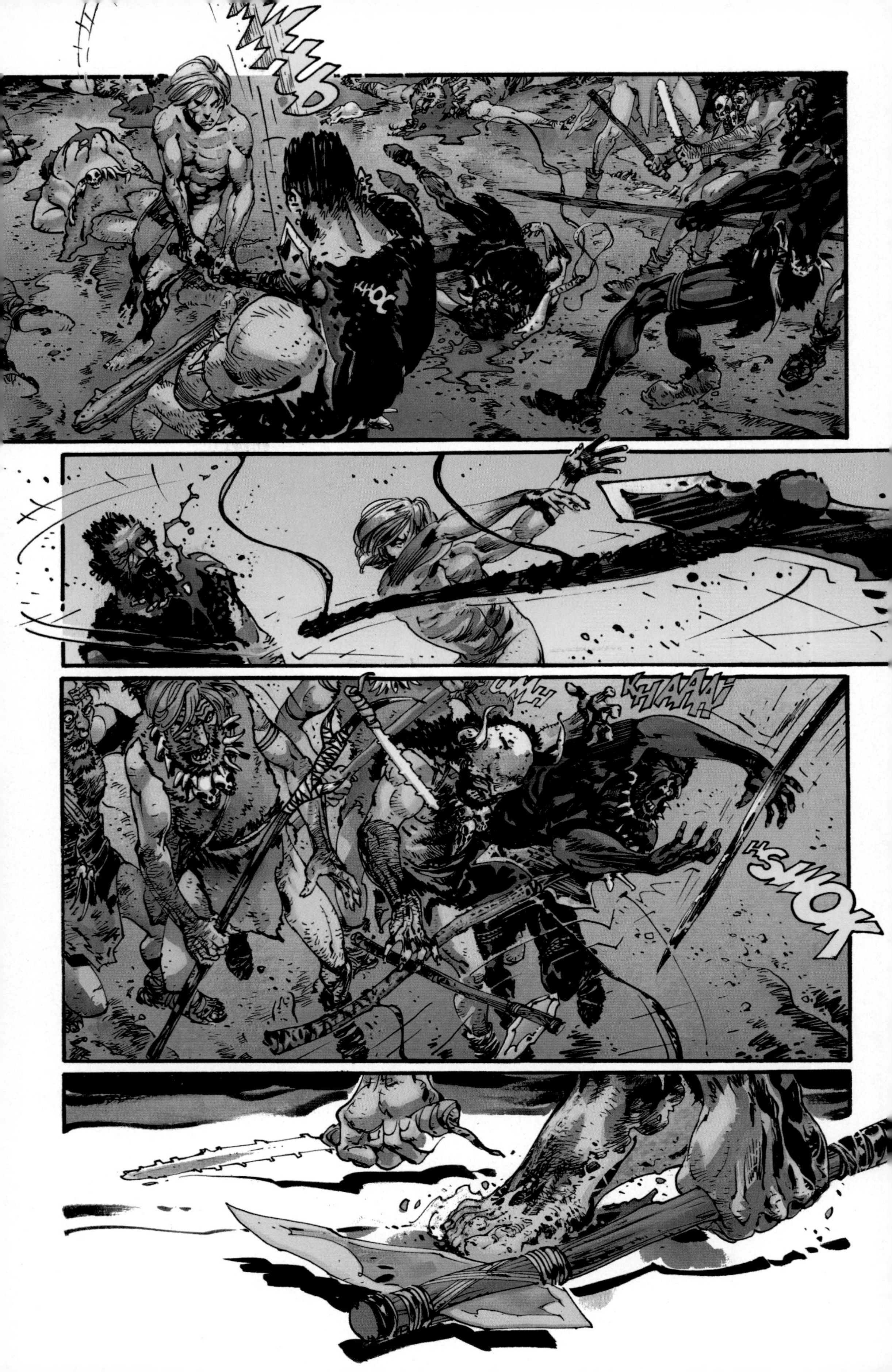
WHUD
KHOC
KHAAA!

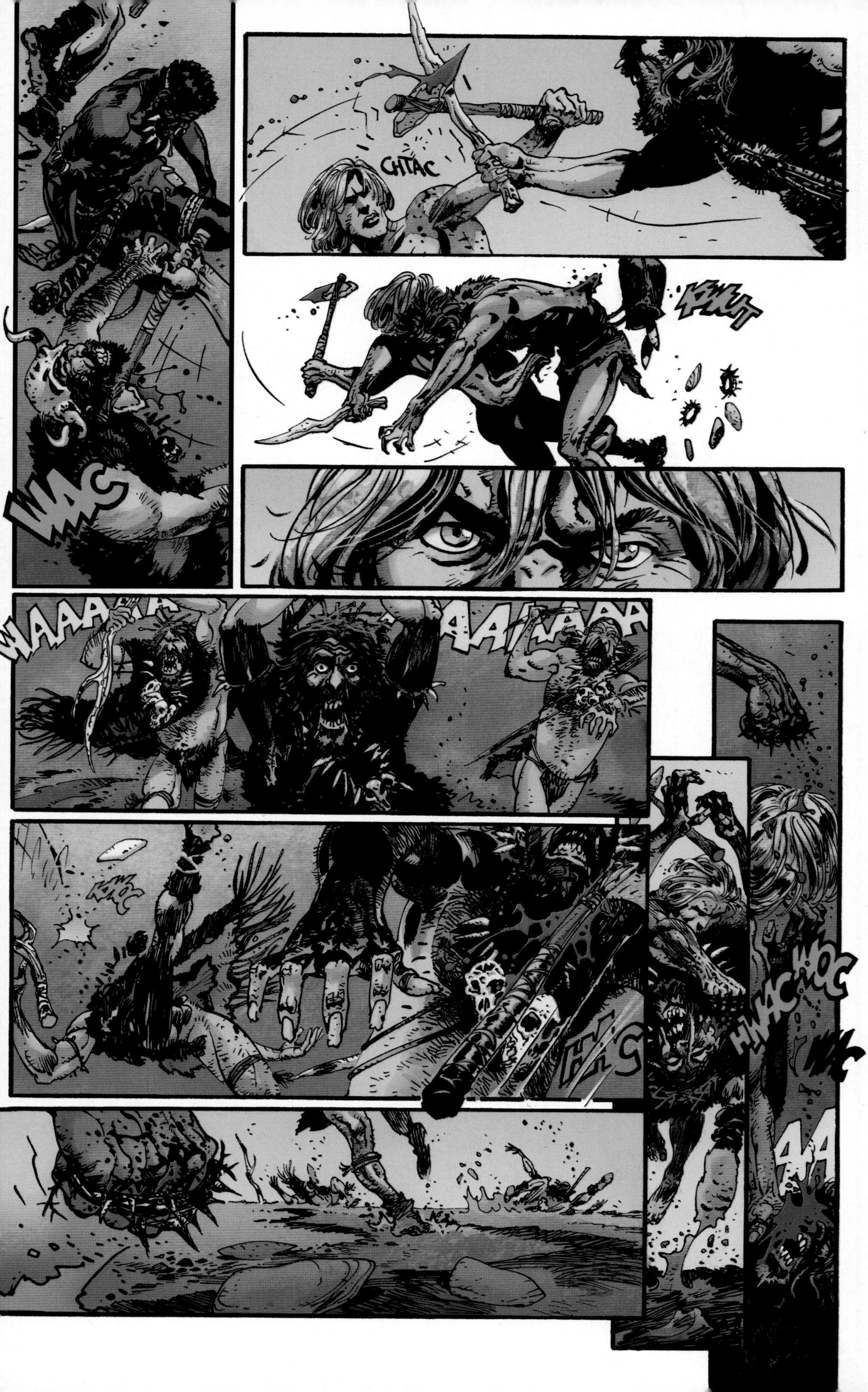

WAC
CHTAC
HAC
HWAC
HOC

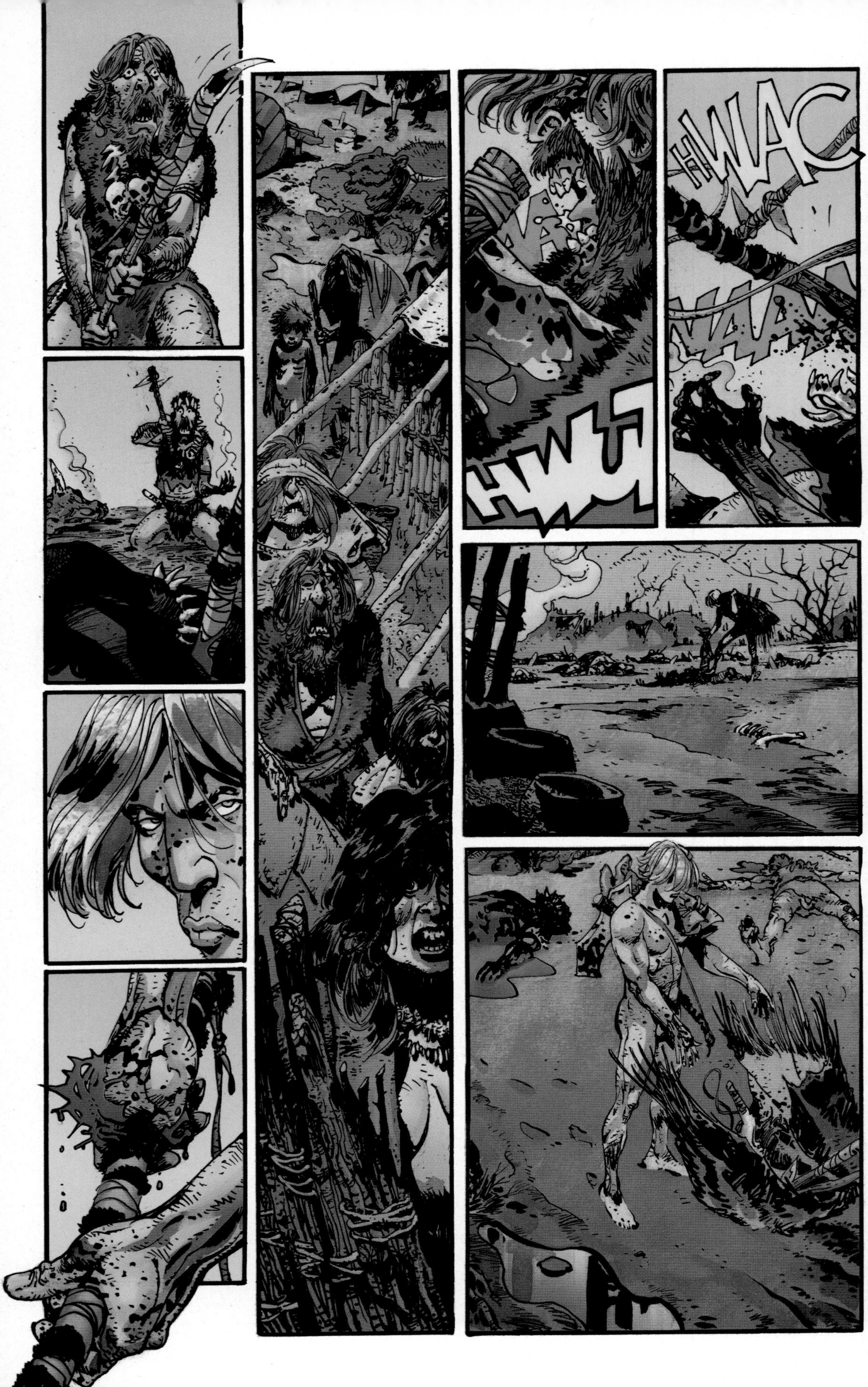
HWUF
HWAC

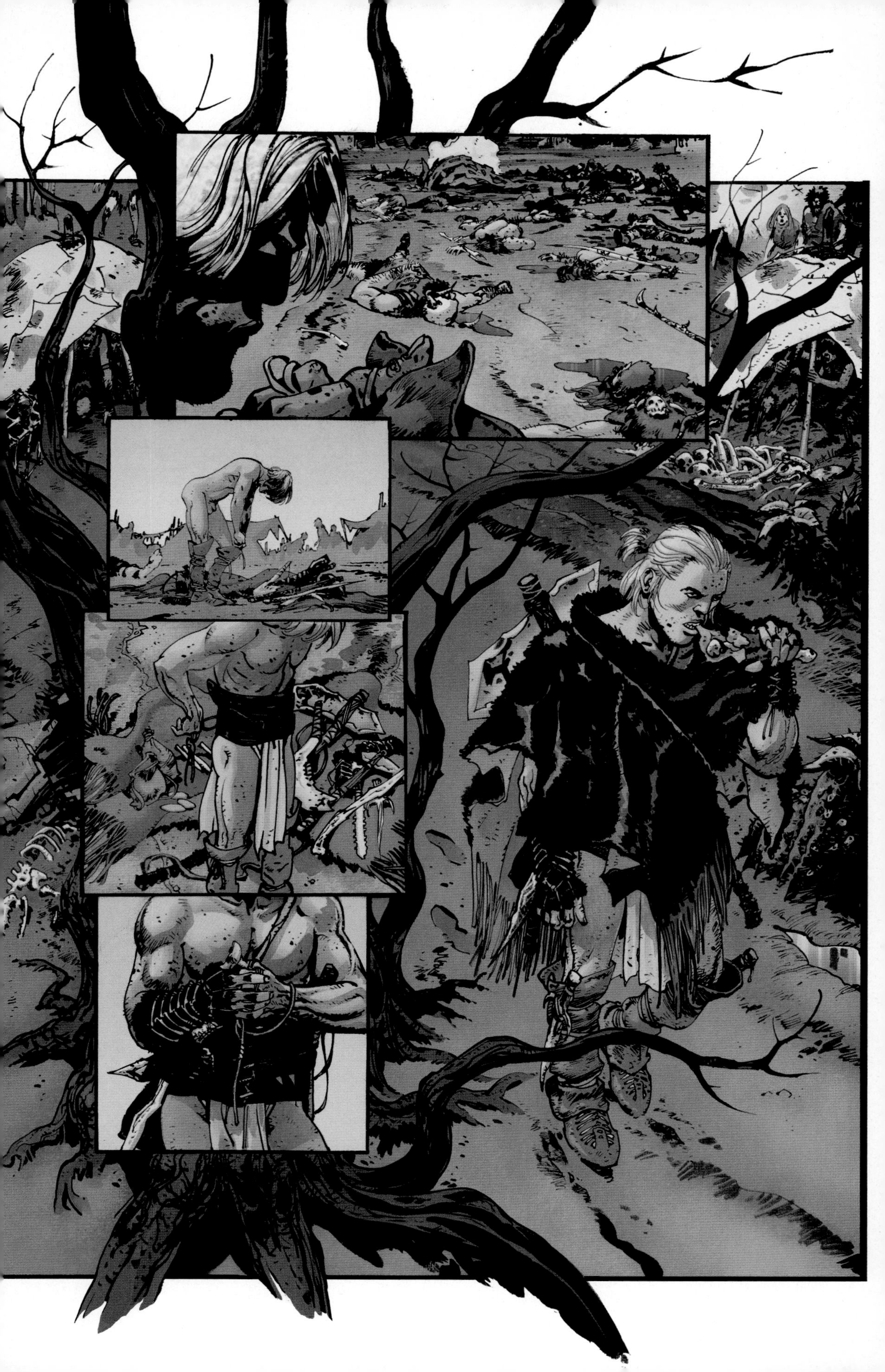

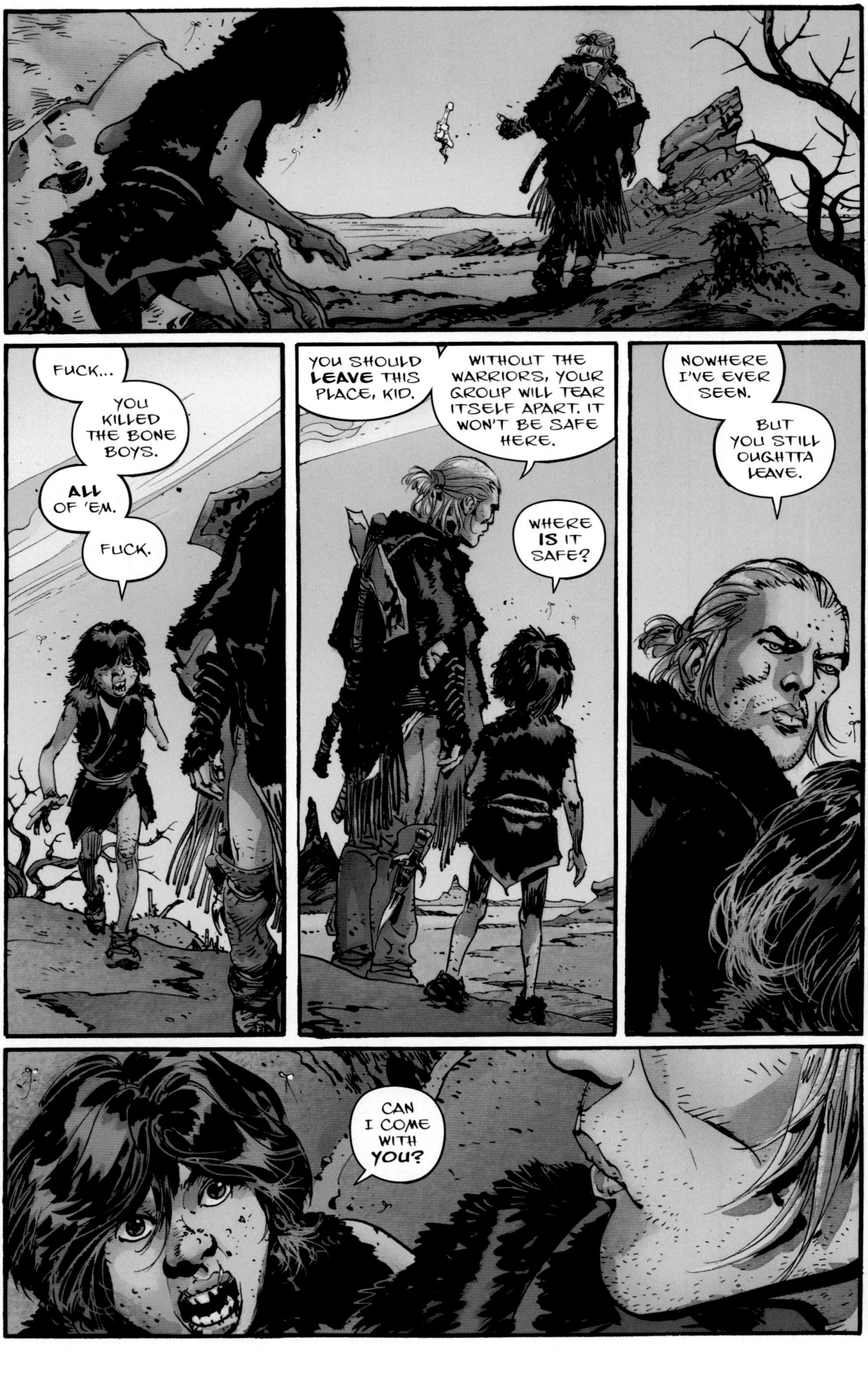
FUCK...
YOU KILLED THE BONE BOYS.
ALL OF 'EM.
FUCK.
YOU SHOULD LEAVE THIS PLACE, KID.
WITHOUT THE WARRIORS, YOUR GROUP WILL TEAR ITSELF APART. IT WON'T BE SAFE HERE.
WHERE IS IT SAFE?
NOWHERE I'VE EVER SEEN.
BUT YOU STILL OUGHTTA LEAVE.
CAN I COME WITH YOU?

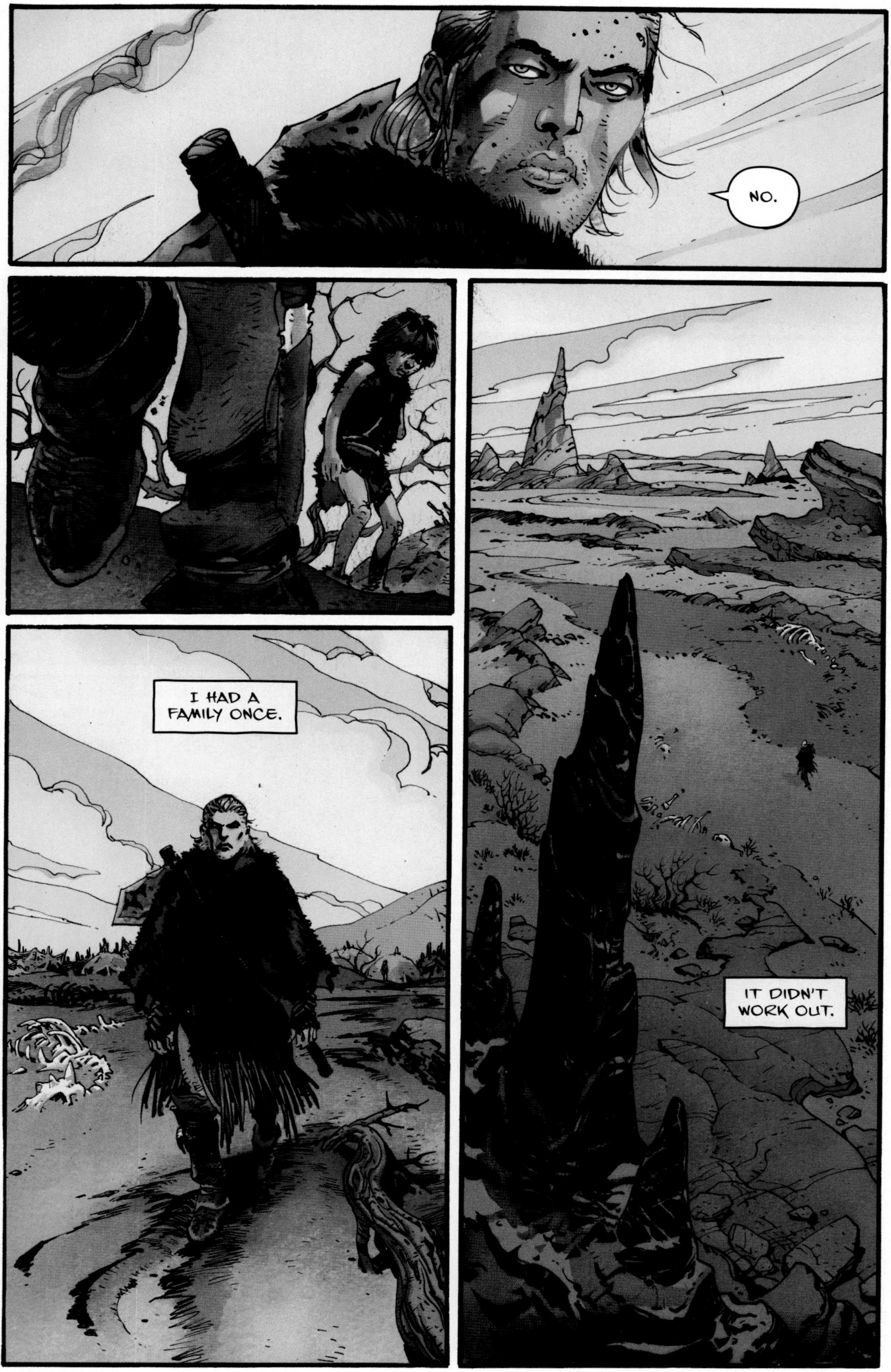
NO.
I HAD A FAMILY ONCE.
IT DIDN'T WORK OUT.

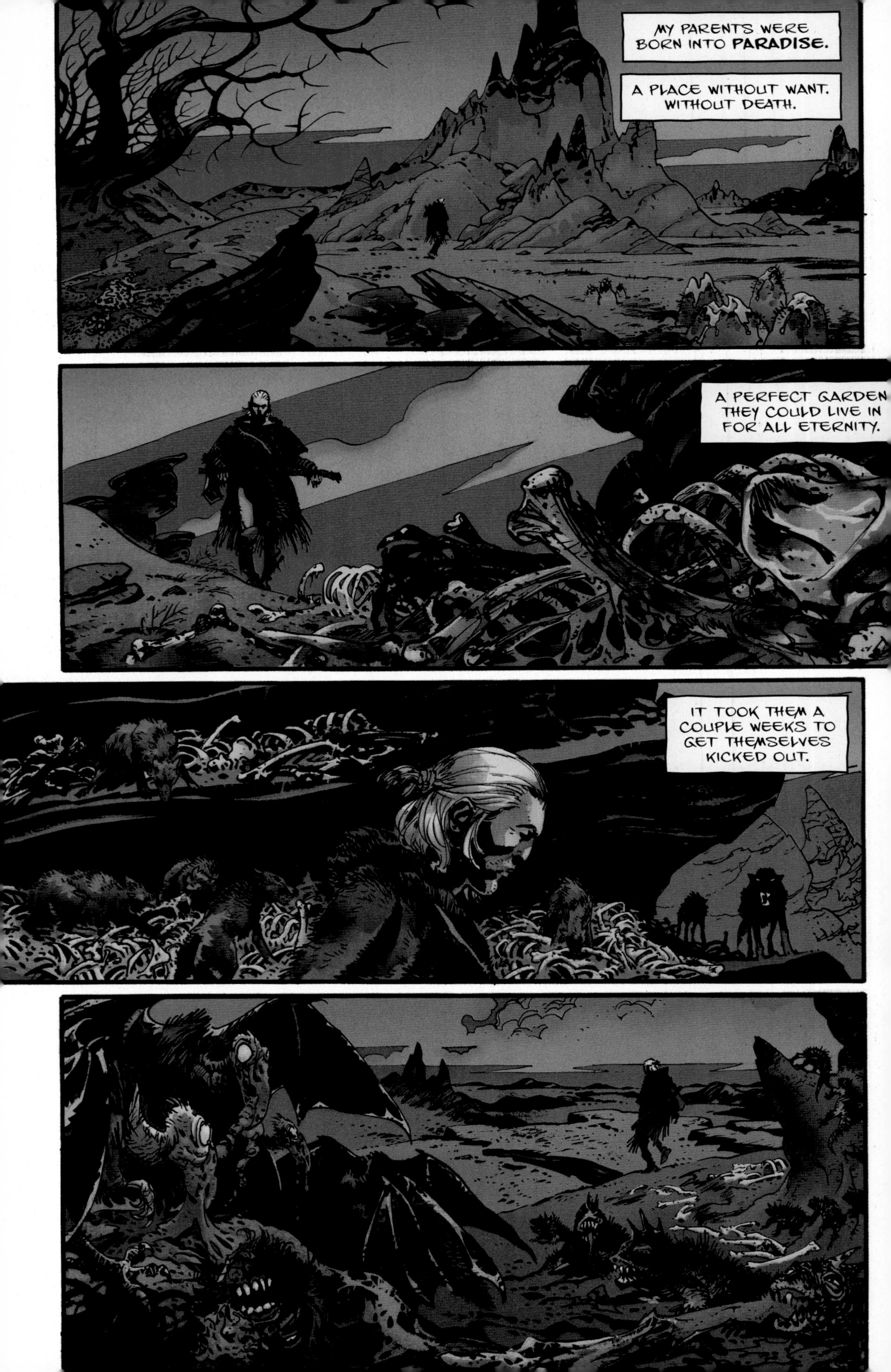
MY PARENTS WERE BORN INTO PARADISE.
A PLACE WITHOUT WANT. WITHOUT DEATH.
A PERFECT GARDEN THEY COULD LIVE IN FOR ALL ETERNITY.
IT TOOK THEM A COUPLE WEEKS TO GET THEMSELVES KICKED OUT.

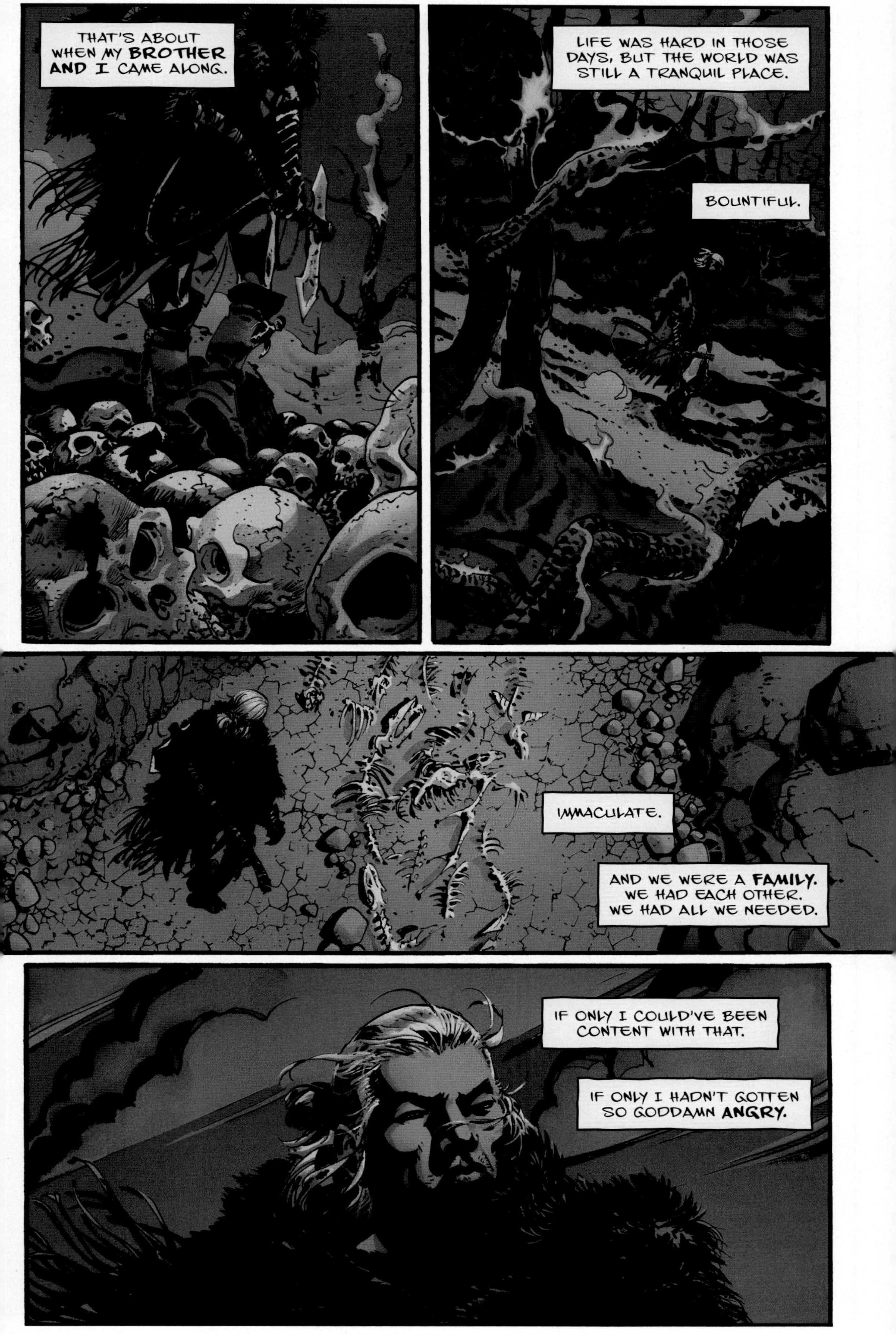
THAT'S ABOUT WHEN MY **BROTHER AND** I CAME ALONG.
LIFE WAS HARD IN THOSE DAYS, BUT THE WORLD WAS STILL A TRANQUIL PLACE.
BOUNTIFUL.
IMMACULATE.
AND WE WERE A **FAMILY.** WE HAD EACH OTHER. WE HAD ALL WE NEEDED.
IF ONLY I COULD'VE BEEN CONTENT WITH THAT.
IF ONLY I HADN'T GOTTEN SO GODDAMN **ANGRY.**

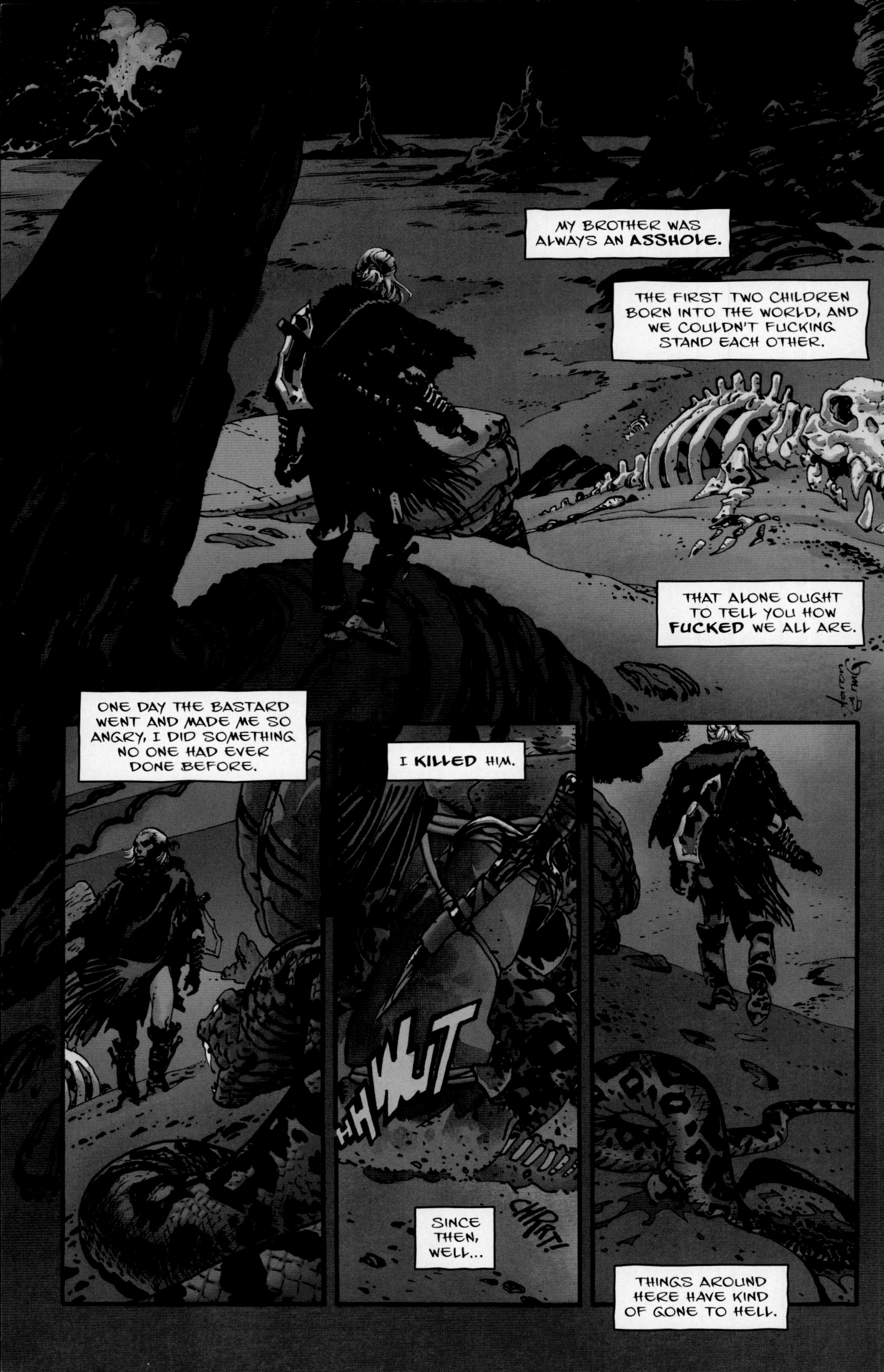
MY BROTHER WAS ALWAYS AN ASSHOLE.
THE FIRST TWO CHILDREN BORN INTO THE WORLD, AND WE COULDN'T FUCKING STAND EACH OTHER.
THAT ALONE OUGHT TO TELL YOU HOW FUCKED WE ALL ARE.
ONE DAY THE BASTARD WENT AND MADE ME SO ANGRY, I DID SOMETHING NO ONE HAD EVER DONE BEFORE.
I KILLED HIM.
CHHWUT
CHRT!
SINCE THEN, WELL...
THINGS AROUND HERE HAVE KIND OF GONE TO HELL.

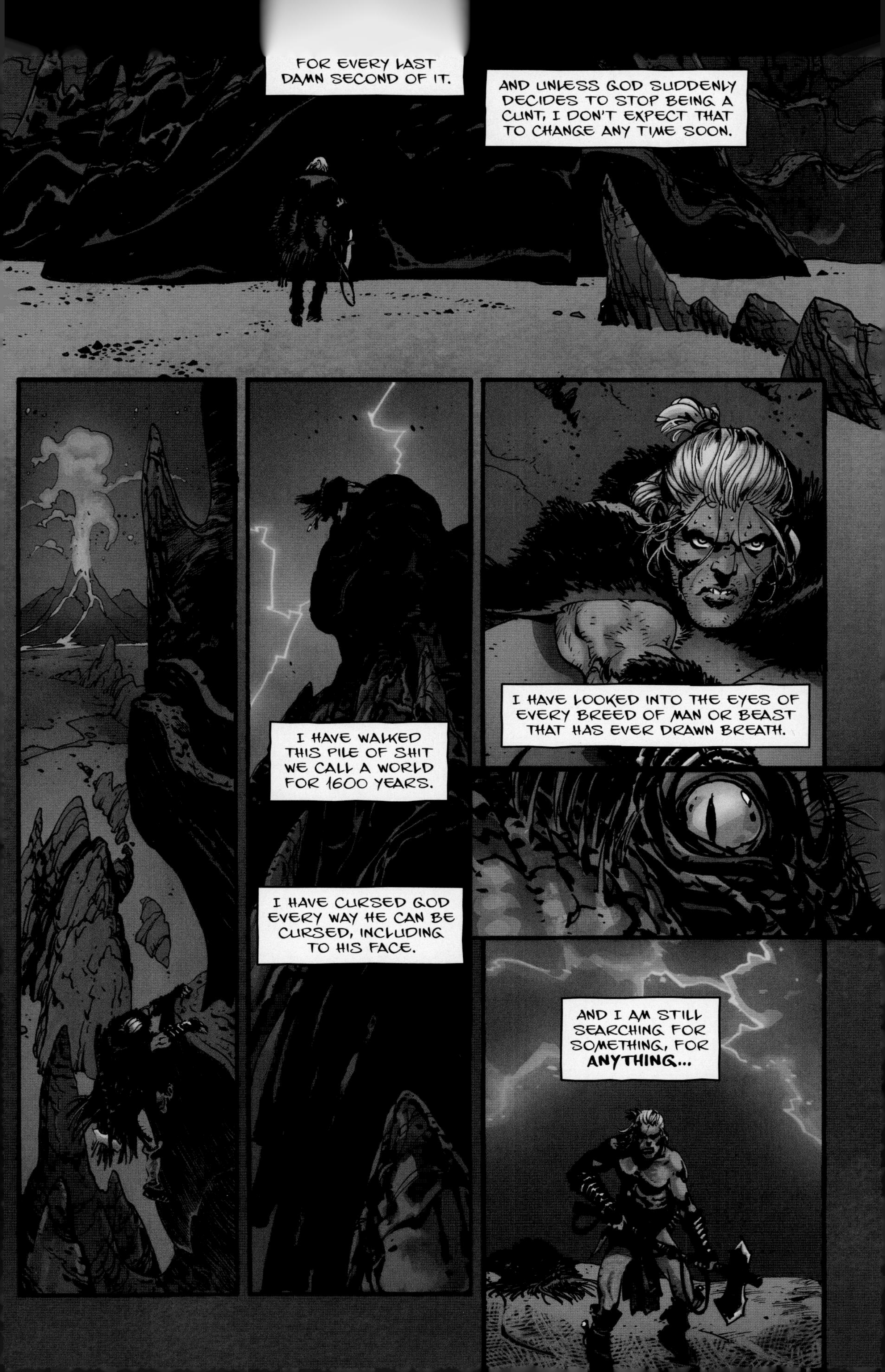
FOR EVERY LAST DAMN SECOND OF IT.
AND UNLESS GOD SUDDENLY DECIDES TO STOP BEING A CUNT, I DON'T EXPECT THAT TO CHANGE ANY TIME SOON.
I HAVE WALKED THIS PILE OF SHIT WE CALL A WORLD FOR 1600 YEARS.
I HAVE CURSED GOD EVERY WAY HE CAN BE CURSED, INCLUDING TO HIS FACE.
I HAVE LOOKED INTO THE EYES OF EVERY BREED OF MAN OR BEAST THAT HAS EVER DRAWN BREATH.
AND I AM STILL SEARCHING FOR SOMETHING, FOR **ANYTHING...**

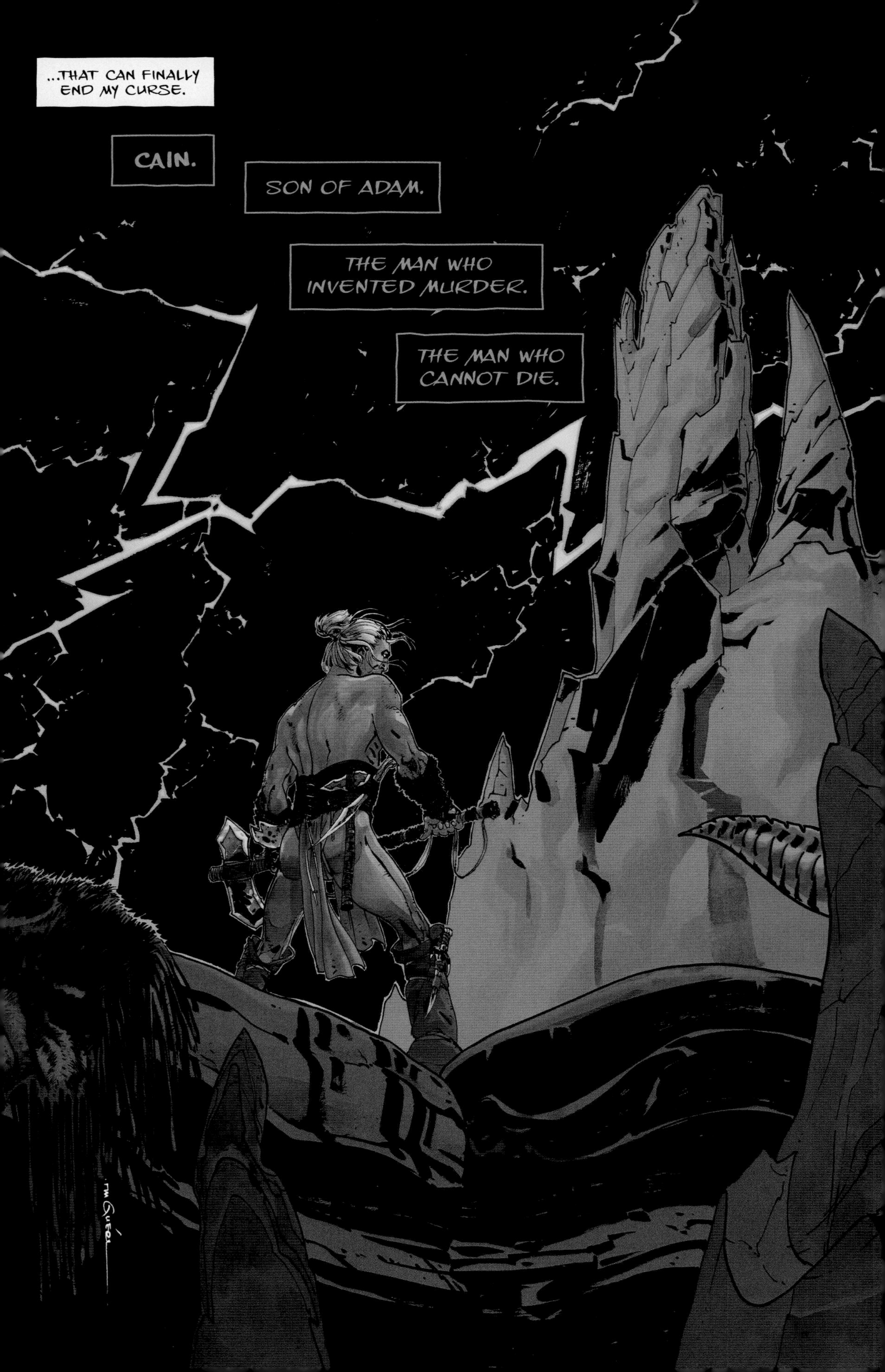
...THAT CAN FINALLY END MY CURSE.
CAIN.
SON OF ADAM.
THE MAN WHO INVENTED MURDER.
THE MAN WHO CANNOT DIE.

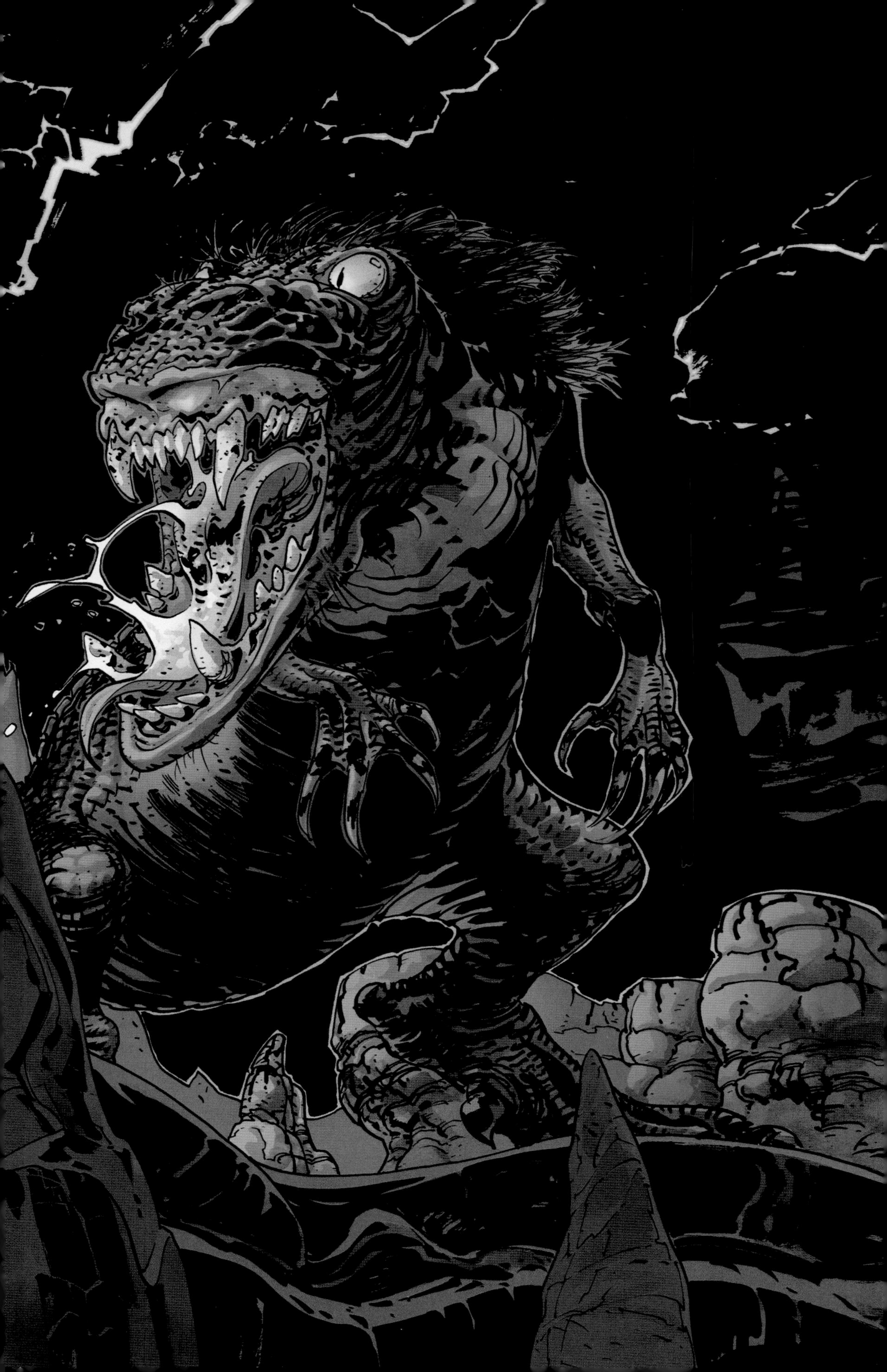

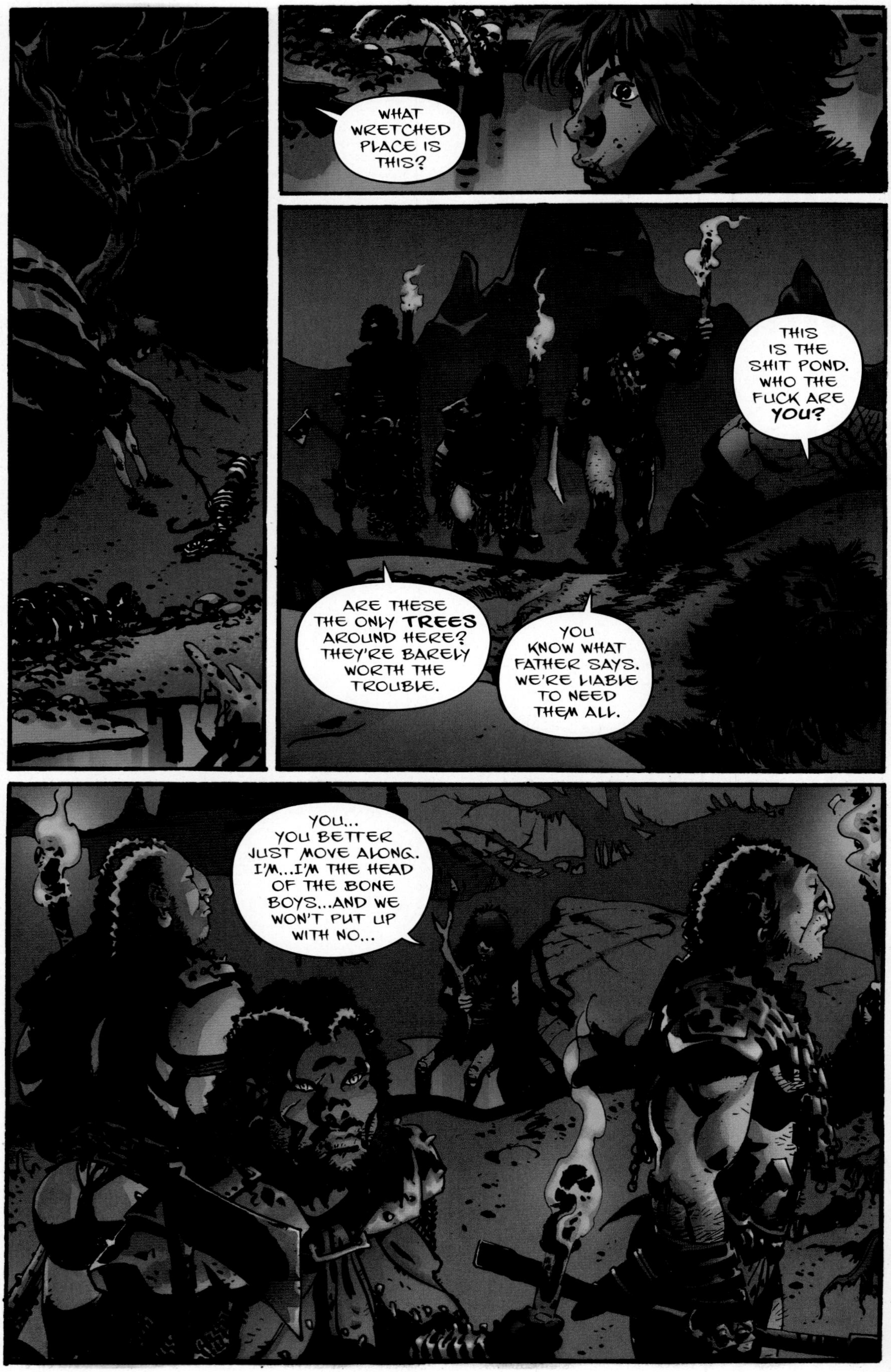
WHAT WRETCHED PLACE IS THIS?
THIS IS THE SHIT POND. WHO THE FUCK ARE YOU?
ARE THESE THE ONLY TREES AROUND HERE? THEY'RE BARELY WORTH THE TROUBLE.
YOU KNOW WHAT FATHER SAYS. WE'RE LIABLE TO NEED THEM ALL.
YOU... YOU BETTER JUST MOVE ALONG. I'M...I'M THE HEAD OF THE BONE BOYS...AND WE WON'T PUT UP WITH NO...

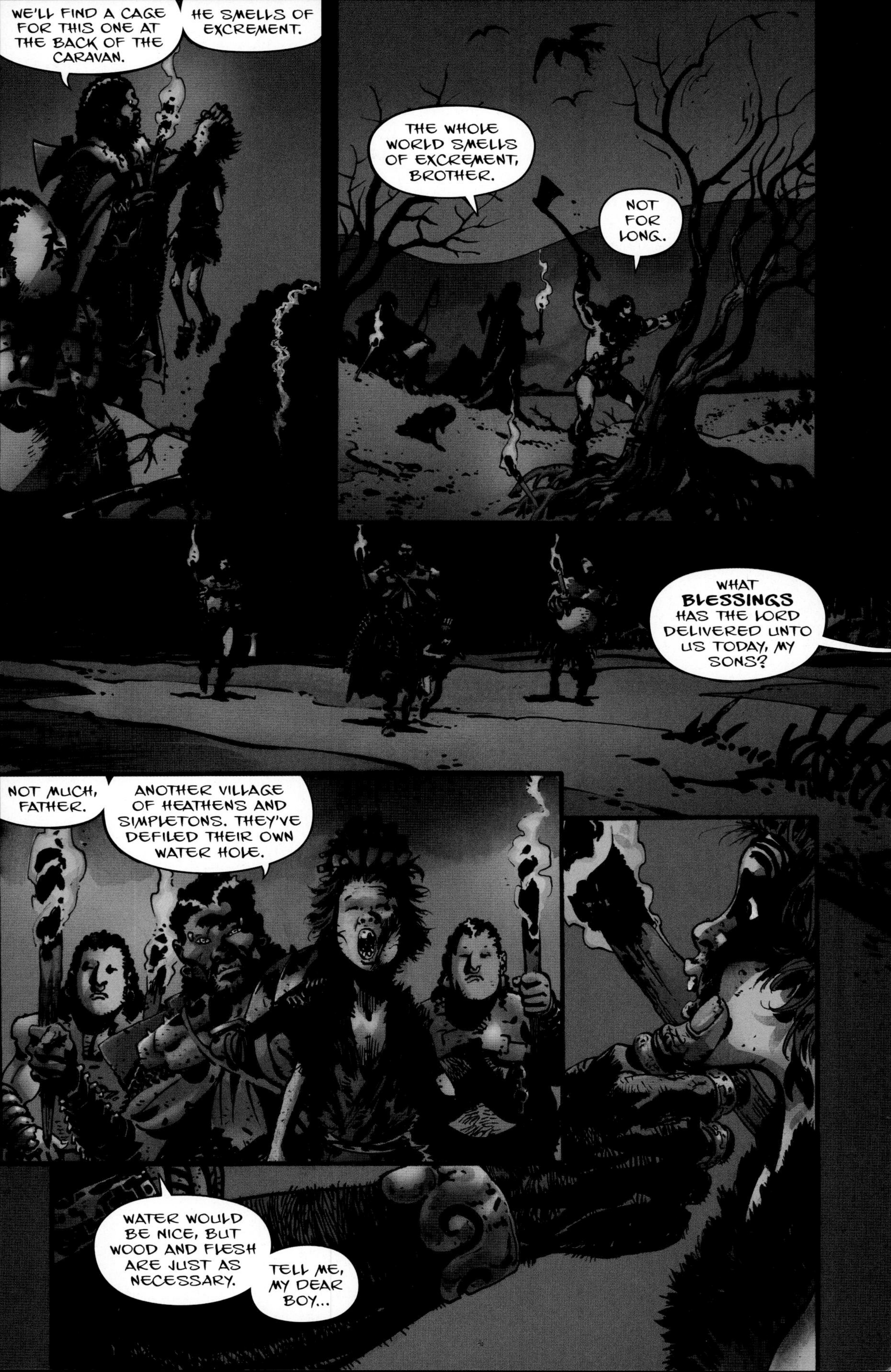
WE'LL FIND A CAGE FOR THIS ONE AT THE BACK OF THE CARAVAN.
HE SMELLS OF EXCREMENT.
THE WHOLE WORLD SMELLS OF EXCREMENT, BROTHER.
NOT FOR LONG.
WHAT BLESSINGS HAS THE LORD DELIVERED UNTO US TODAY, MY SONS?
NOT MUCH, FATHER.
ANOTHER VILLAGE OF HEATHENS AND SIMPLETONS. THEY'VE DEFILED THEIR OWN WATER HOLE.
WATER WOULD BE NICE, BUT WOOD AND FLESH ARE JUST AS NECESSARY.
TELL ME, MY DEAR BOY...

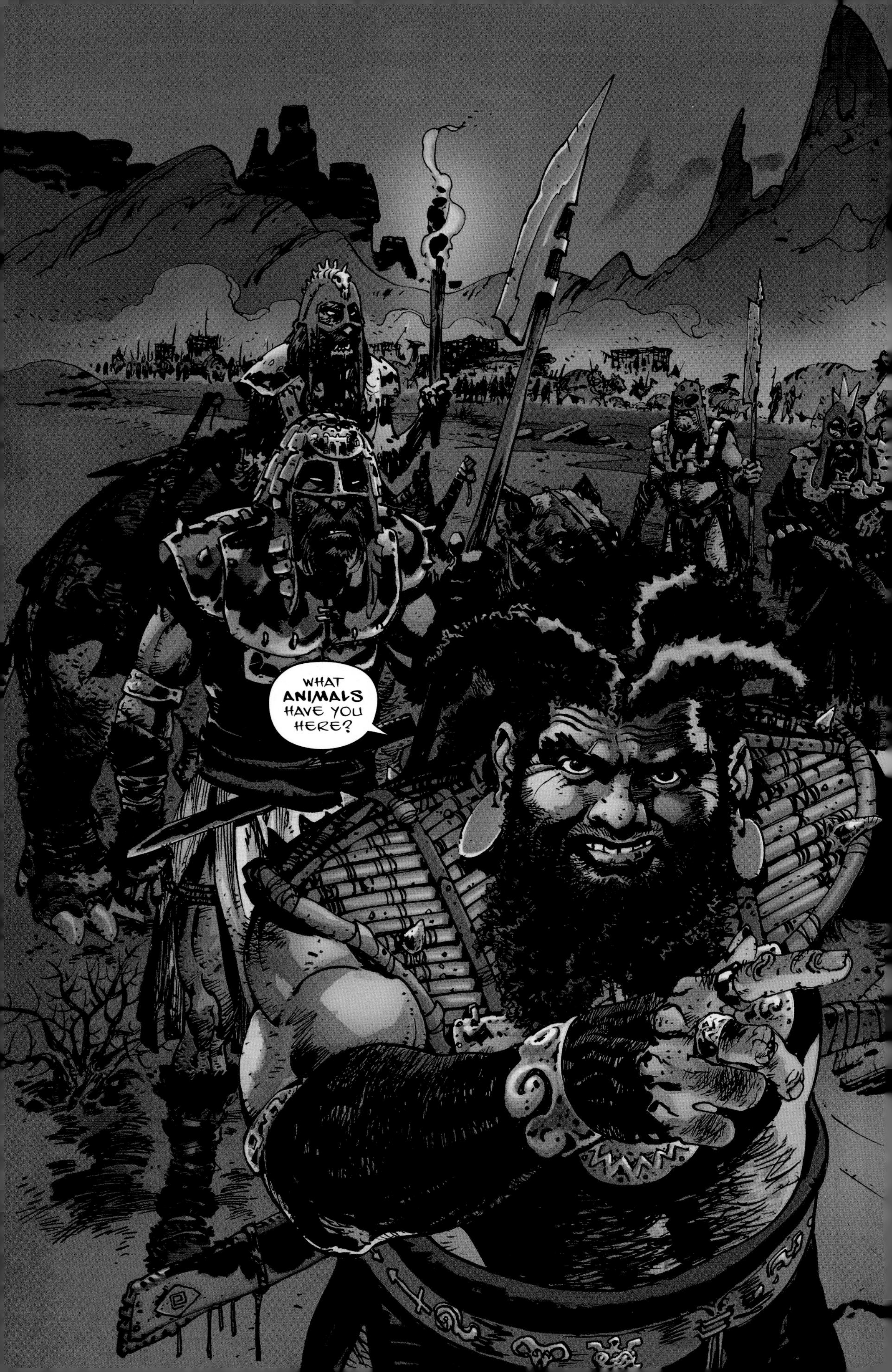
WHAT ANIMALS HAVE YOU HERE?

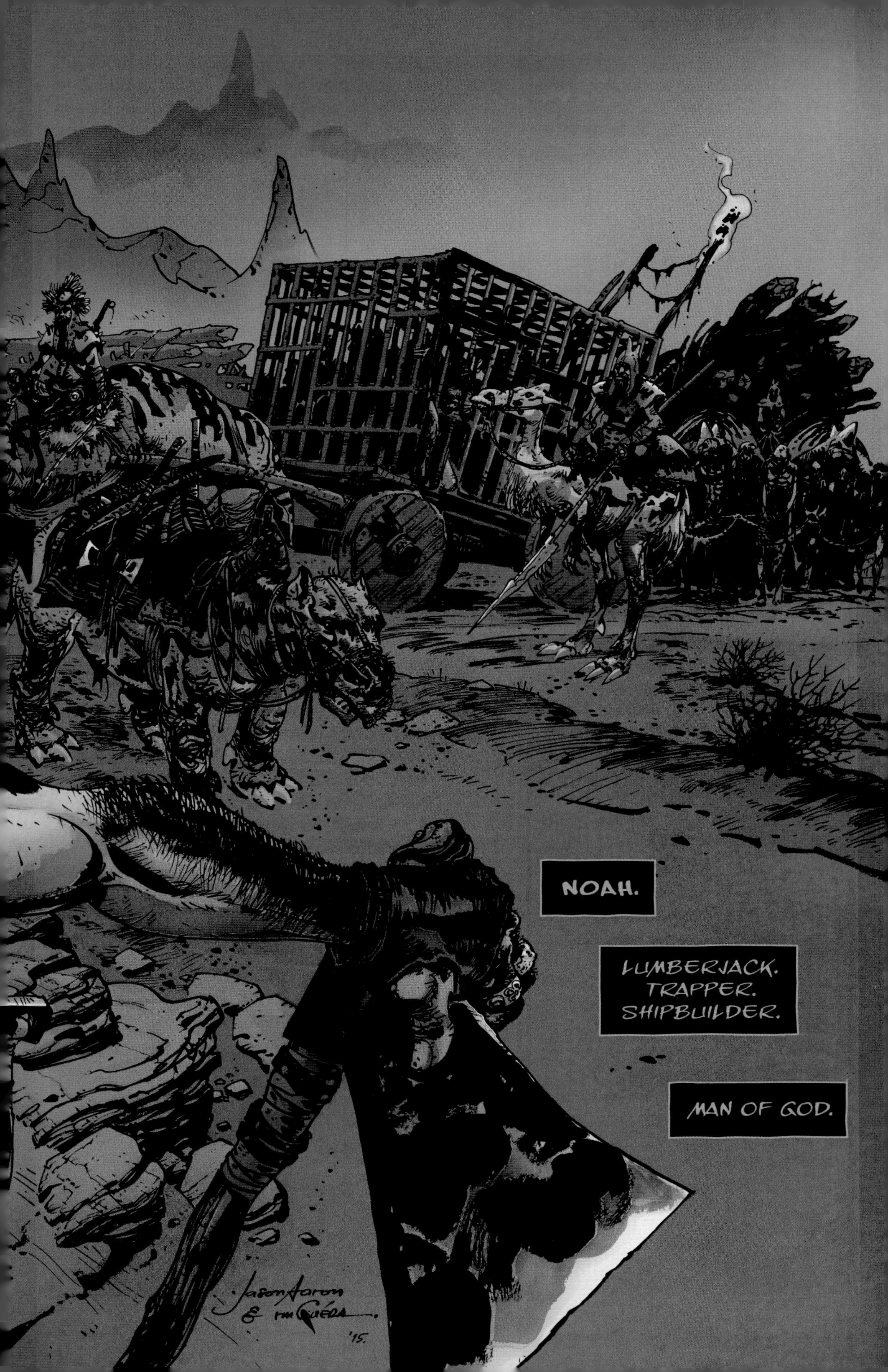
NOAH.
LUMBERJACK. TRAPPER. SHIPBUILDER.
MAN OF GOD.
Jason Aaron & RM Guéra '15.

chapter two

The Beasts of the Field

AND THE EARTH WAS
FILLED WITH VIOLENCE.

GENESIS 6:11

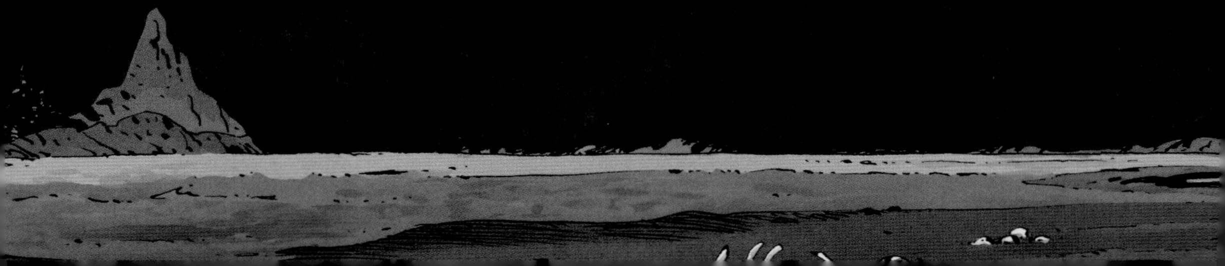

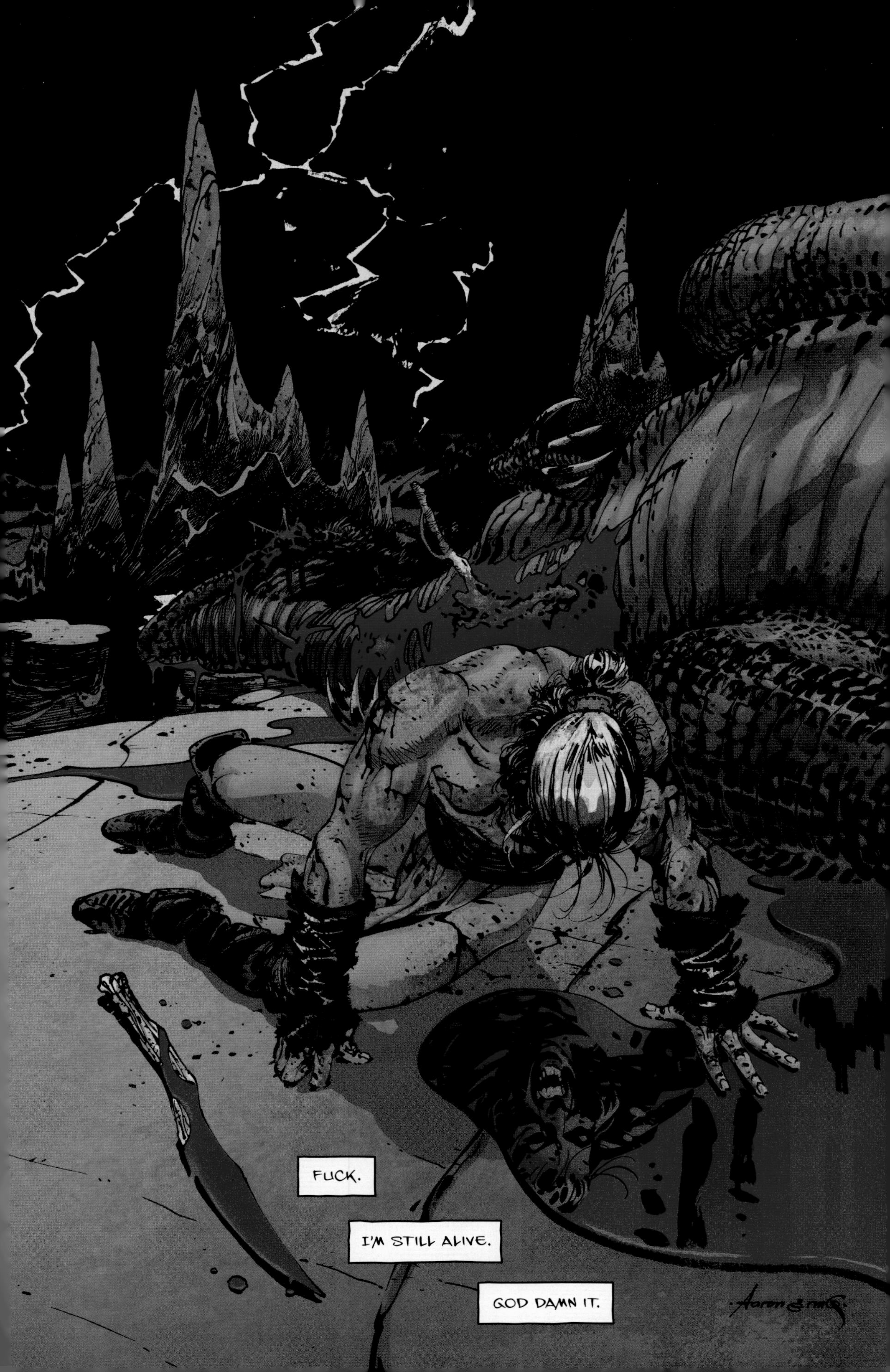
FUCK.
I'M STILL ALIVE.
GOD DAMN IT.

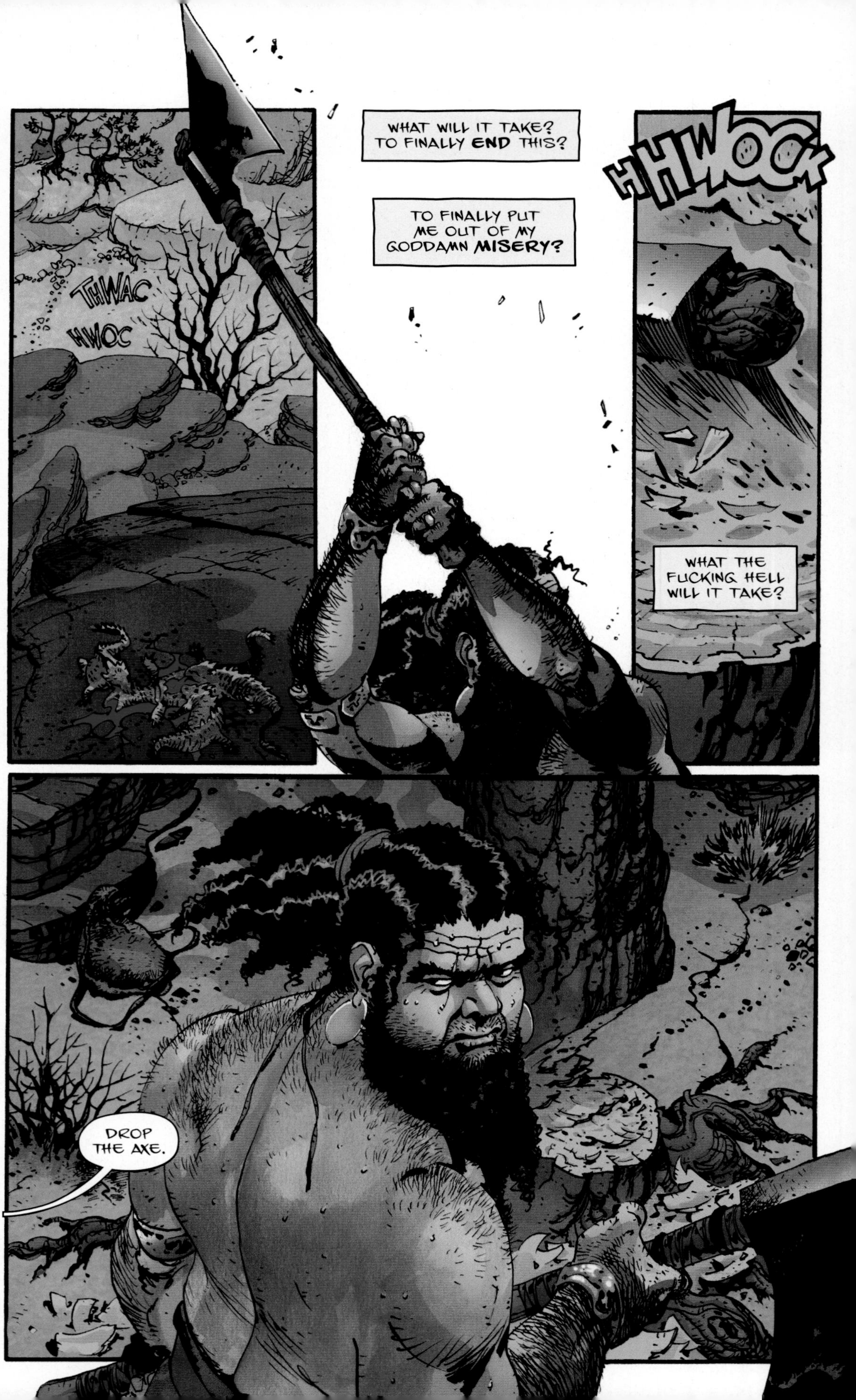
THWAC
HWOC
WHAT WILL IT TAKE? TO FINALLY END THIS?
TO FINALLY PUT ME OUT OF MY GODDAMN MISERY?
HHWOCK
WHAT THE FUCKING HELL WILL IT TAKE?
DROP THE AXE.

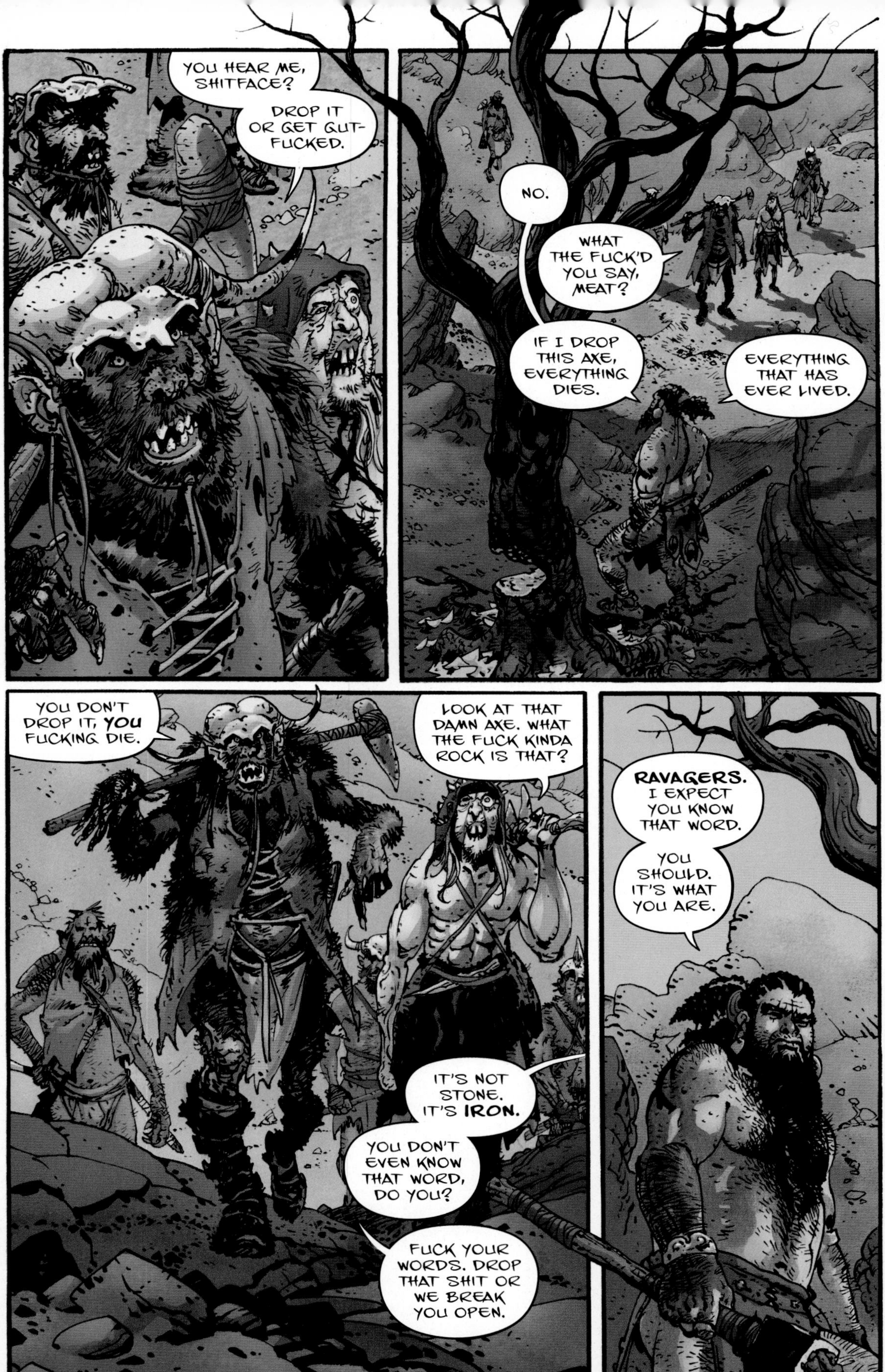
YOU HEAR ME, SHITFACE?
DROP IT OR GET GUT-FUCKED.
NO.
WHAT THE FUCK'D YOU SAY, MEAT?
IF I DROP THIS AXE, EVERYTHING DIES.
EVERYTHING THAT HAS EVER LIVED.
YOU DON'T DROP IT, YOU FUCKING DIE.
LOOK AT THAT DAMN AXE. WHAT THE FUCK KINDA ROCK IS THAT?
IT'S NOT STONE. IT'S IRON.
YOU DON'T EVEN KNOW THAT WORD, DO YOU?
FUCK YOUR WORDS. DROP THAT SHIT OR WE BREAK YOU OPEN.
RAVAGERS. I EXPECT YOU KNOW THAT WORD.
YOU SHOULD. IT'S WHAT YOU ARE.

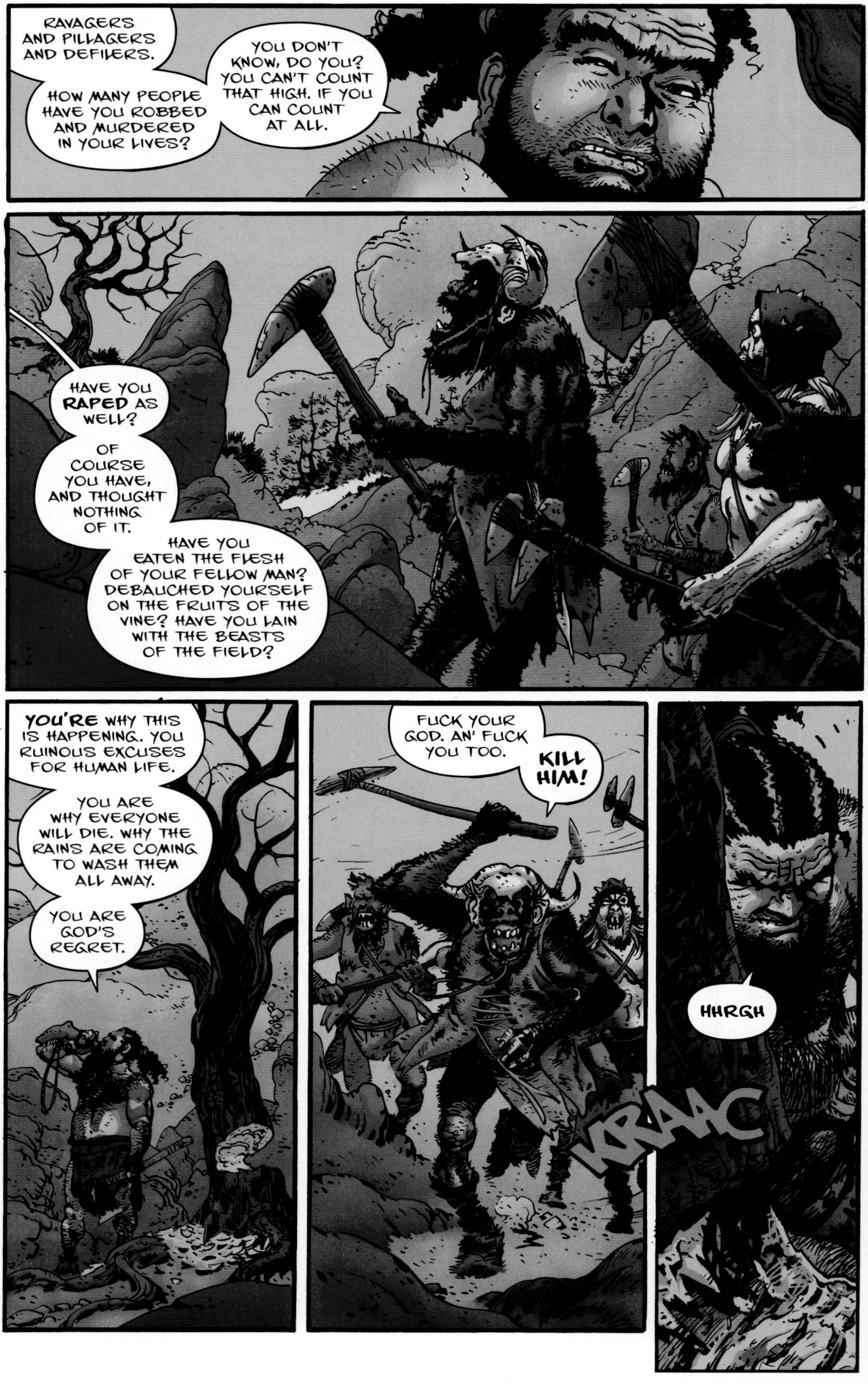
RAVAGERS AND PILLAGERS AND DEFILERS.
HOW MANY PEOPLE HAVE YOU ROBBED AND MURDERED IN YOUR LIVES?
YOU DON'T KNOW, DO YOU? YOU CAN'T COUNT THAT HIGH. IF YOU CAN COUNT AT ALL.
HAVE YOU **RAPED** AS WELL?
OF COURSE YOU HAVE, AND THOUGHT NOTHING OF IT.
HAVE YOU EATEN THE FLESH OF YOUR FELLOW MAN? DEBAUCHED YOURSELF ON THE FRUITS OF THE VINE? HAVE YOU LAIN WITH THE BEASTS OF THE FIELD?
YOU'RE WHY THIS IS HAPPENING. YOU RUINOUS EXCUSES FOR HUMAN LIFE.
YOU ARE WHY EVERYONE WILL DIE. WHY THE RAINS ARE COMING TO WASH THEM ALL AWAY.
YOU ARE GOD'S REGRET.
FUCK YOUR GOD. AN' FUCK YOU TOO.
KILL HIM!
KRAAC
HHRGH

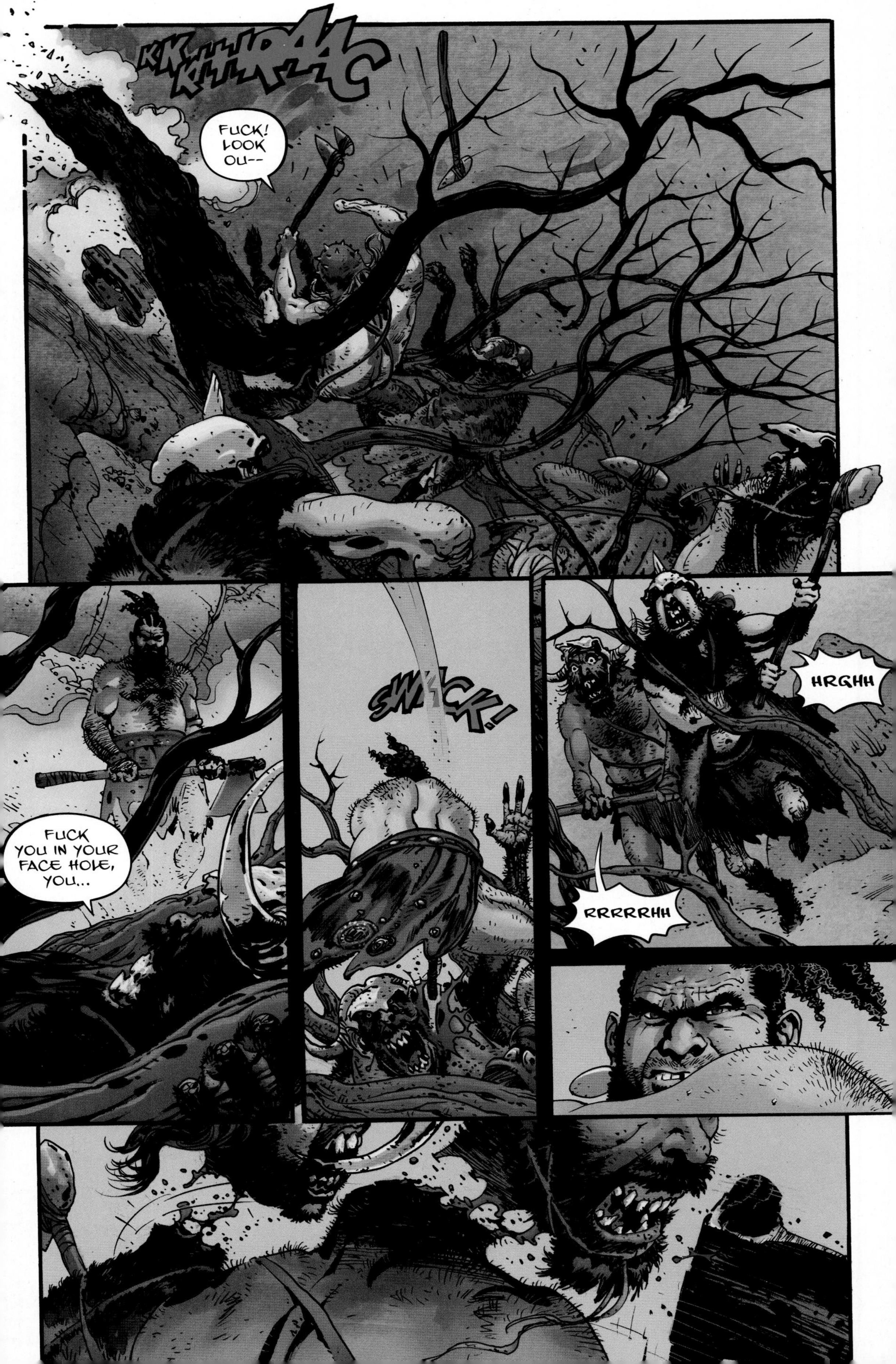
FUCK! LOOK OU--
FUCK YOU IN YOUR FACE HOLE, YOU...
SWACK!
HRGHH
RRRRRHH

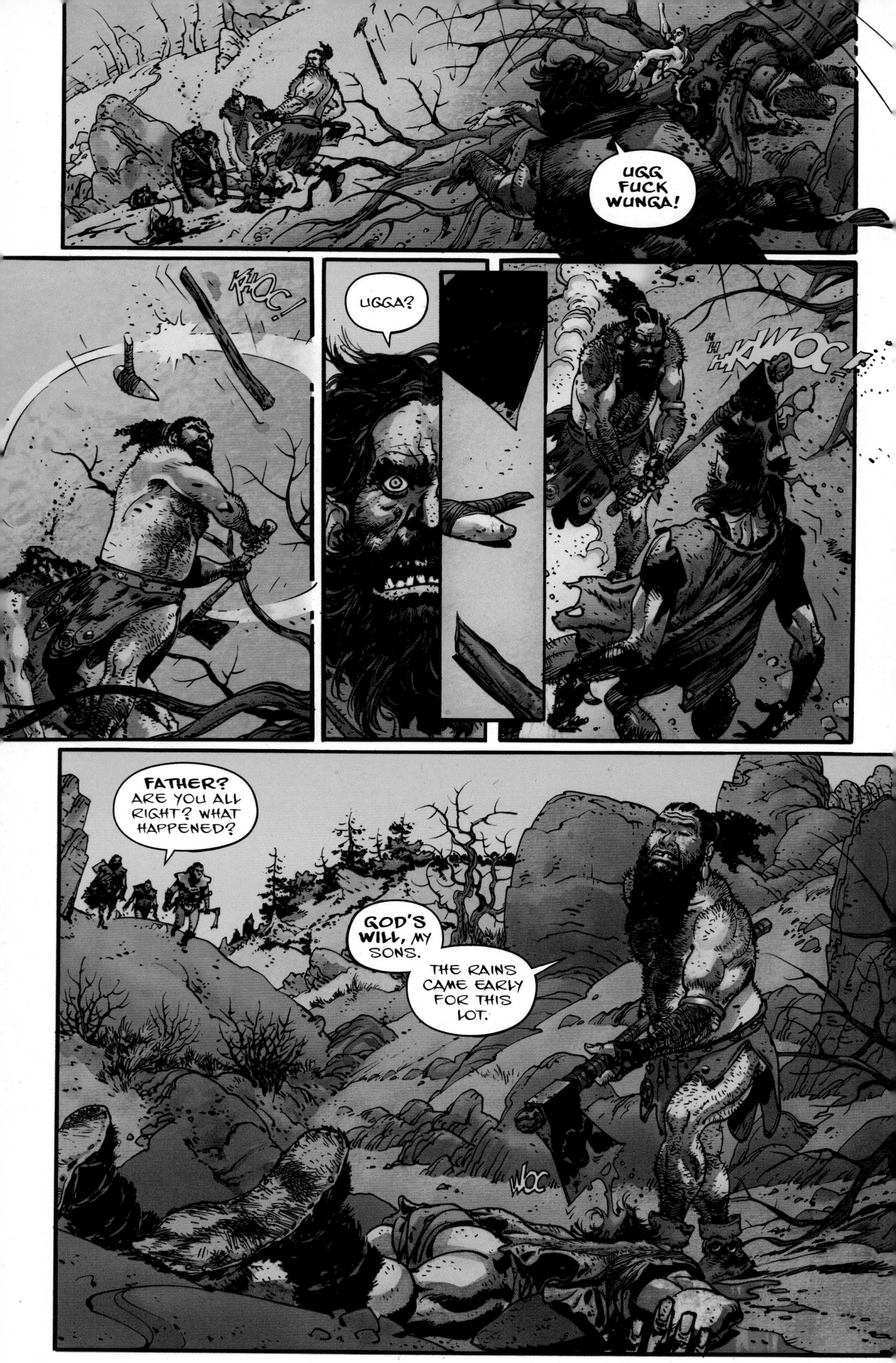
UGG FUCK WUNGA!
KHOC!
UGGA?
HHHKWOC!
FATHER? ARE YOU ALL RIGHT? WHAT HAPPENED?
GOD'S WILL, MY SONS.
THE RAINS CAME EARLY FOR THIS LOT.
WOC

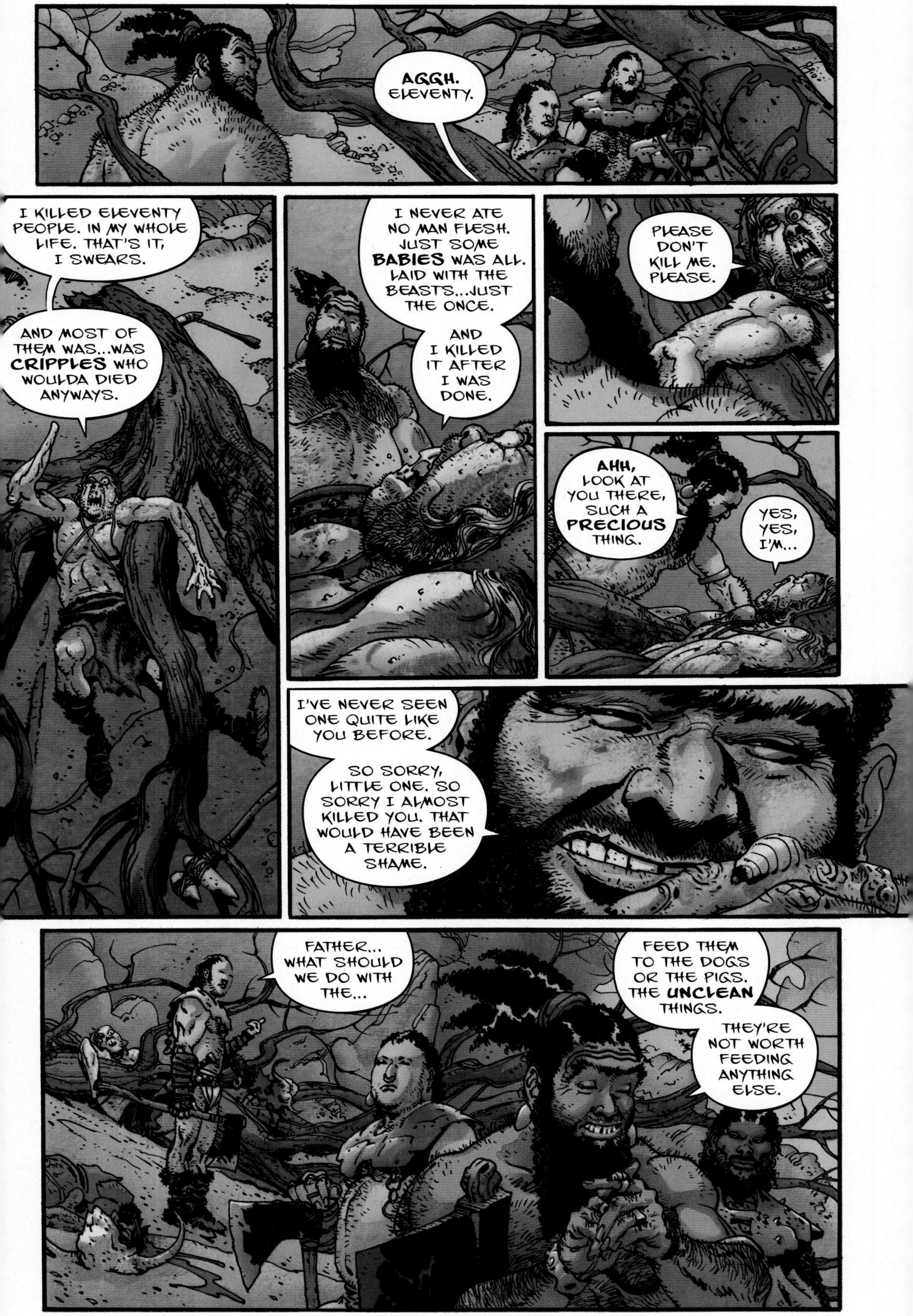
AGGH. ELEVENTY.
I KILLED ELEVENTY PEOPLE. IN MY WHOLE LIFE. THAT'S IT, I SWEARS.
AND MOST OF THEM WAS...WAS **CRIPPLES** WHO WOULDA DIED ANYWAYS.
I NEVER ATE NO MAN FLESH. JUST SOME **BABIES** WAS ALL. LAID WITH THE BEASTS...JUST THE ONCE.
AND I KILLED IT AFTER I WAS DONE.
PLEASE DON'T KILL ME. PLEASE.
AHH, LOOK AT YOU THERE, SUCH A **PRECIOUS** THING.
YES, YES, I'M...
I'VE NEVER SEEN ONE QUITE LIKE YOU BEFORE.
SO SORRY, LITTLE ONE. SO SORRY I ALMOST KILLED YOU. THAT WOULD HAVE BEEN A TERRIBLE SHAME.
FATHER... WHAT SHOULD WE DO WITH THE...
FEED THEM TO THE DOGS OR THE PIGS. THE **UNCLEAN** THINGS.
THEY'RE NOT WORTH FEEDING ANYTHING ELSE.

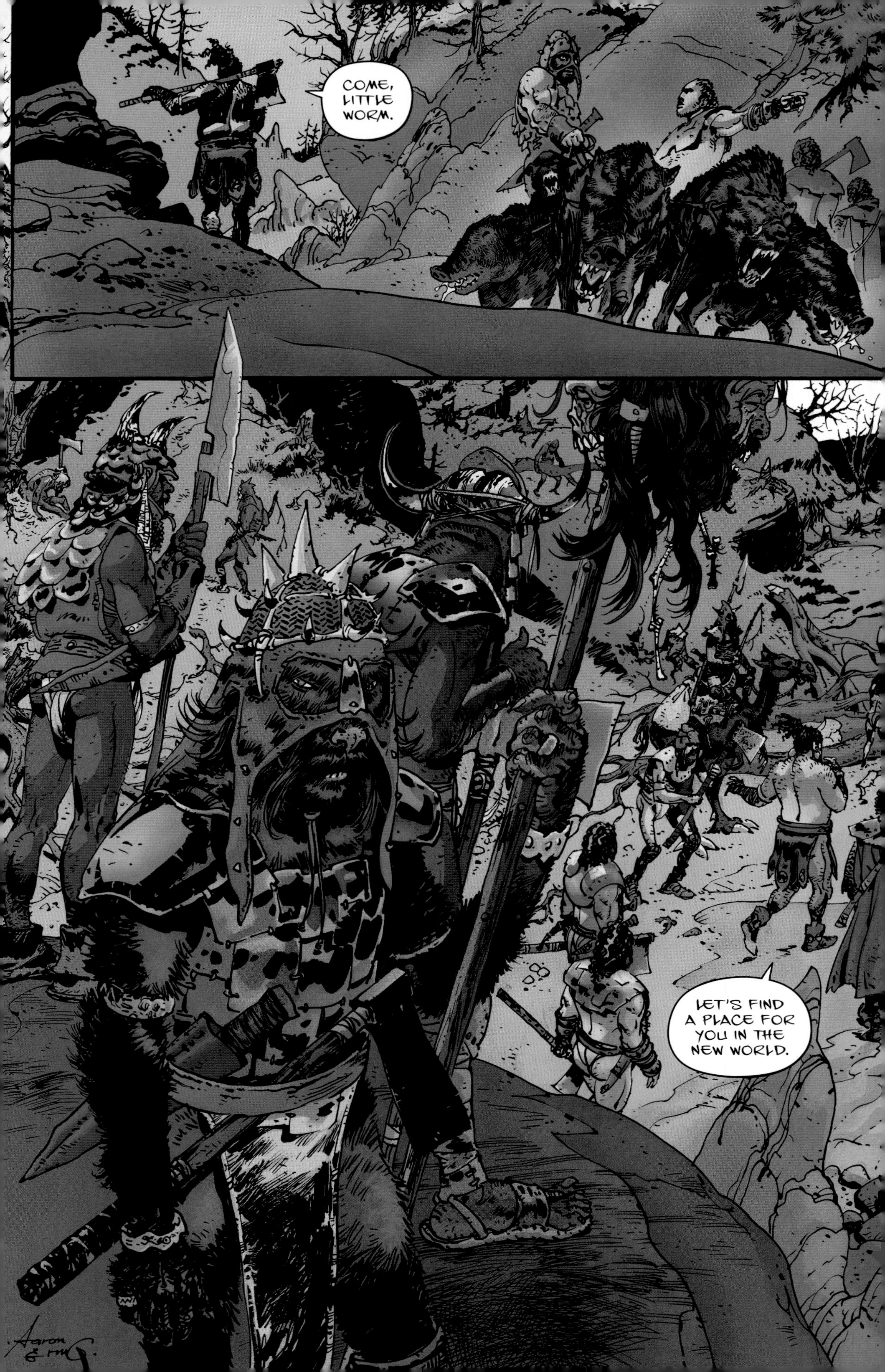
COME, LITTLE WORM.
LET'S FIND A PLACE FOR YOU IN THE NEW WORLD.

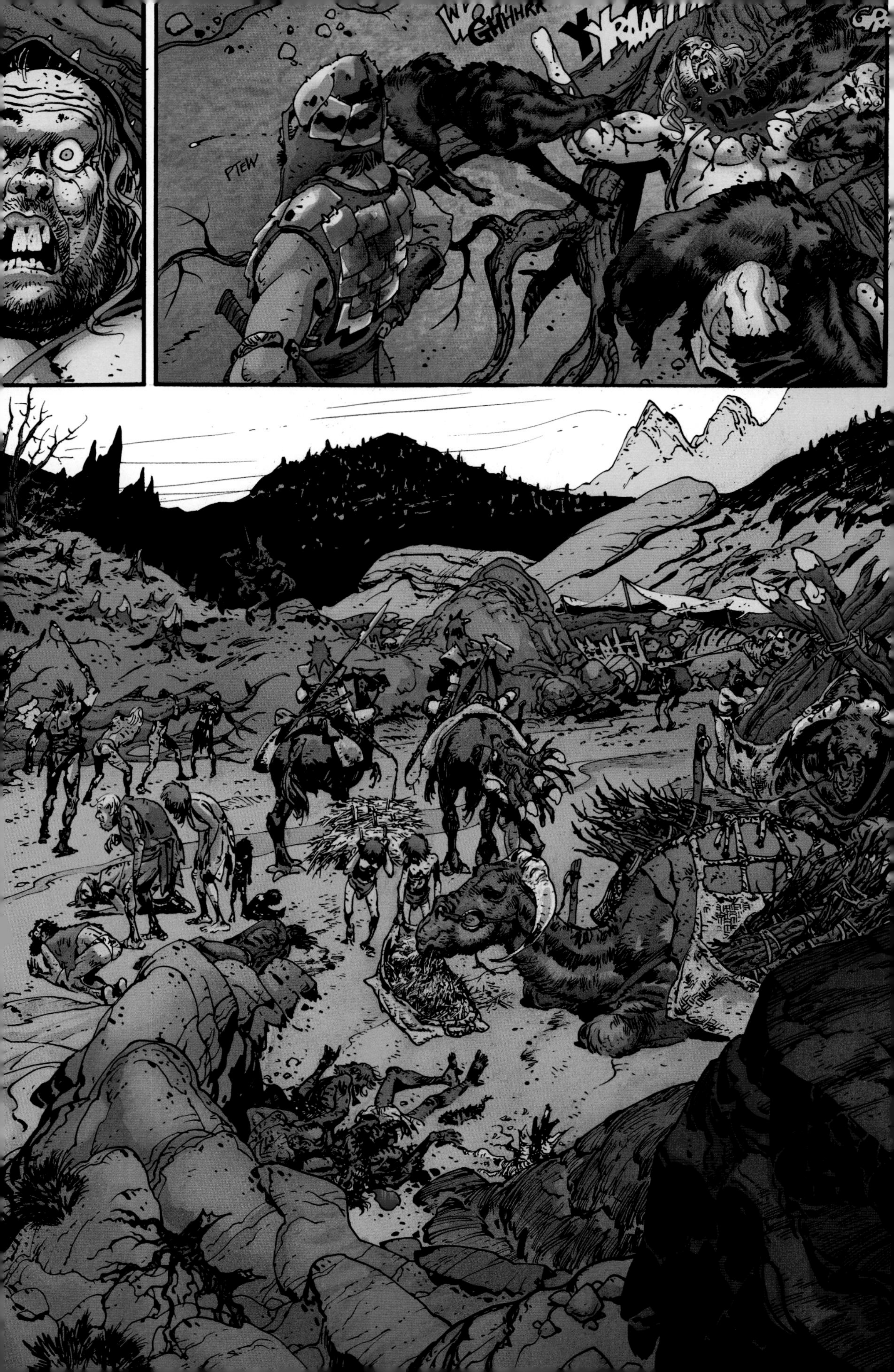
PTEW

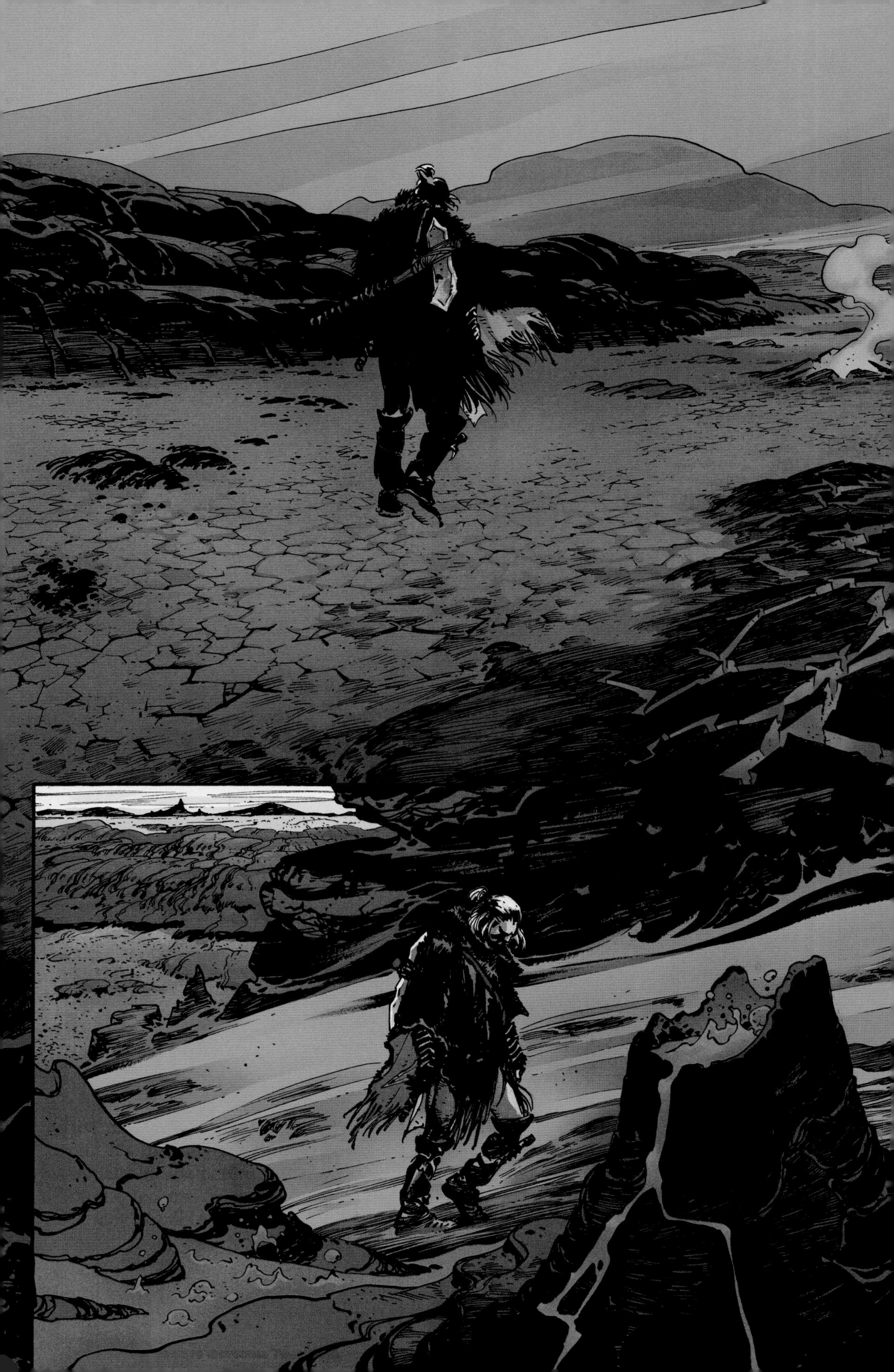

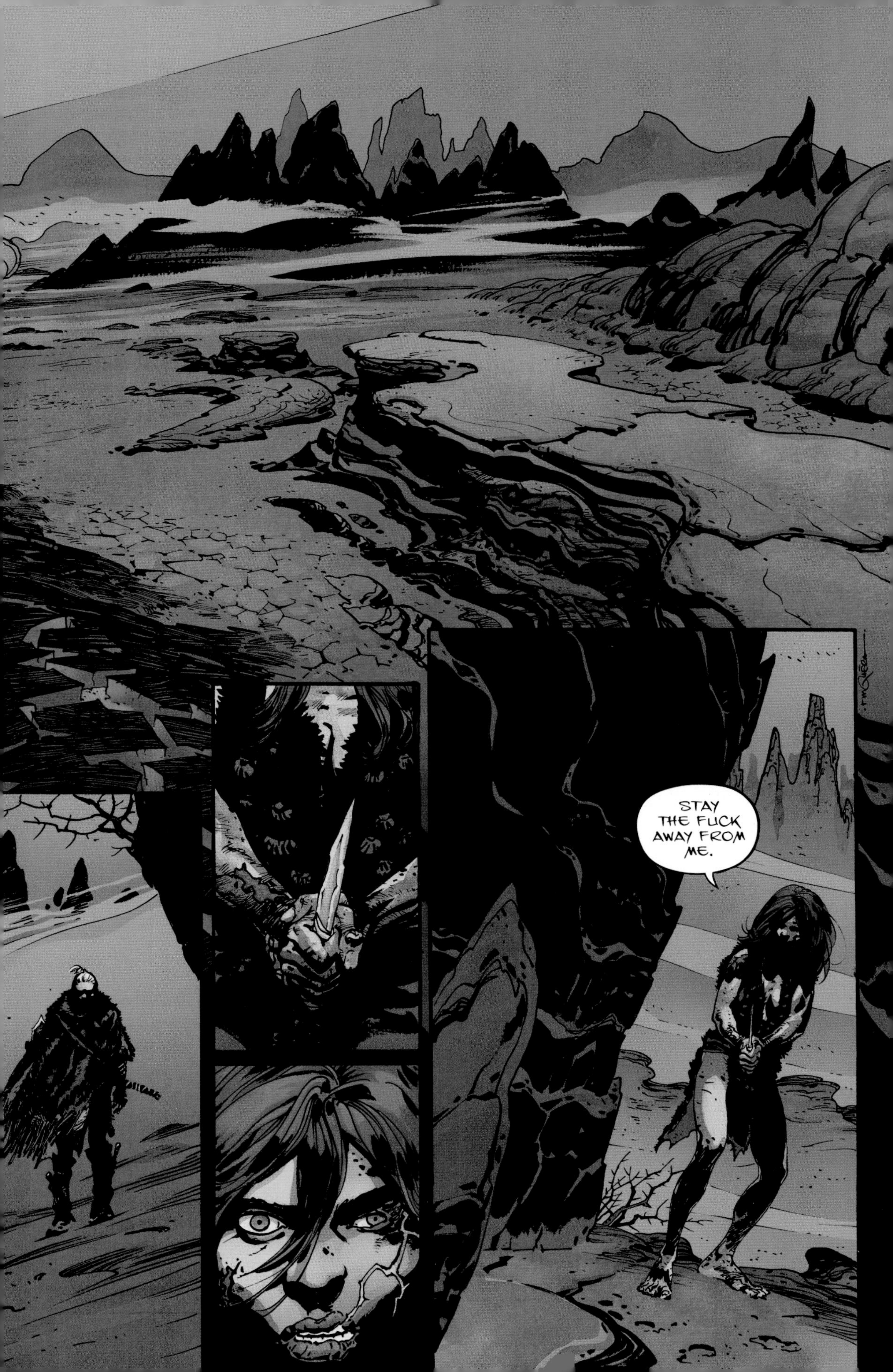
STAY THE FUCK AWAY FROM ME.

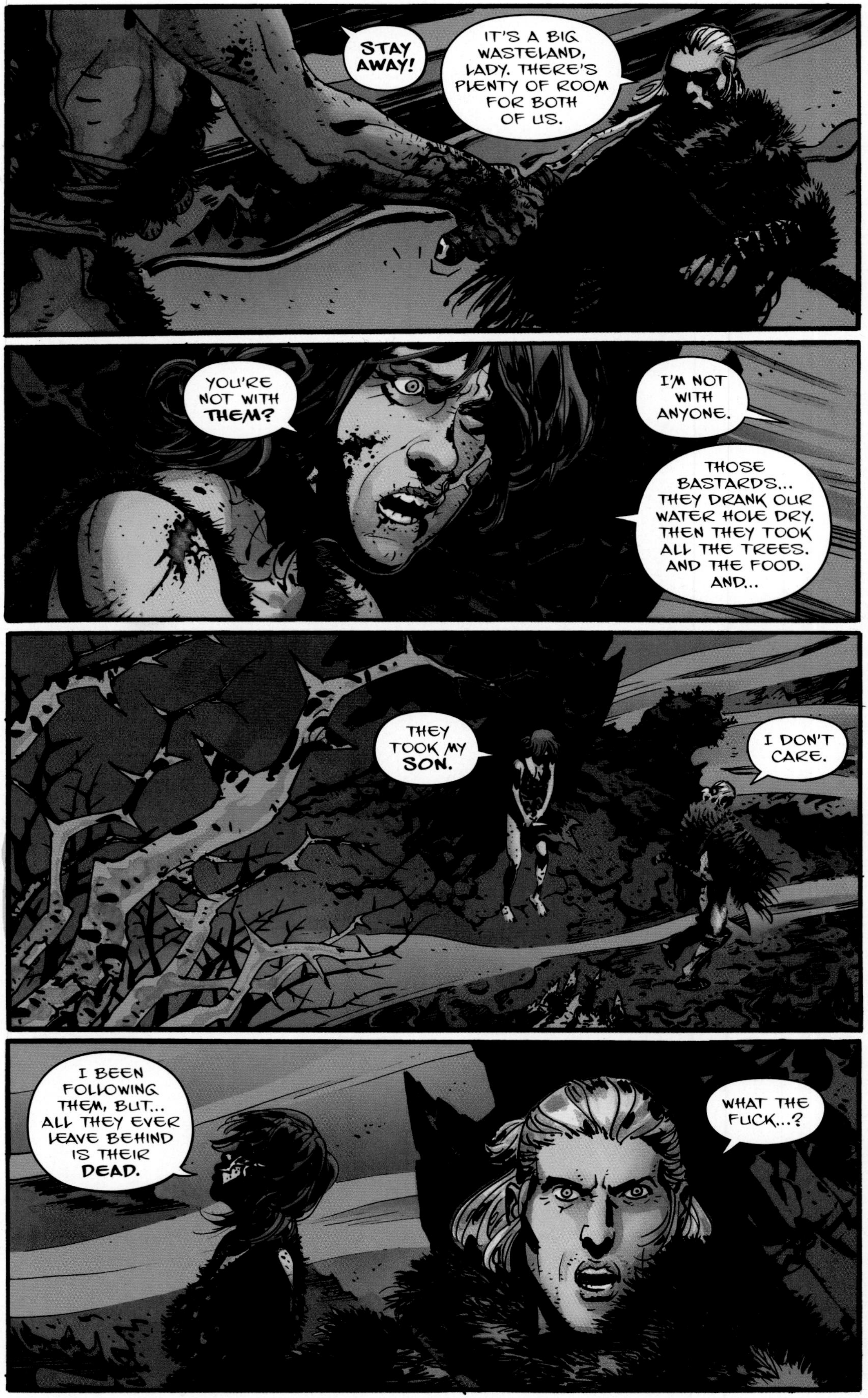
STAY AWAY!
IT'S A BIG WASTELAND, LADY. THERE'S PLENTY OF ROOM FOR BOTH OF US.
YOU'RE NOT WITH THEM?
I'M NOT WITH ANYONE.
THOSE BASTARDS... THEY DRANK OUR WATER HOLE DRY. THEN THEY TOOK ALL THE TREES. AND THE FOOD. AND...
THEY TOOK MY SON.
I DON'T CARE.
I BEEN FOLLOWING THEM, BUT... ALL THEY EVER LEAVE BEHIND IS THEIR DEAD.
WHAT THE FUCK...?

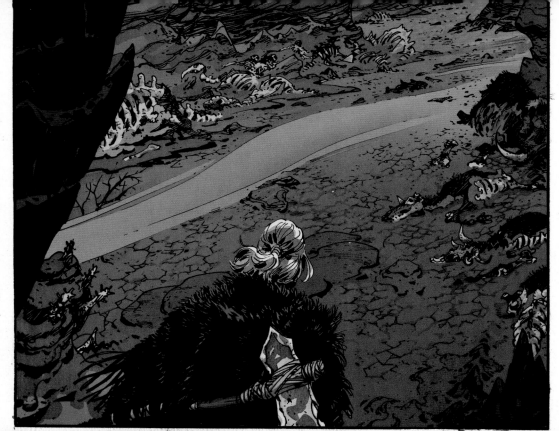

THESE **ANIMALS**... CAME FROM **VERY** FAR AWAY.

THERE WERE MORE.

MORE BEASTS THAN I KNEW THERE WERE IN THE WORLD.

SOME WERE IN CAGES. SOME THEY RODE.

MOVING CAGES? YOU MEAN THEY HAD **WHEELS**?

WHAT ARE WHEELS?

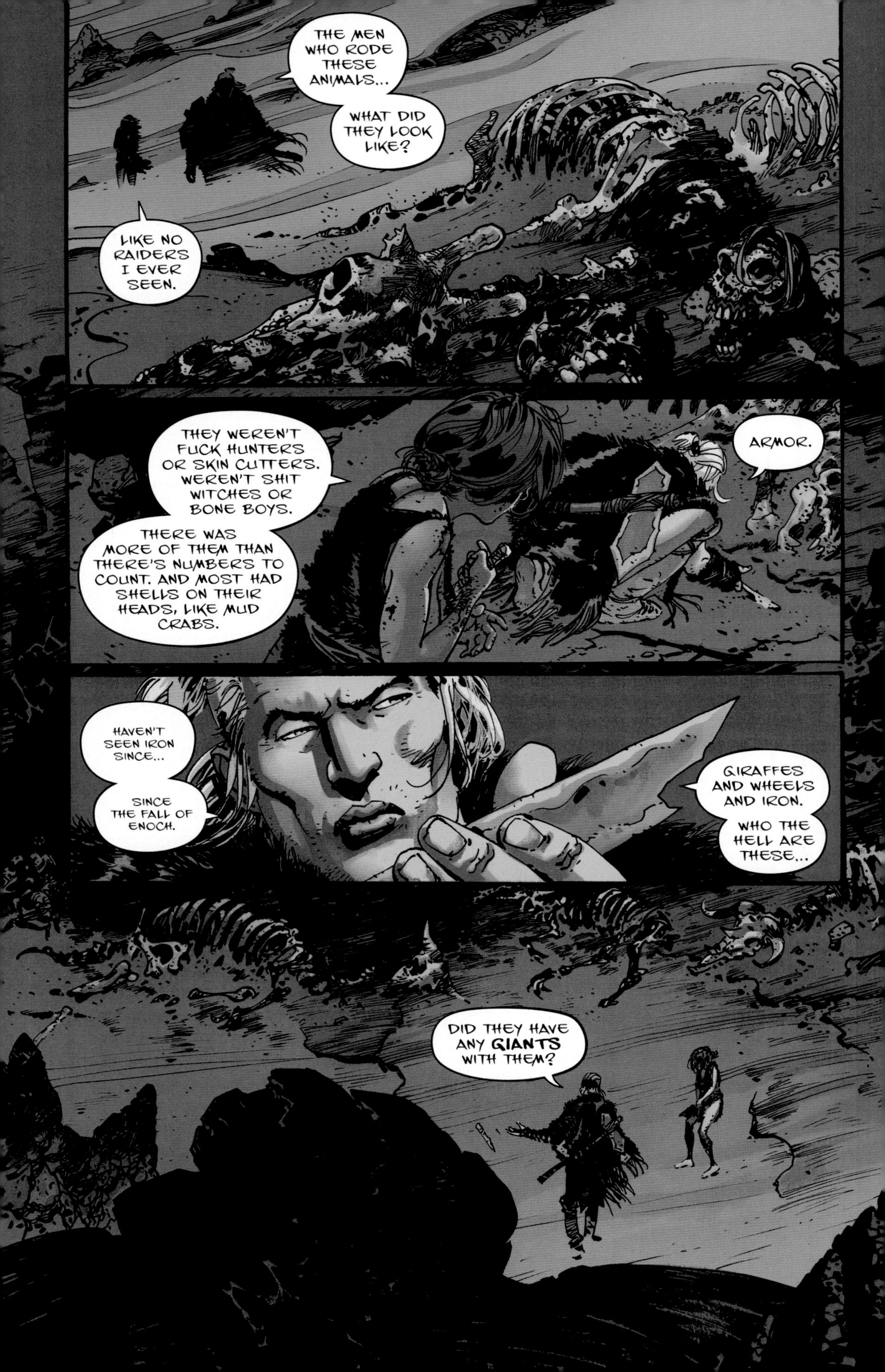
THE MEN WHO RODE THESE ANIMALS...
WHAT DID THEY LOOK LIKE?
LIKE NO RAIDERS I EVER SEEN.
THEY WEREN'T FUCK HUNTERS OR SKIN CUTTERS. WEREN'T SHIT WITCHES OR BONE BOYS.
THERE WAS MORE OF THEM THAN THERE'S NUMBERS TO COUNT. AND MOST HAD SHELLS ON THEIR HEADS, LIKE MUD CRABS.
ARMOR.
HAVEN'T SEEN IRON SINCE...
SINCE THE FALL OF ENOCH.
GIRAFFES AND WHEELS AND IRON.
WHO THE HELL ARE THESE...
DID THEY HAVE ANY **GIANTS** WITH THEM?

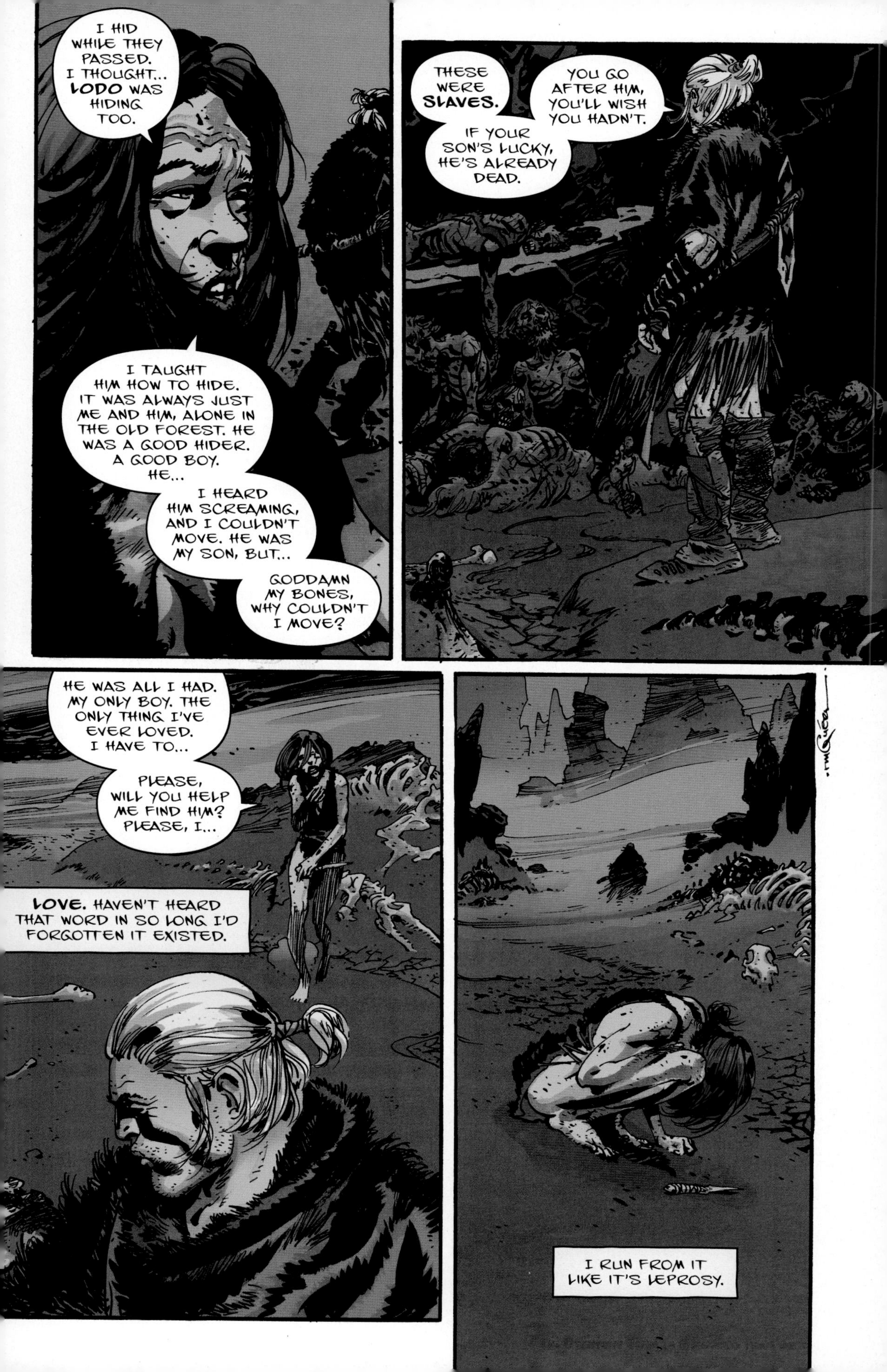
I HID WHILE THEY PASSED. I THOUGHT... LODO WAS HIDING TOO.
I TAUGHT HIM HOW TO HIDE. IT WAS ALWAYS JUST ME AND HIM, ALONE IN THE OLD FOREST. HE WAS A GOOD HIDER. A GOOD BOY. HE...
I HEARD HIM SCREAMING, AND I COULDN'T MOVE. HE WAS MY SON, BUT...
GODDAMN MY BONES, WHY COULDN'T I MOVE?
THESE WERE SLAVES.
IF YOUR SON'S LUCKY, HE'S ALREADY DEAD.
YOU GO AFTER HIM, YOU'LL WISH YOU HADN'T.
HE WAS ALL I HAD. MY ONLY BOY. THE ONLY THING I'VE EVER LOVED. I HAVE TO...
PLEASE, WILL YOU HELP ME FIND HIM? PLEASE, I...
LOVE. HAVEN'T HEARD THAT WORD IN SO LONG I'D FORGOTTEN IT EXISTED.
I RUN FROM IT LIKE IT'S LEPROSY.

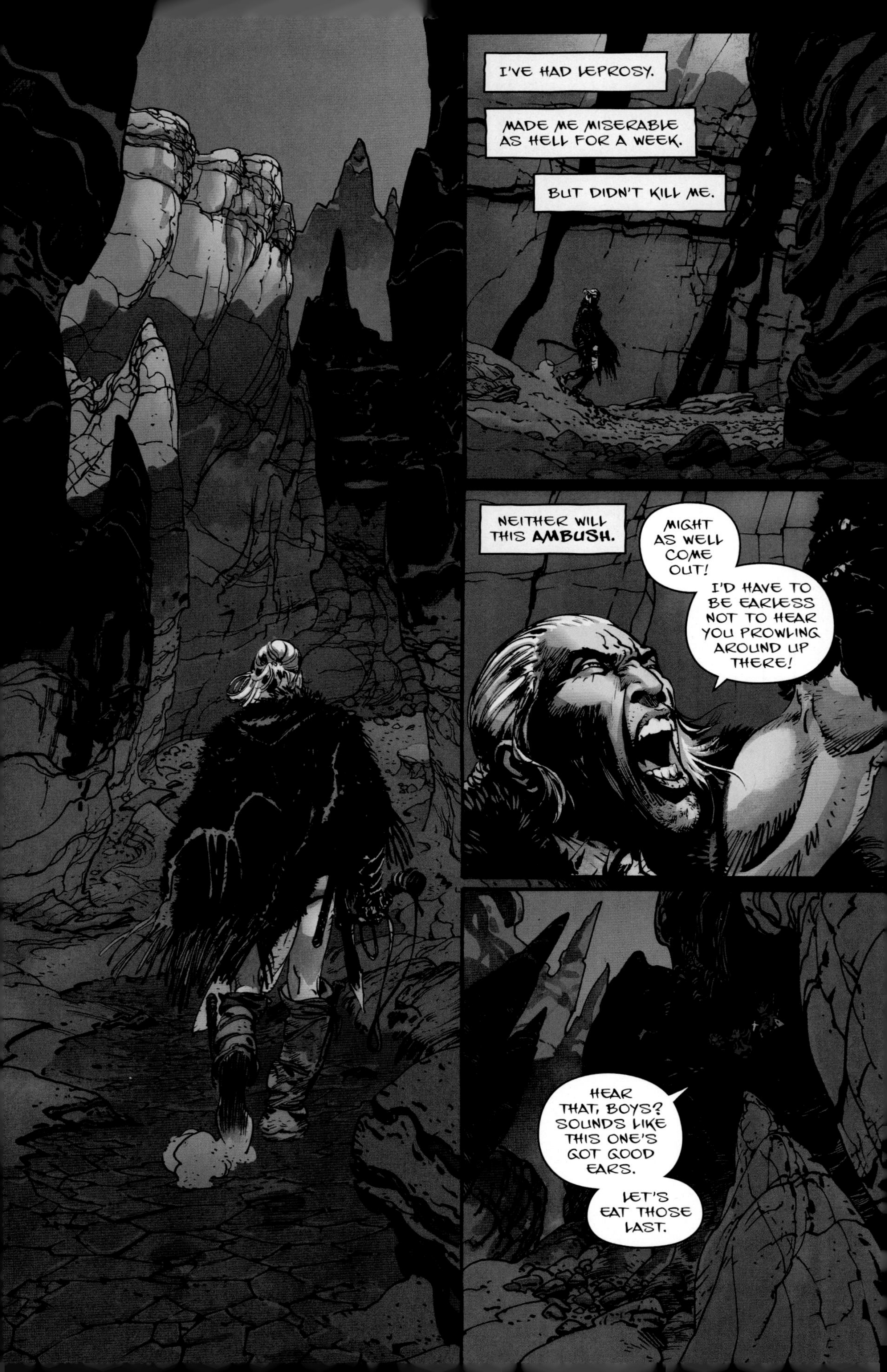
I'VE HAD LEPROSY.
MADE ME MISERABLE AS HELL FOR A WEEK.
BUT DIDN'T KILL ME.
NEITHER WILL THIS AMBUSH.
MIGHT AS WELL COME OUT!
I'D HAVE TO BE EARLESS NOT TO HEAR YOU PROWLING AROUND UP THERE!
HEAR THAT, BOYS? SOUNDS LIKE THIS ONE'S GOT GOOD EARS.
LET'S EAT THOSE LAST.

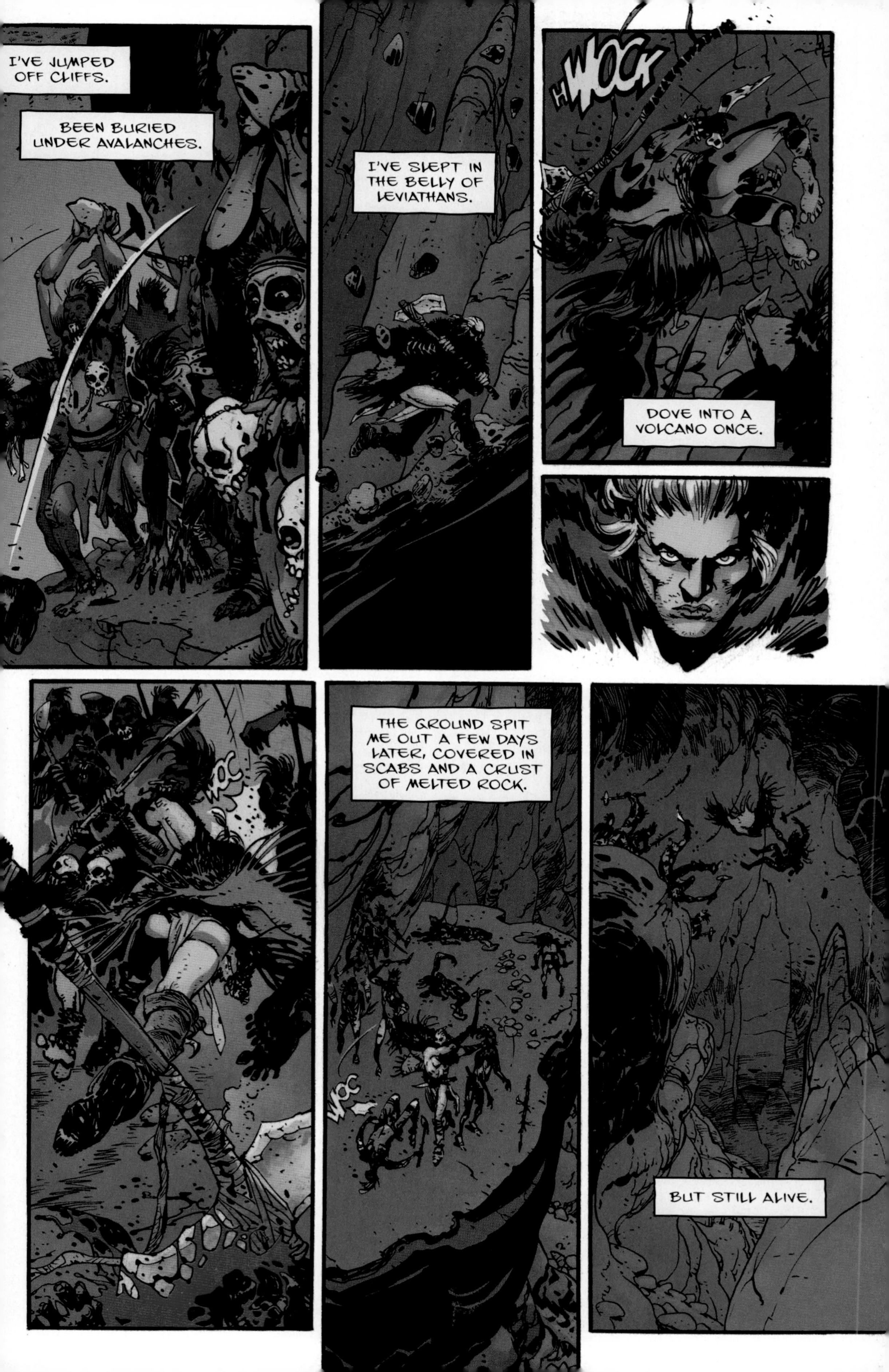
I'VE JUMPED OFF CLIFFS.
BEEN BURIED UNDER AVALANCHES.
I'VE SLEPT IN THE BELLY OF LEVIATHANS.
HWOCK
DOVE INTO A VOLCANO ONCE.
WOC
THE GROUND SPIT ME OUT A FEW DAYS LATER, COVERED IN SCABS AND A CRUST OF MELTED ROCK.
WOC
BUT STILL ALIVE.

I'VE SEEN EVERYTHING THIS WORLD HAS TO OFFER.

EVERY DEPRAVITY. EVERY DANGER. EVERY MONSTER, HUMAN OR OTHERWISE.

AND **NONE** OF IT COULD KILL ME.

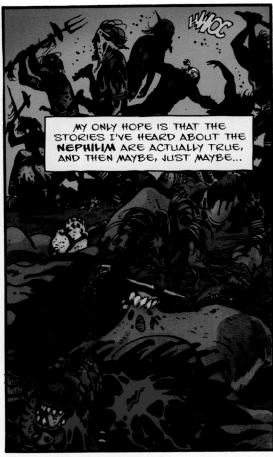

MY ONLY HOPE IS THAT THE STORIES I'VE HEARD ABOUT THE **NEPHILIM** ARE ACTUALLY TRUE, AND THEN MAYBE, JUST MAYBE...

HWWOC

I CAN FINALLY PUT AN END TO THIS FUCKING CURSE.

FINALLY KNOW WHAT IT'S LIKE TO BE MURDERED.

PLEASE, FUCKING GODDAMN GOD, LET ME BE MURDERED.

THE FUCKER'S CUTTING US TO PIECES!

BRING OUT THE FUCKING **DOGS!**

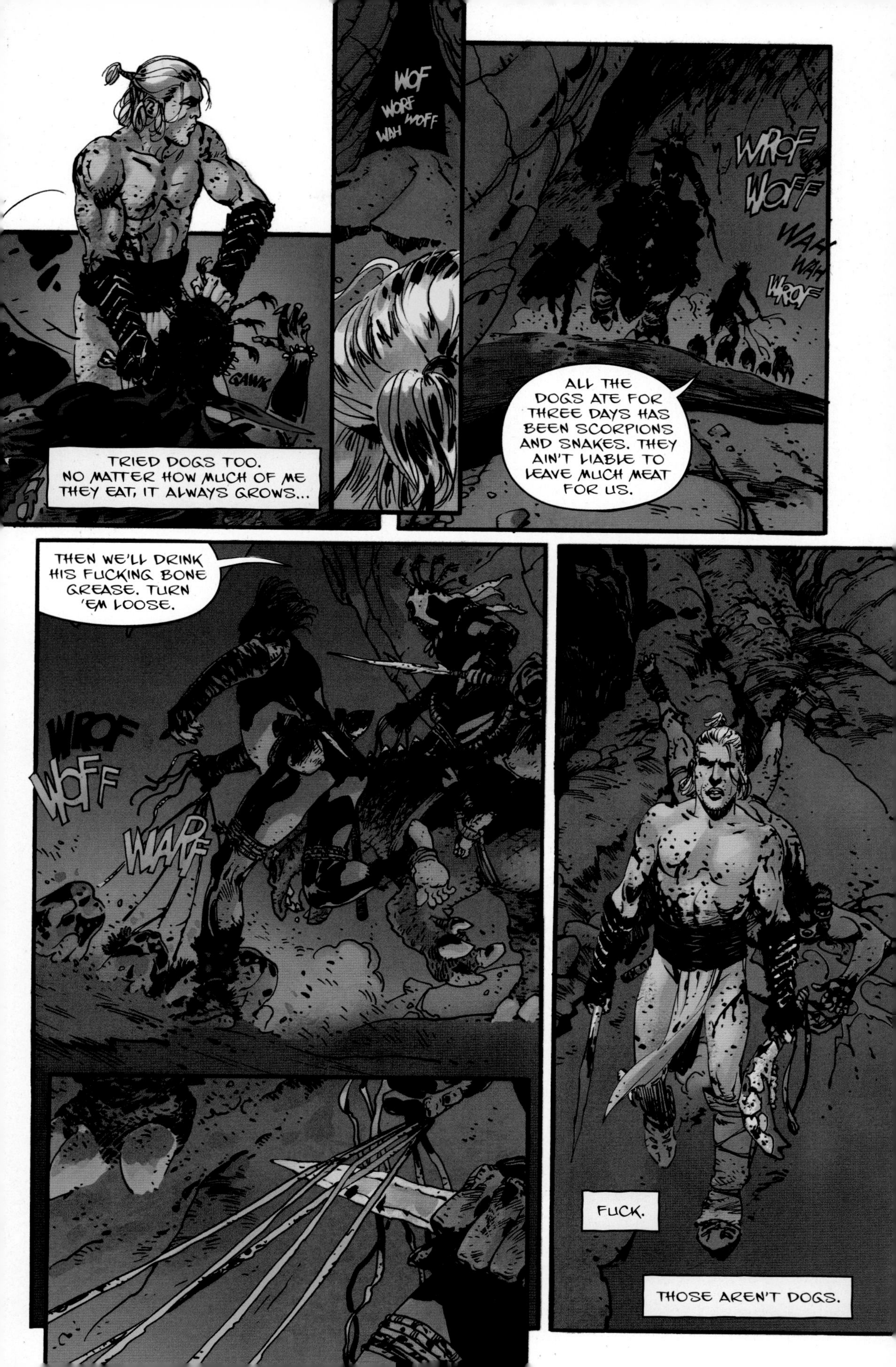
GAWK
TRIED DOGS TOO. NO MATTER HOW MUCH OF ME THEY EAT, IT ALWAYS GROWS...
WOF
WORF
WOFF
WAH
WROF
WOFF
WAH
WAH
WROF
ALL THE DOGS ATE FOR THREE DAYS HAS BEEN SCORPIONS AND SNAKES. THEY AIN'T LIABLE TO LEAVE MUCH MEAT FOR US.
THEN WE'LL DRINK HIS FUCKING BONE GREASE. TURN 'EM LOOSE.
WROF
WOFF
WARF
FUCK.
THOSE AREN'T DOGS.

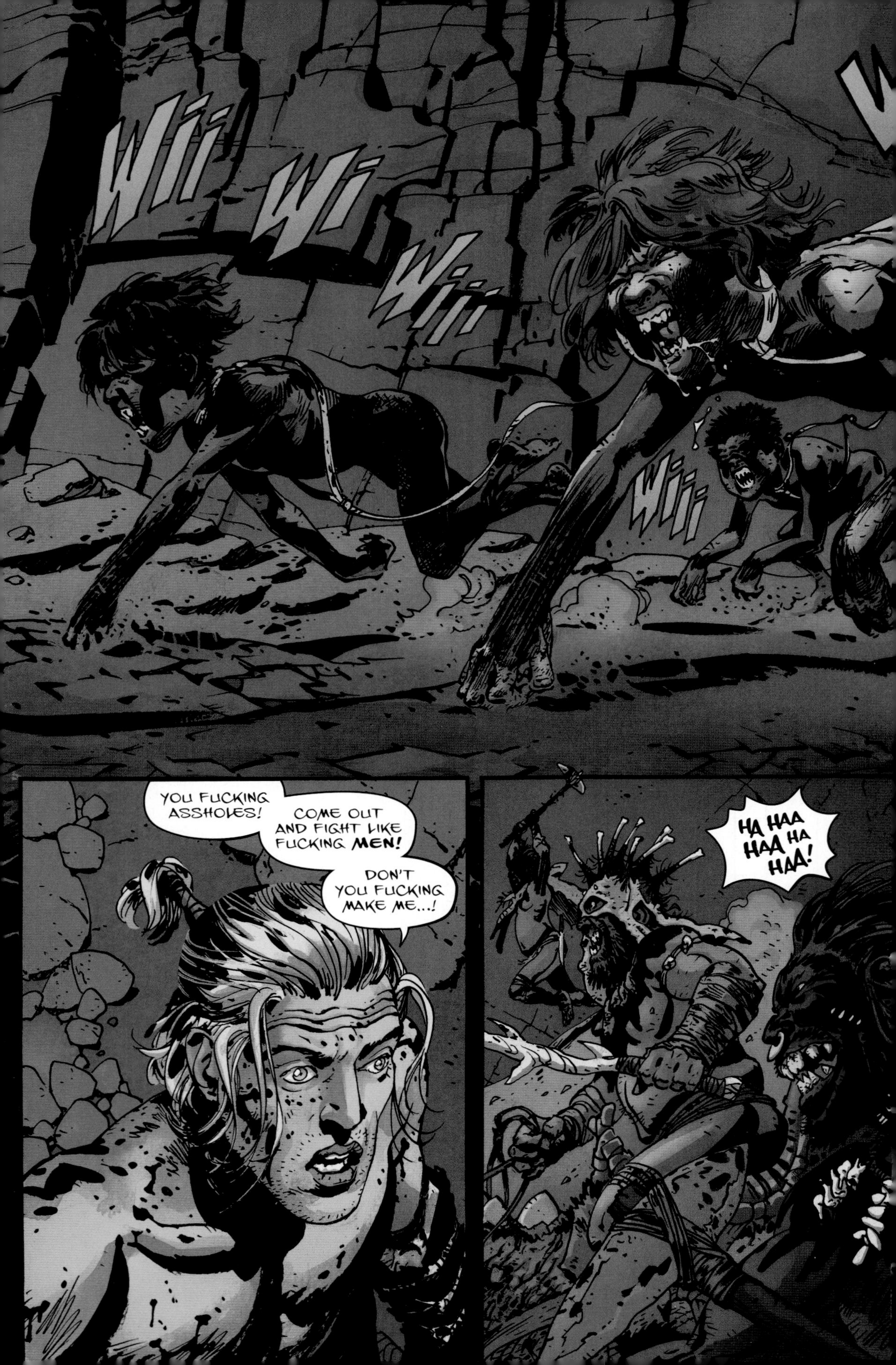

WIII
WI
WIII
WIII
YOU FUCKING ASSHOLES!
COME OUT AND FIGHT LIKE FUCKING MEN!
DON'T YOU FUCKING MAKE ME...!
HA HAA HAA HA HAA!

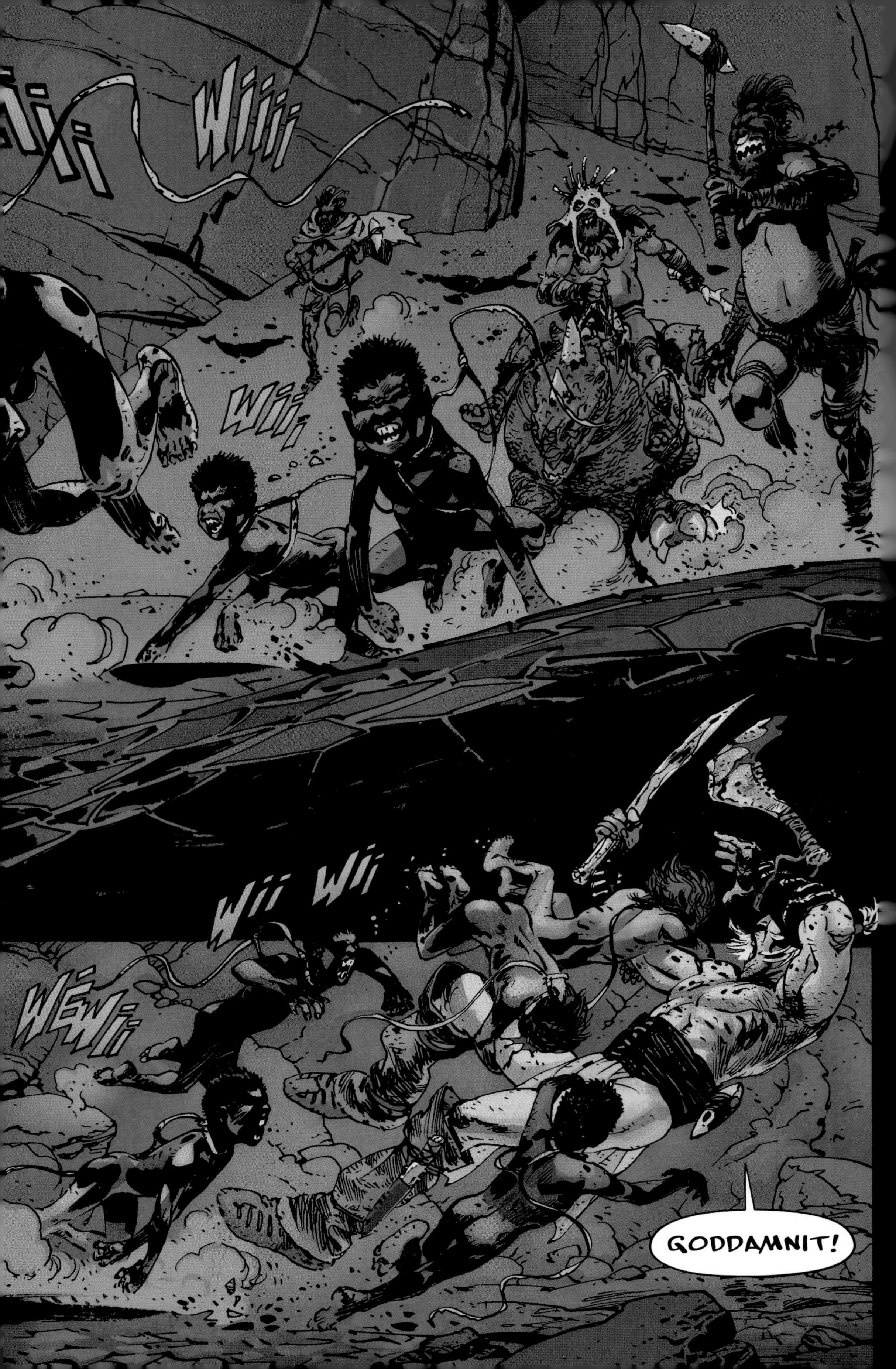
WIII
WII
WII WII
WEWII
GODDAMNIT!

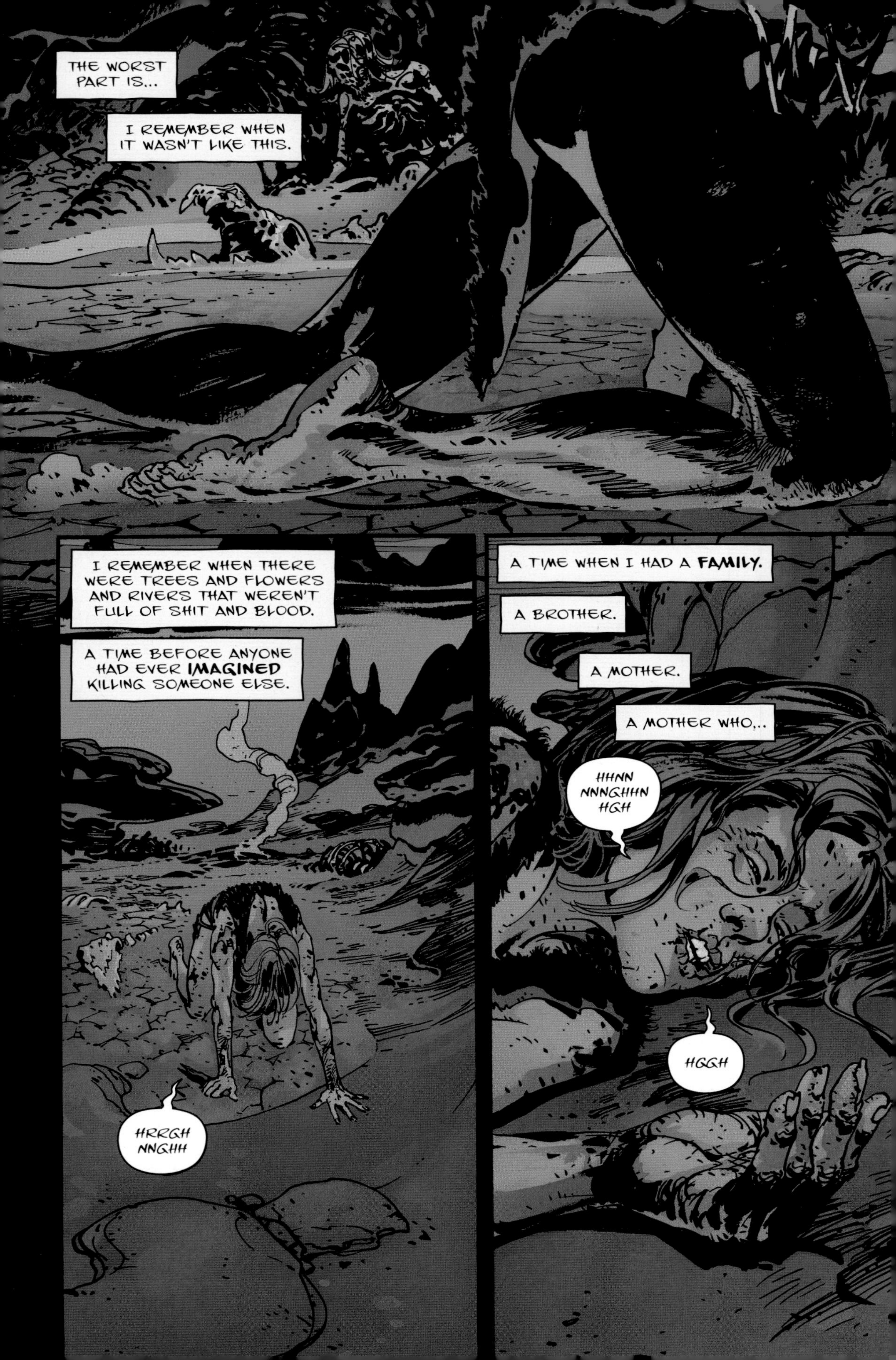
THE WORST PART IS...
I REMEMBER WHEN IT WASN'T LIKE THIS.
I REMEMBER WHEN THERE WERE TREES AND FLOWERS AND RIVERS THAT WEREN'T FULL OF SHIT AND BLOOD.
A TIME BEFORE ANYONE HAD EVER **IMAGINED** KILLING SOMEONE ELSE.
HRRGH NNGHH
A TIME WHEN I HAD A **FAMILY.**
A BROTHER.
A MOTHER.
A MOTHER WHO...
HHNN NNNGHHN HGH
HGGH

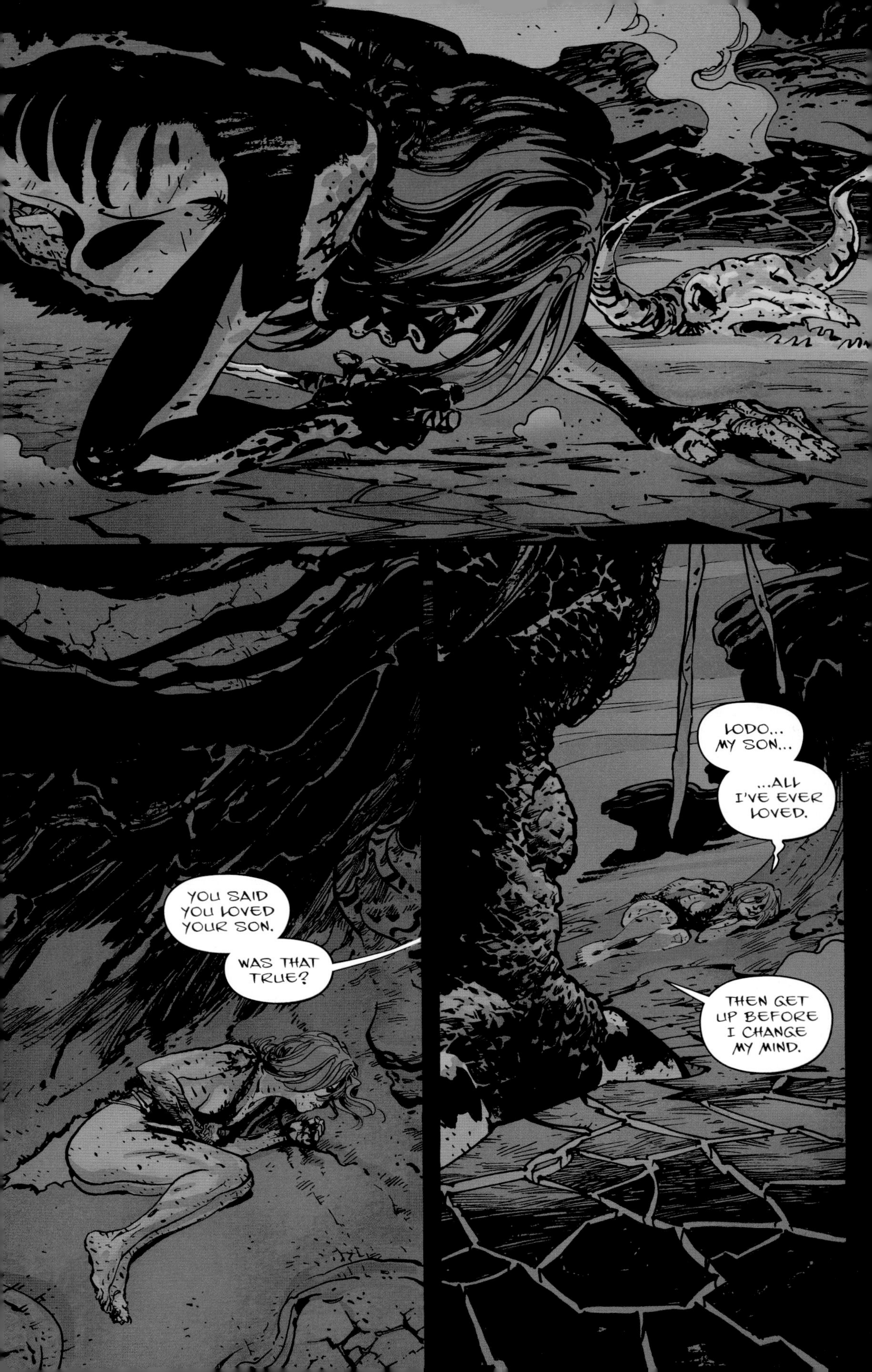
LODO... MY SON...
...ALL I'VE EVER LOVED.
YOU SAID YOU LOVED YOUR SON.
WAS THAT TRUE?
THEN GET UP BEFORE I CHANGE MY MIND.

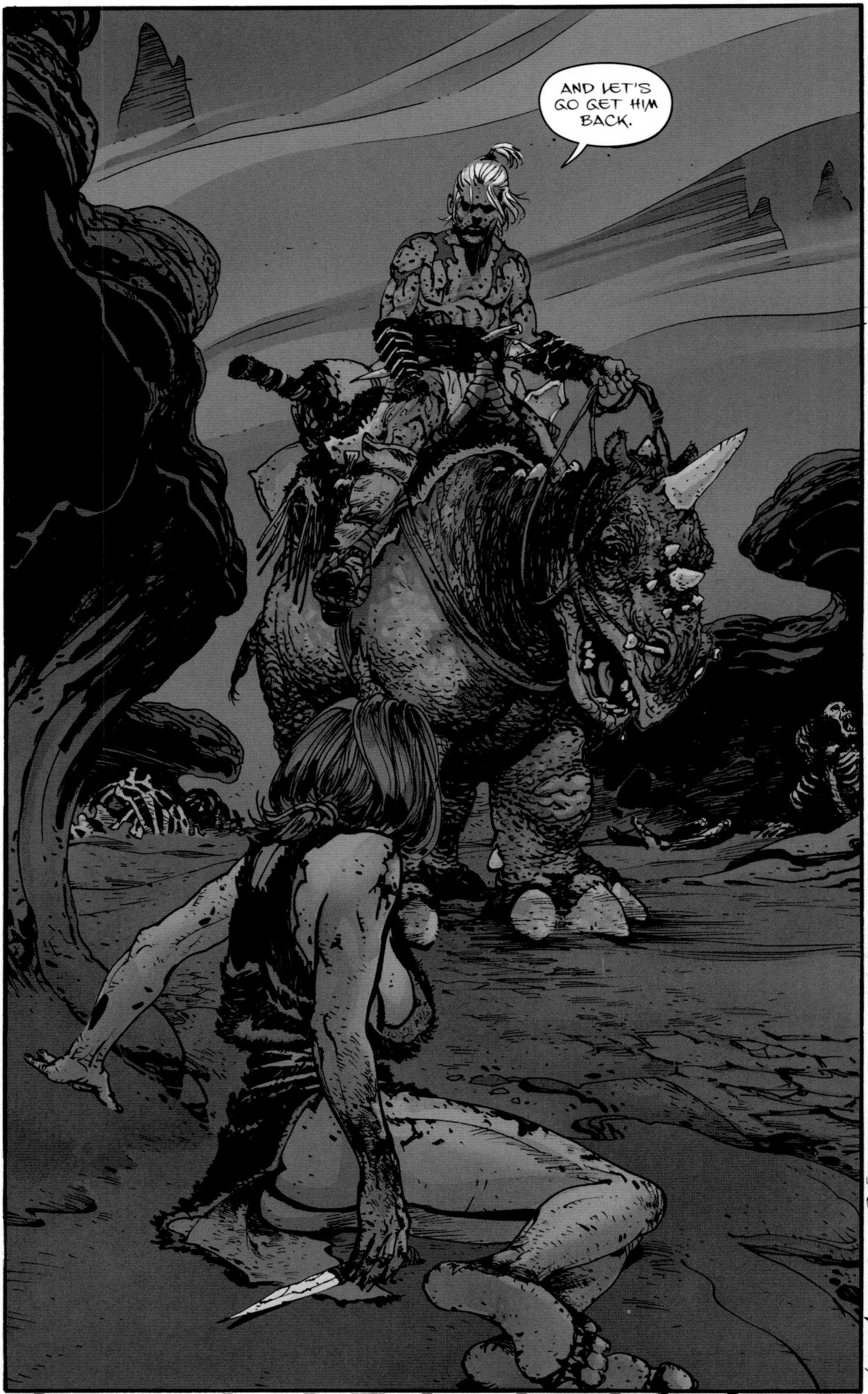
AND LET'S GO GET HIM BACK.

chapter three

The Children of Eden

AND GOD BLESSED THEM,
AND GOD SAID UNTO THEM,
BE FRUITFUL, AND MULTIPLY,
AND REPLENISH THE EARTH,
AND SUBDUE IT.

GENESIS 1:28

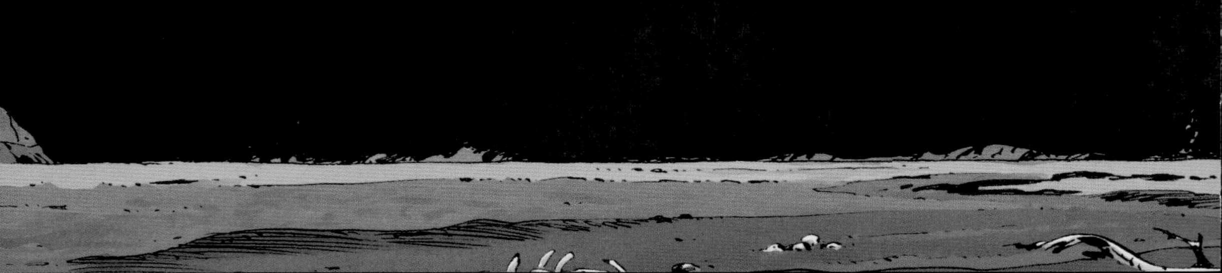

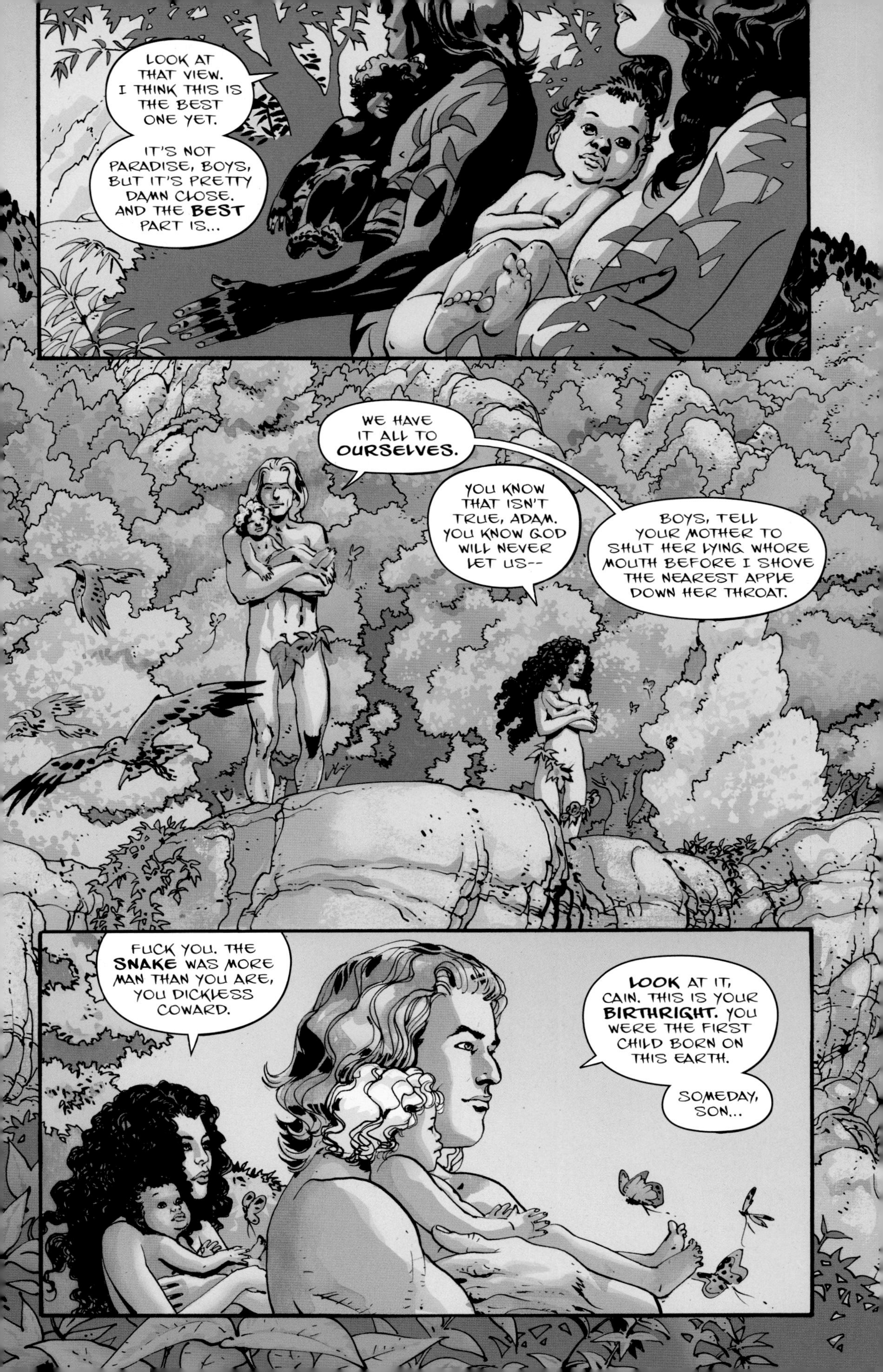
LOOK AT THAT VIEW. I THINK THIS IS THE BEST ONE YET.
IT'S NOT PARADISE, BOYS, BUT IT'S PRETTY DAMN CLOSE. AND THE **BEST** PART IS...
WE HAVE IT ALL TO **OURSELVES.**
YOU KNOW THAT ISN'T TRUE, ADAM. YOU KNOW GOD WILL NEVER LET US--
BOYS, TELL YOUR MOTHER TO SHUT HER LYING WHORE MOUTH BEFORE I SHOVE THE NEAREST APPLE DOWN HER THROAT.
FUCK YOU. THE **SNAKE** WAS MORE MAN THAN YOU ARE, YOU DICKLESS COWARD.
LOOK AT IT, CAIN. THIS IS YOUR **BIRTHRIGHT.** YOU WERE THE FIRST CHILD BORN ON THIS EARTH.
SOMEDAY, SON...

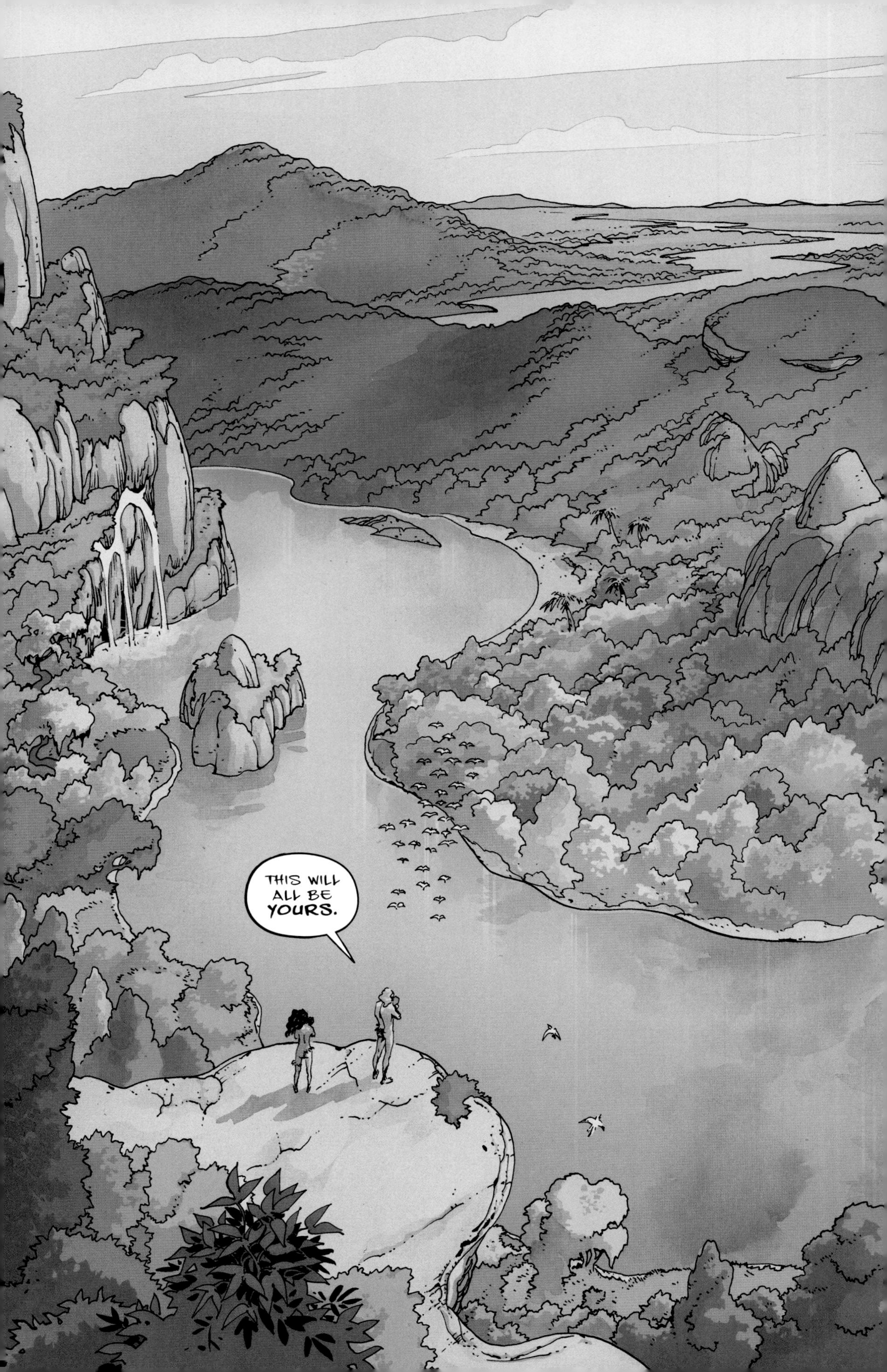
THIS WILL ALL BE YOURS.

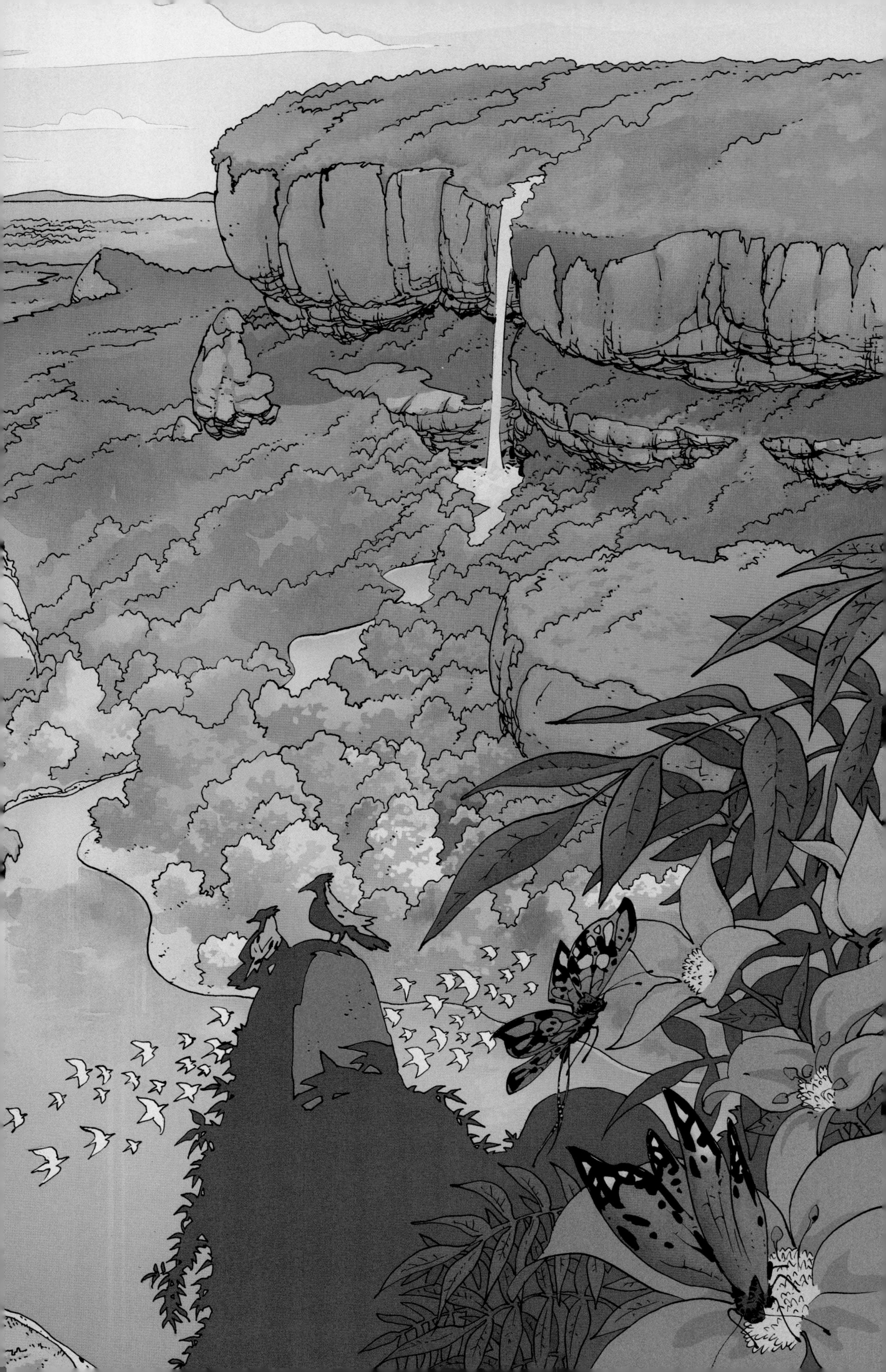

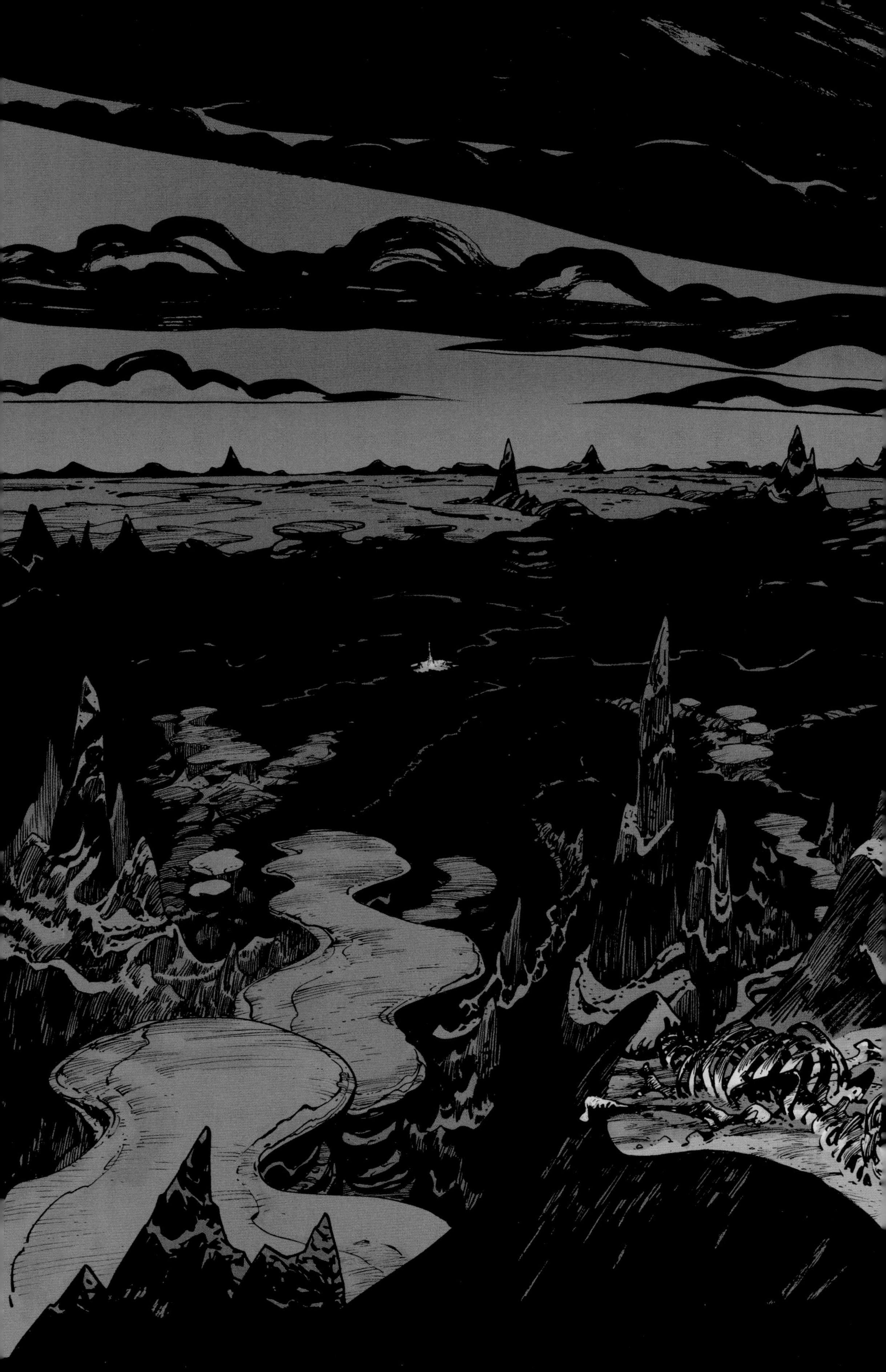

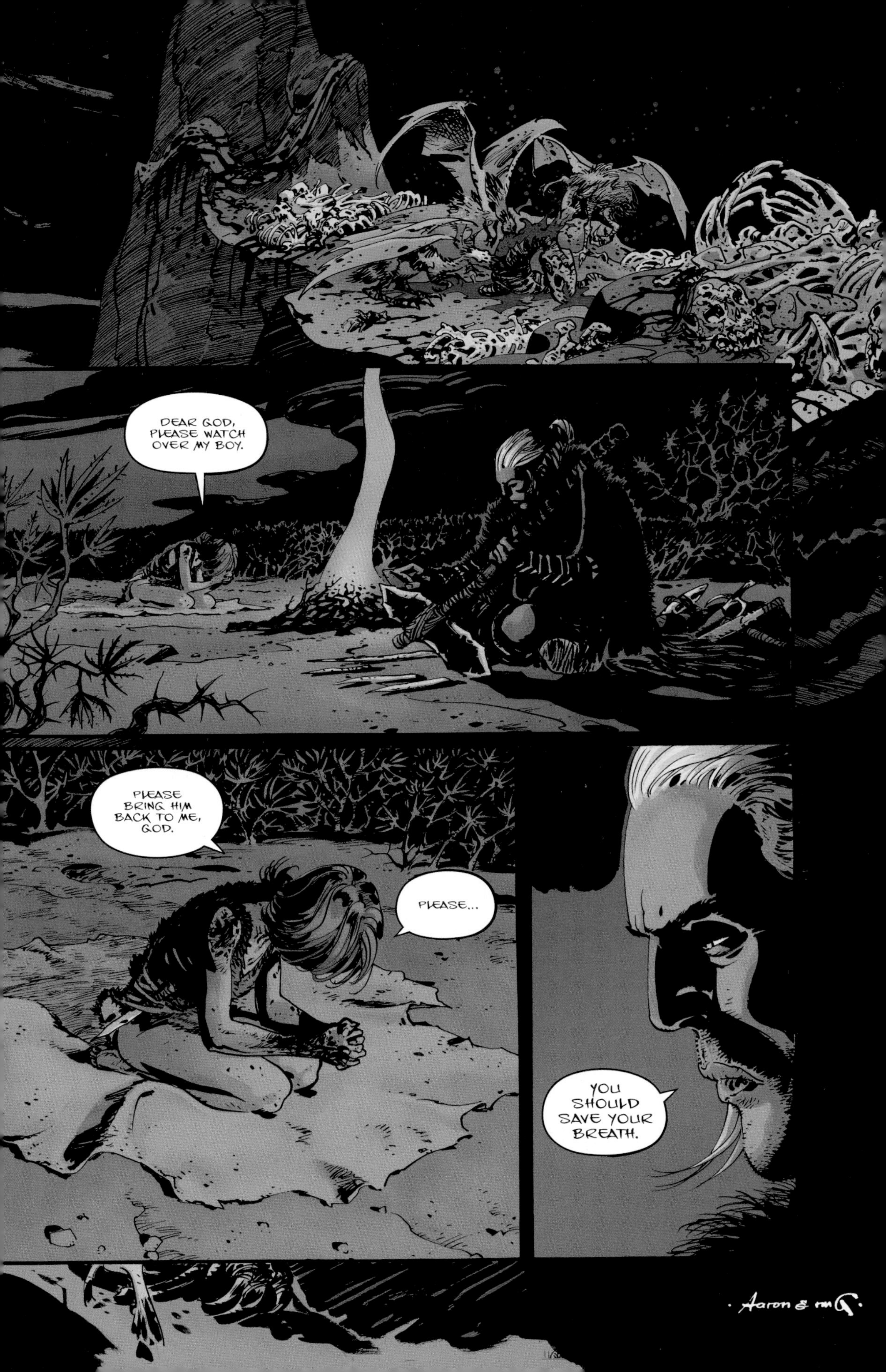
DEAR GOD, PLEASE WATCH OVER MY BOY.
PLEASE BRING HIM BACK TO ME, GOD.
PLEASE...
YOU SHOULD SAVE YOUR BREATH.
Aaron & rmG

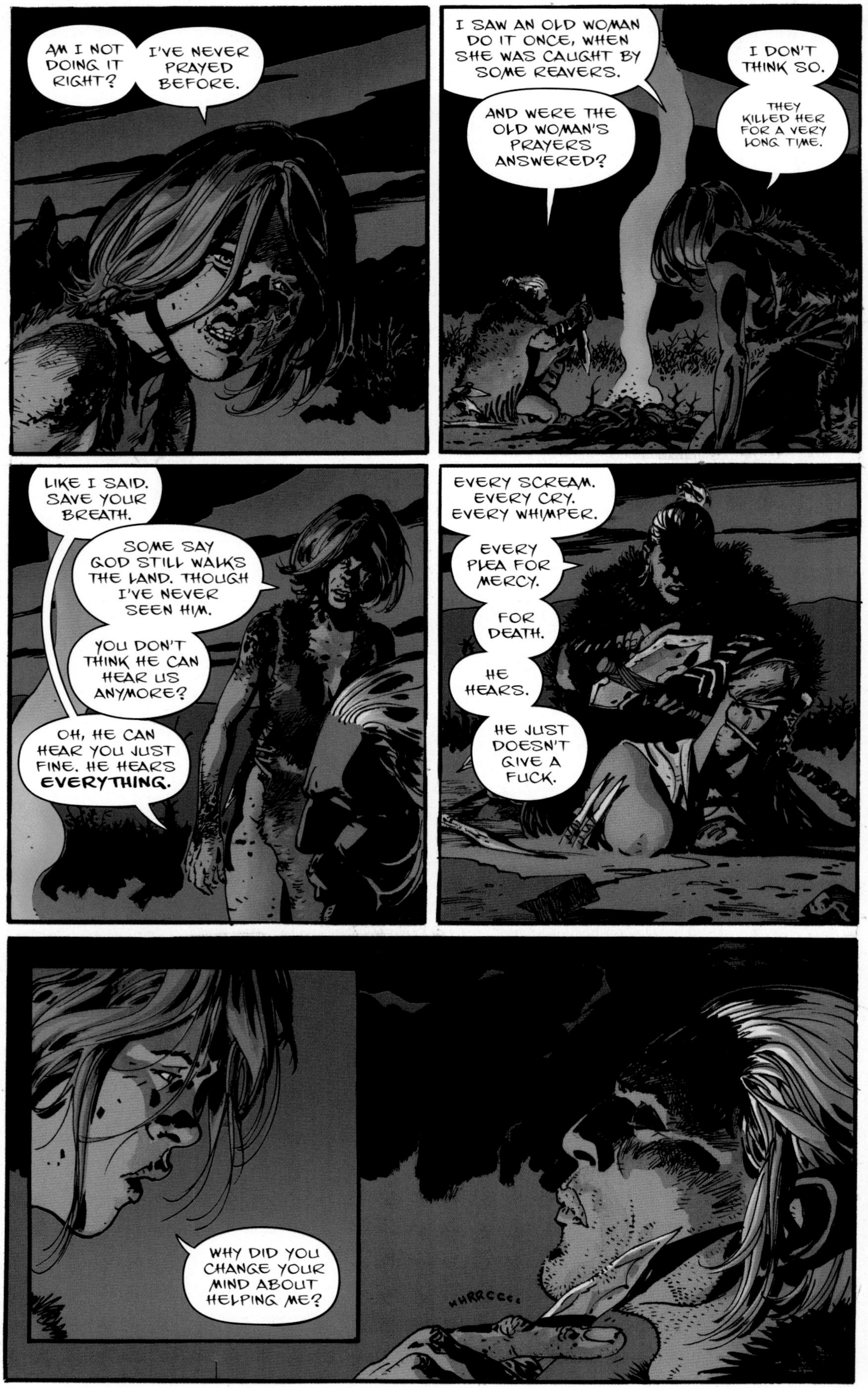

AM I NOT DOING IT RIGHT?
I'VE NEVER PRAYED BEFORE.
I SAW AN OLD WOMAN DO IT ONCE, WHEN SHE WAS CAUGHT BY SOME REAVERS.
AND WERE THE OLD WOMAN'S PRAYERS ANSWERED?
I DON'T THINK SO.
THEY KILLED HER FOR A VERY LONG TIME.
LIKE I SAID. SAVE YOUR BREATH.
SOME SAY GOD STILL WALKS THE LAND. THOUGH I'VE NEVER SEEN HIM.
YOU DON'T THINK HE CAN HEAR US ANYMORE?
OH, HE CAN HEAR YOU JUST FINE. HE HEARS **EVERYTHING.**
EVERY SCREAM. EVERY CRY. EVERY WHIMPER.
EVERY PLEA FOR MERCY.
FOR DEATH.
HE HEARS.
HE JUST DOESN'T GIVE A FUCK.
WHY DID YOU CHANGE YOUR MIND ABOUT HELPING ME?
WHRRCCCc

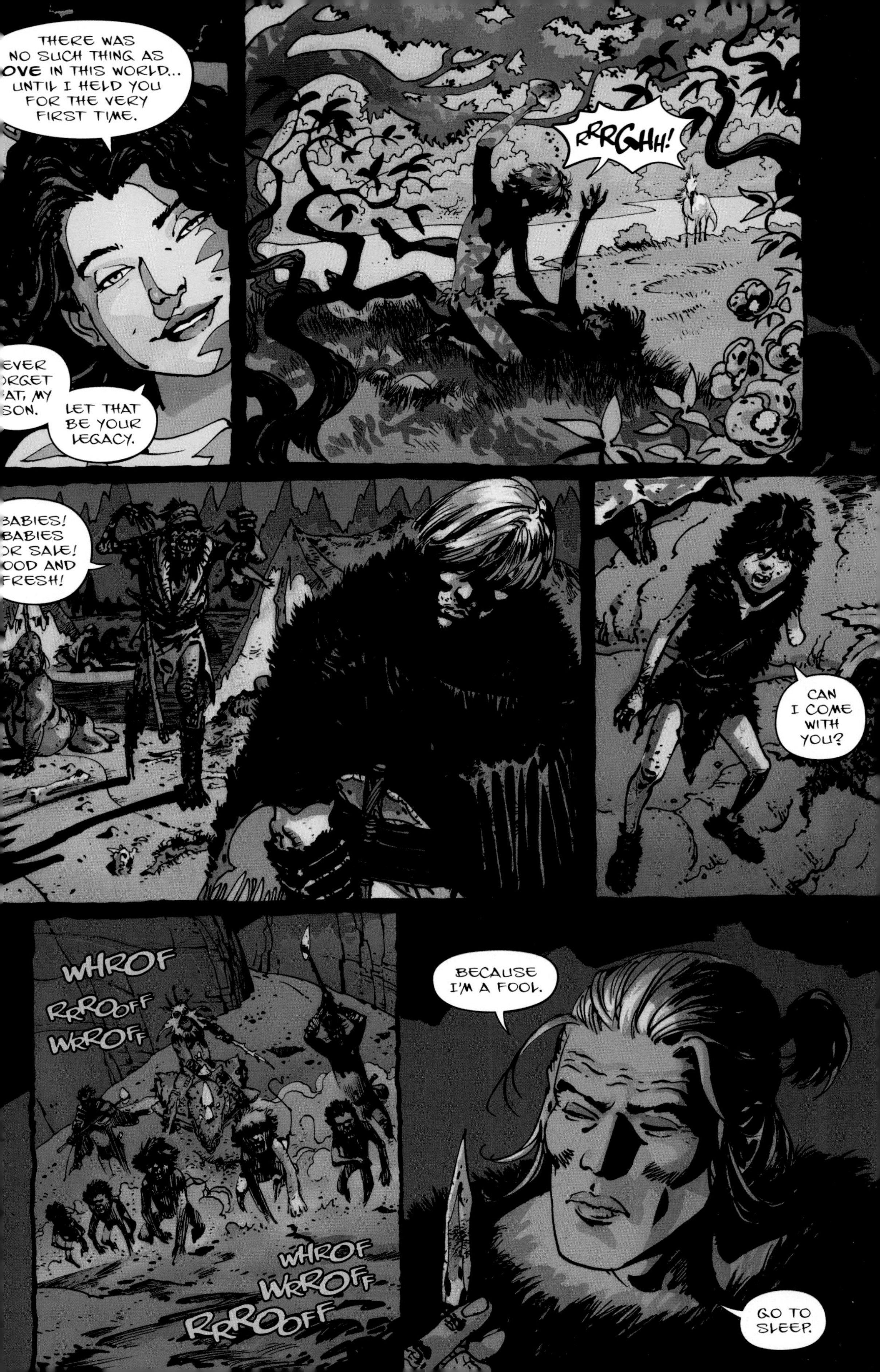
THERE WAS NO SUCH THING AS LOVE IN THIS WORLD... UNTIL I HELD YOU FOR THE VERY FIRST TIME.
EVER ORGET AT, MY SON.
LET THAT BE YOUR LEGACY.
RRRGHH!
BABIES! BABIES OR SALE! OOD AND FRESH!
CAN I COME WITH YOU?
WHROF
RRROOFF
WRROFF
WHROF
WRROFF
RRROOFF
BECAUSE I'M A FOOL.
GO TO SLEEP.

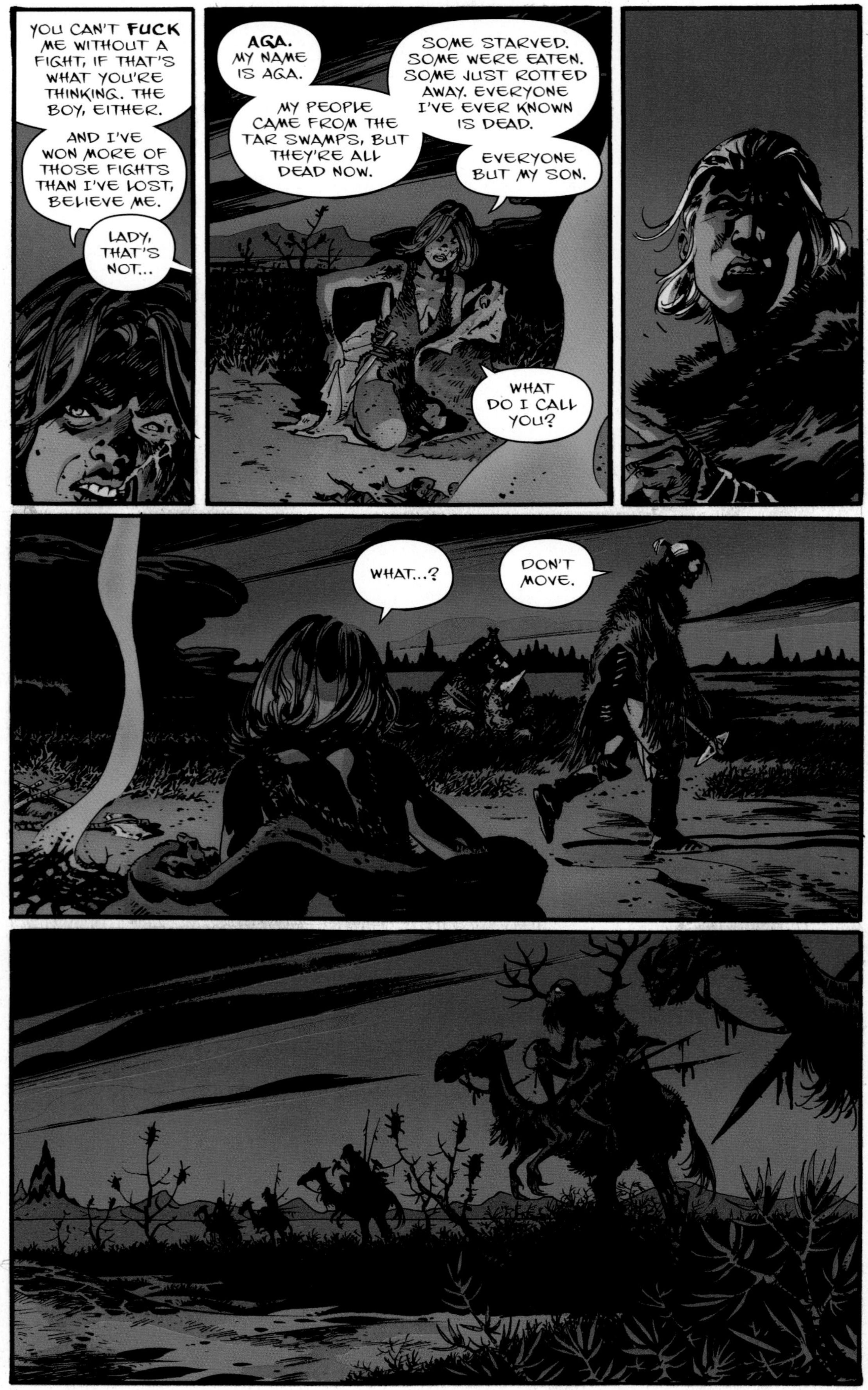
YOU CAN'T FUCK ME WITHOUT A FIGHT, IF THAT'S WHAT YOU'RE THINKING. THE BOY, EITHER.
AND I'VE WON MORE OF THOSE FIGHTS THAN I'VE LOST, BELIEVE ME.
LADY, THAT'S NOT...
AGA. MY NAME IS AGA.
MY PEOPLE CAME FROM THE TAR SWAMPS, BUT THEY'RE ALL DEAD NOW.
SOME STARVED. SOME WERE EATEN. SOME JUST ROTTED AWAY. EVERYONE I'VE EVER KNOWN IS DEAD.
EVERYONE BUT MY SON.
WHAT DO I CALL YOU?
WHAT...?
DON'T MOVE.

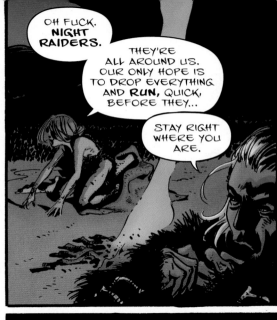

OH FUCK. **NIGHT RAIDERS.**

THEY'RE ALL AROUND US. OUR ONLY HOPE IS TO DROP EVERYTHING AND **RUN,** QUICK, BEFORE THEY...

STAY RIGHT WHERE YOU ARE.

BUT... WHAT ARE YOU...

...

HE'S **CRAZY.**

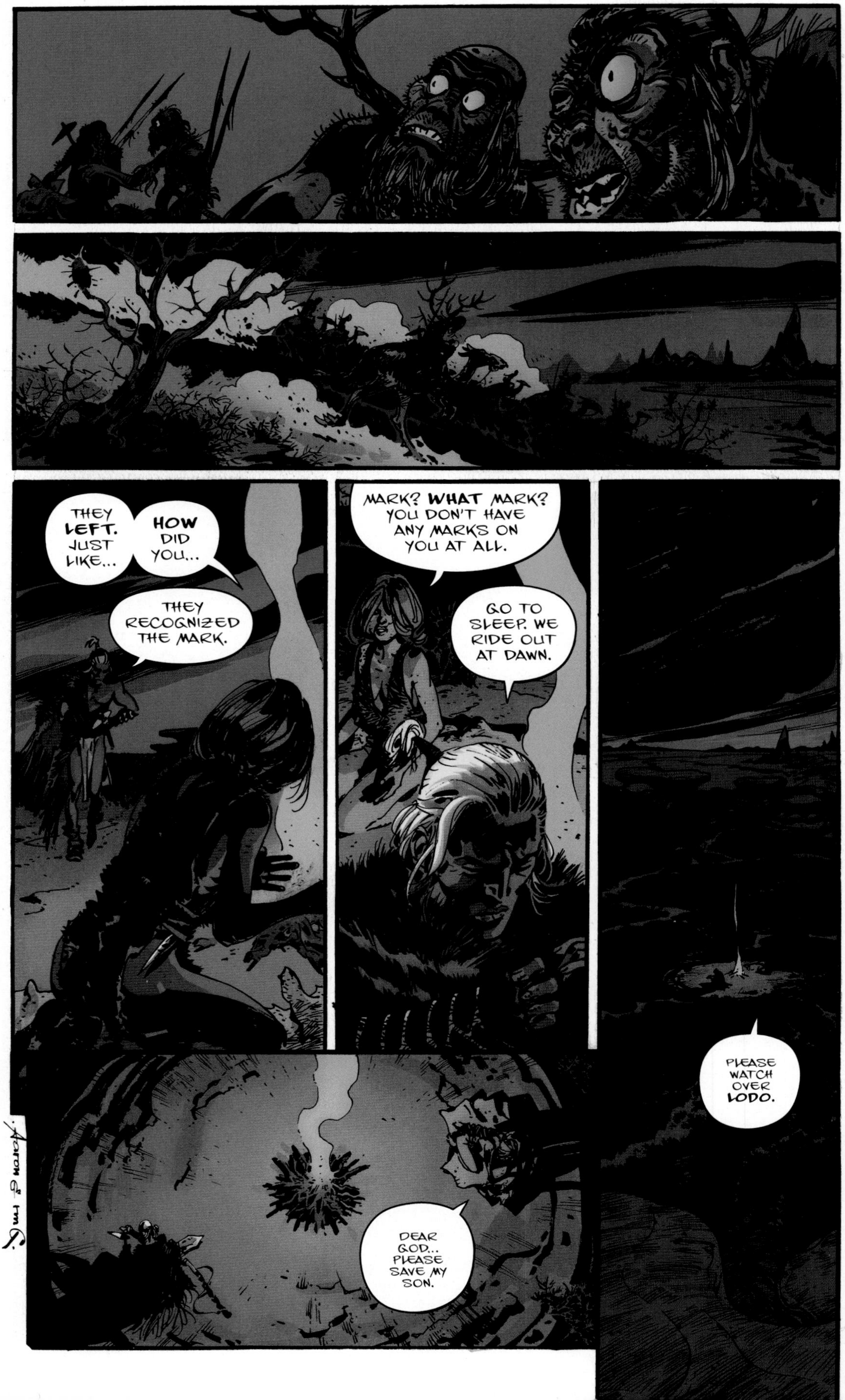
THEY LEFT. JUST LIKE...
HOW DID YOU...
THEY RECOGNIZED THE MARK.
MARK? WHAT MARK? YOU DON'T HAVE ANY MARKS ON YOU AT ALL.
GO TO SLEEP. WE RIDE OUT AT DAWN.
DEAR GOD... PLEASE SAVE MY SON.
PLEASE WATCH OVER LODO.

MY...MY NAME IS LODO.

AND I DON'T KNOW WHY I'M HERE.

HEH.

NEW BOYS ALWAYS THINK WE GIVE A SHIT WHAT THEIR FUCKING NAMES ARE. MAKES ME LAUGH EVERY TIME.

NO ONE CARES WHAT YOU USED TO BE CALLED, SHIT-FACE. YOU'RE A FEEDER NOW.

ALL NEW BOYS ARE FEEDERS.

HEH. SHOW THE LITTLE MUD-LICKER WHAT THE MEAT WAGON'S SERVING TODAY.

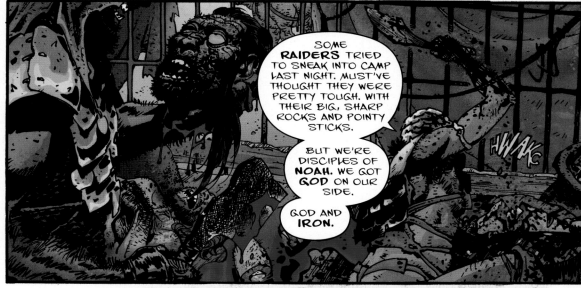

SOME RAIDERS TRIED TO SNEAK INTO CAMP LAST NIGHT. MUST'VE THOUGHT THEY WERE PRETTY TOUGH. WITH THEIR BIG, SHARP ROCKS AND POINTY STICKS.

BUT WE'RE DISCIPLES OF NOAH. WE GOT GOD ON OUR SIDE.

GOD AND IRON.

HWAKC

MAKE SURE EVERY ANIMAL GETS FED. OR TOMORROW YOU WON'T BE CARRYING THE SACK...

YOU'LL BE IN IT.

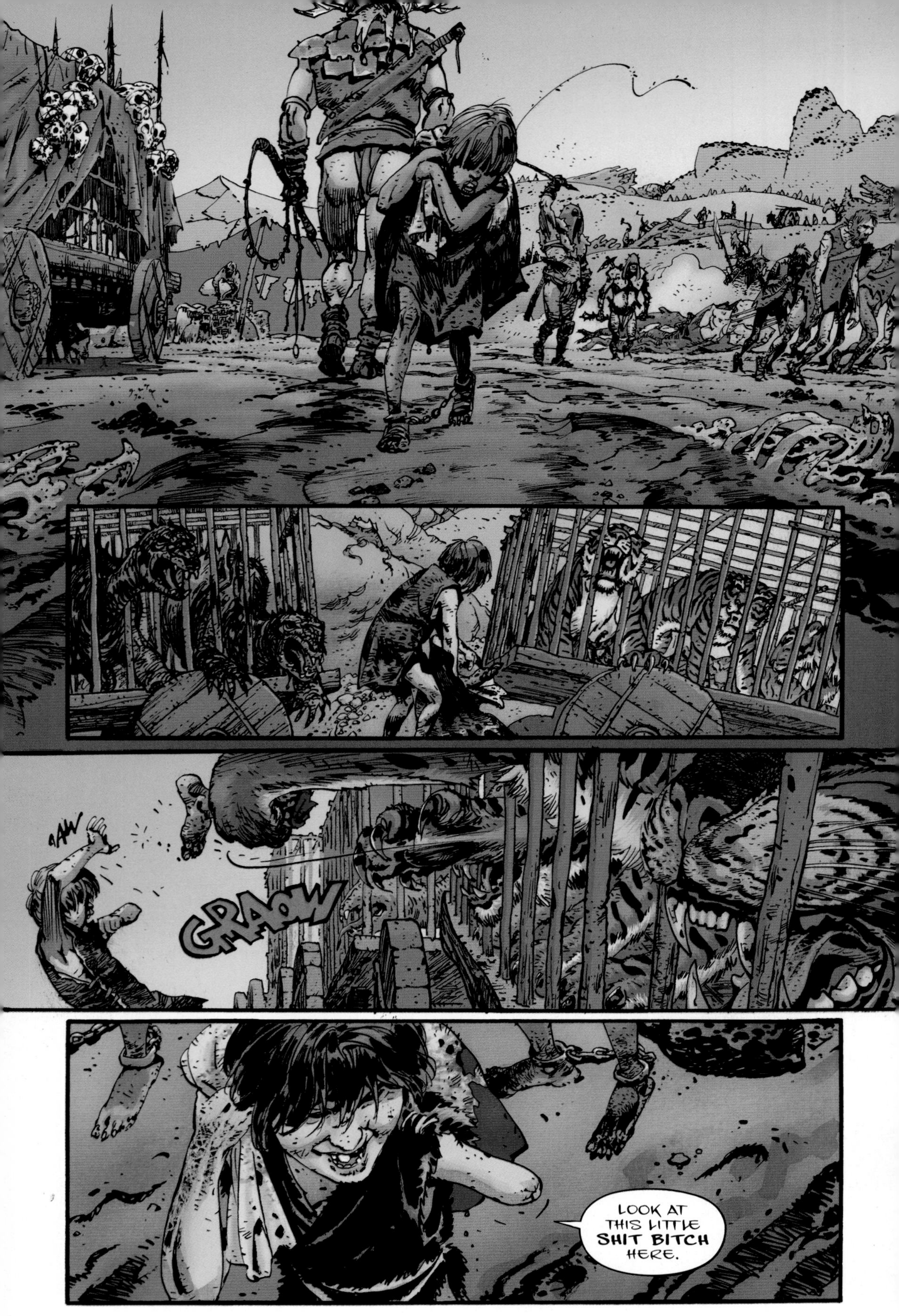
AAW
GRAOW
LOOK AT THIS LITTLE SHIT BITCH HERE.

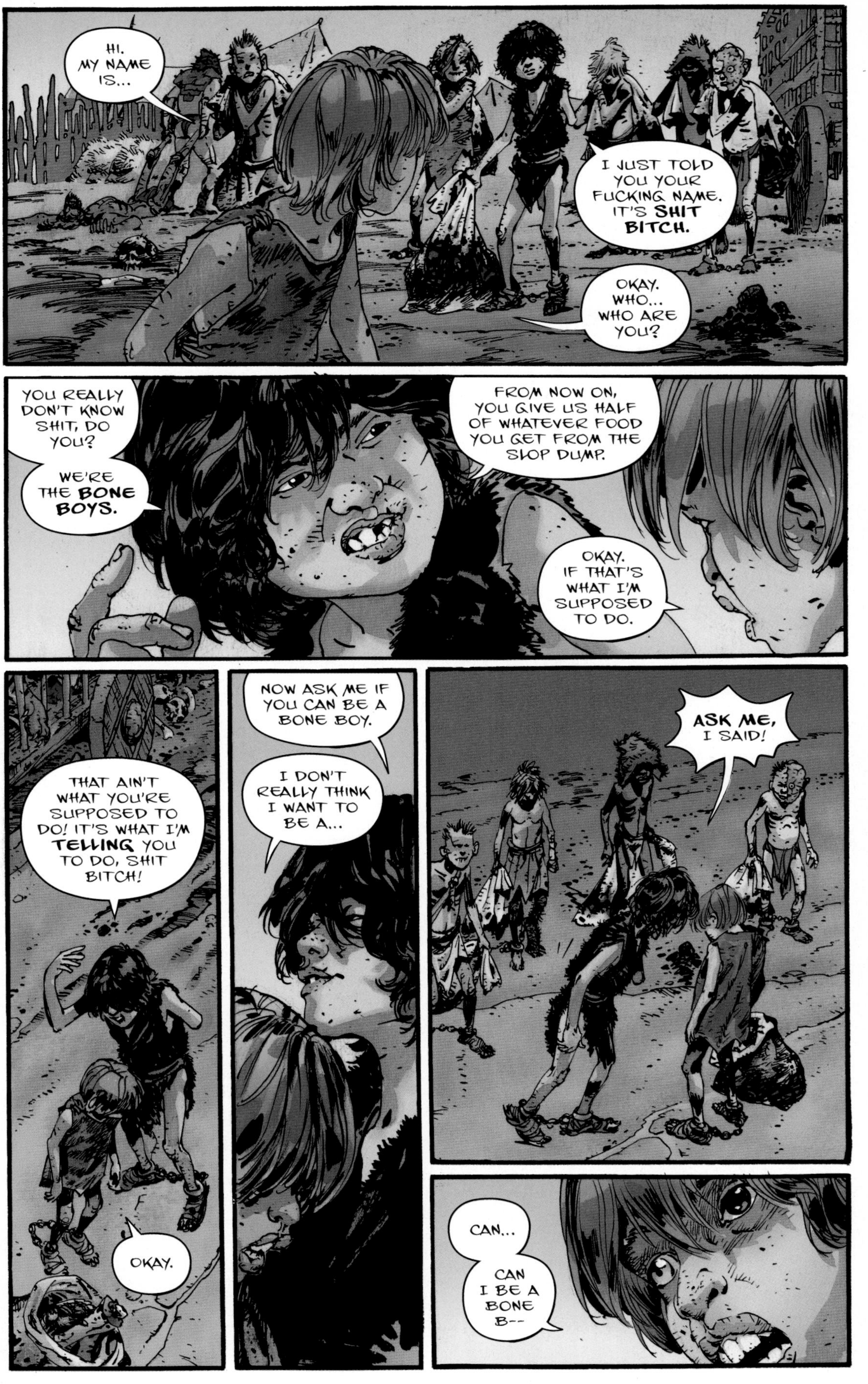
HI. MY NAME IS...
I JUST TOLD YOU YOUR FUCKING NAME. IT'S SHIT BITCH.
OKAY. WHO... WHO ARE YOU?
YOU REALLY DON'T KNOW SHIT, DO YOU?
WE'RE THE BONE BOYS.
FROM NOW ON, YOU GIVE US HALF OF WHATEVER FOOD YOU GET FROM THE SLOP DUMP.
OKAY. IF THAT'S WHAT I'M SUPPOSED TO DO.
THAT AIN'T WHAT YOU'RE SUPPOSED TO DO! IT'S WHAT I'M TELLING YOU TO DO, SHIT BITCH!
OKAY.
NOW ASK ME IF YOU CAN BE A BONE BOY.
I DON'T REALLY THINK I WANT TO BE A...
ASK ME, I SAID!
CAN...
CAN I BE A BONE B--

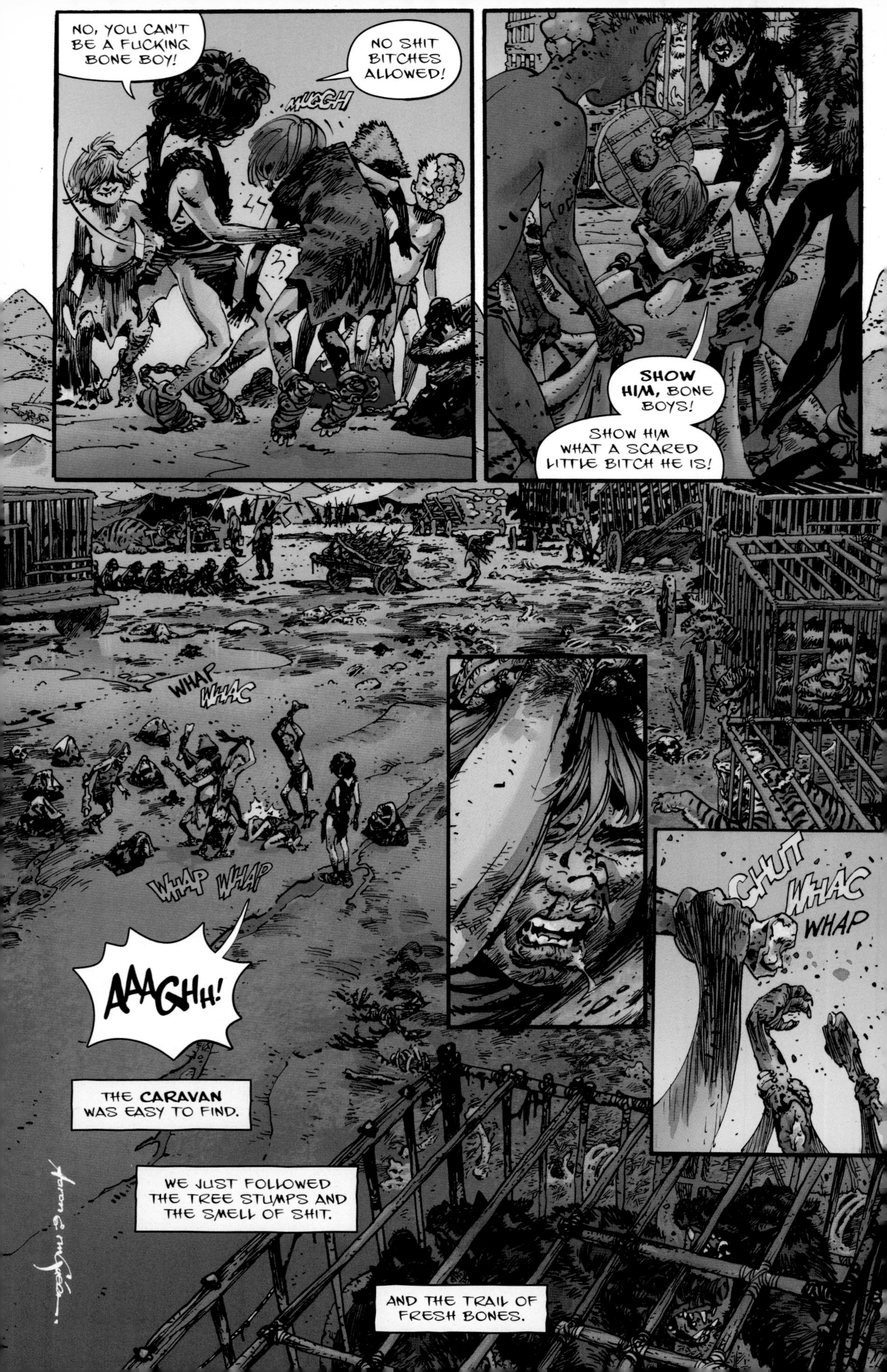
NO, YOU CAN'T BE A FUCKING BONE BOY!
NO SHIT BITCHES ALLOWED!
MMUGH
SHOW HIM, BONE BOYS!
SHOW HIM WHAT A SCARED LITTLE BITCH HE IS!
WHAP
WHAC
WHAP WHAP
AAAGHH!
CHUT
WHAC
WHAP
THE CARAVAN WAS EASY TO FIND.
WE JUST FOLLOWED THE TREE STUMPS AND THE SMELL OF SHIT.
AND THE TRAIL OF FRESH BONES.

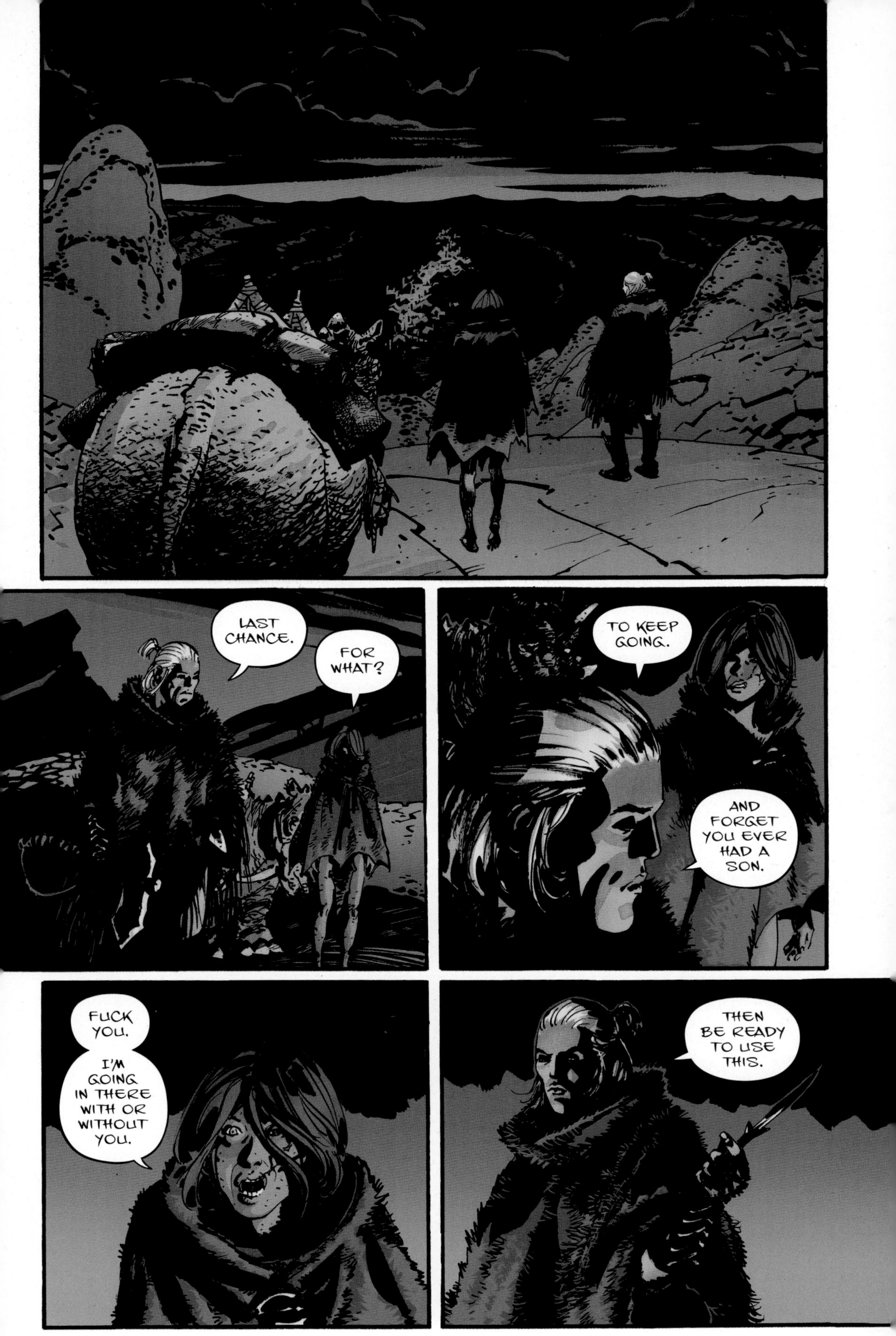
LAST CHANCE.
FOR WHAT?
TO KEEP GOING.
AND FORGET YOU EVER HAD A SON.
FUCK YOU.
I'M GOING IN THERE WITH OR WITHOUT YOU.
THEN BE READY TO USE THIS.

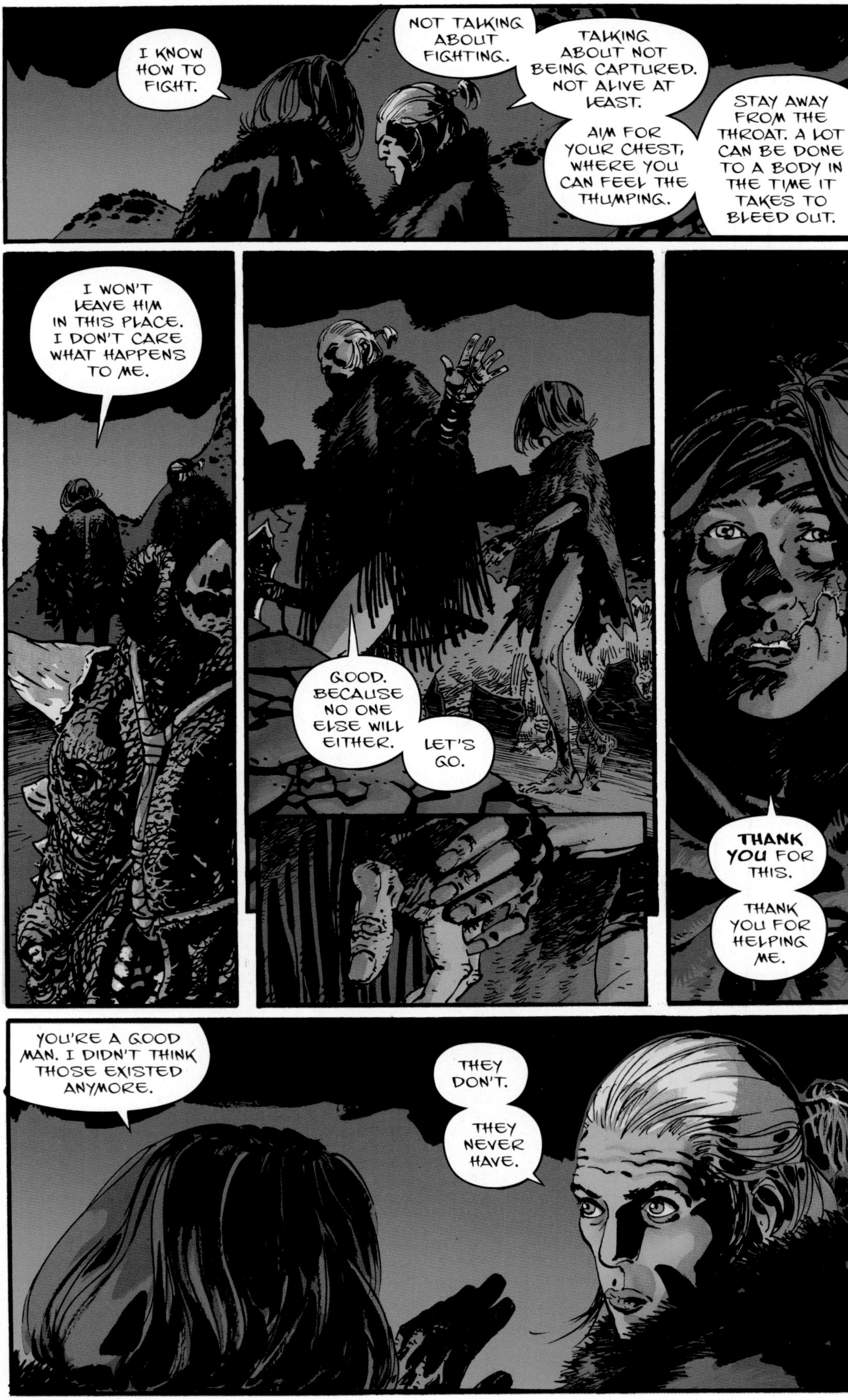
I KNOW HOW TO FIGHT.
NOT TALKING ABOUT FIGHTING.
TALKING ABOUT NOT BEING CAPTURED. NOT ALIVE AT LEAST.
AIM FOR YOUR CHEST, WHERE YOU CAN FEEL THE THUMPING.
STAY AWAY FROM THE THROAT. A LOT CAN BE DONE TO A BODY IN THE TIME IT TAKES TO BLEED OUT.
I WON'T LEAVE HIM IN THIS PLACE. I DON'T CARE WHAT HAPPENS TO ME.
GOOD. BECAUSE NO ONE ELSE WILL EITHER.
LET'S GO.
THANK YOU FOR THIS.
THANK YOU FOR HELPING ME.
YOU'RE A GOOD MAN. I DIDN'T THINK THOSE EXISTED ANYMORE.
THEY DON'T.
THEY NEVER HAVE.

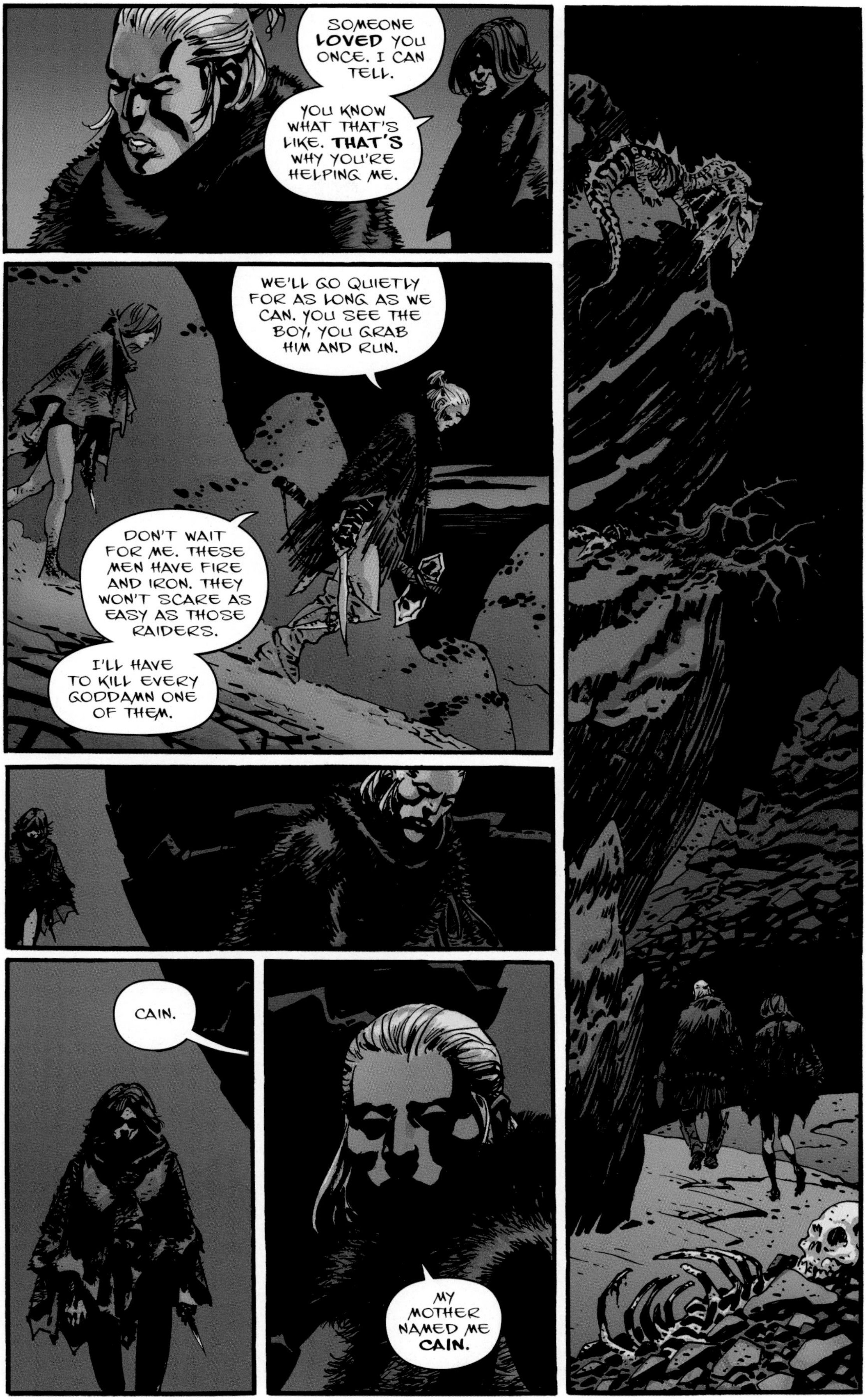
SOMEONE LOVED YOU ONCE. I CAN TELL.
YOU KNOW WHAT THAT'S LIKE. THAT'S WHY YOU'RE HELPING ME.
WE'LL GO QUIETLY FOR AS LONG AS WE CAN. YOU SEE THE BOY, YOU GRAB HIM AND RUN.
DON'T WAIT FOR ME. THESE MEN HAVE FIRE AND IRON. THEY WON'T SCARE AS EASY AS THOSE RAIDERS.
I'LL HAVE TO KILL EVERY GODDAMN ONE OF THEM.
CAIN.
MY MOTHER NAMED ME CAIN.

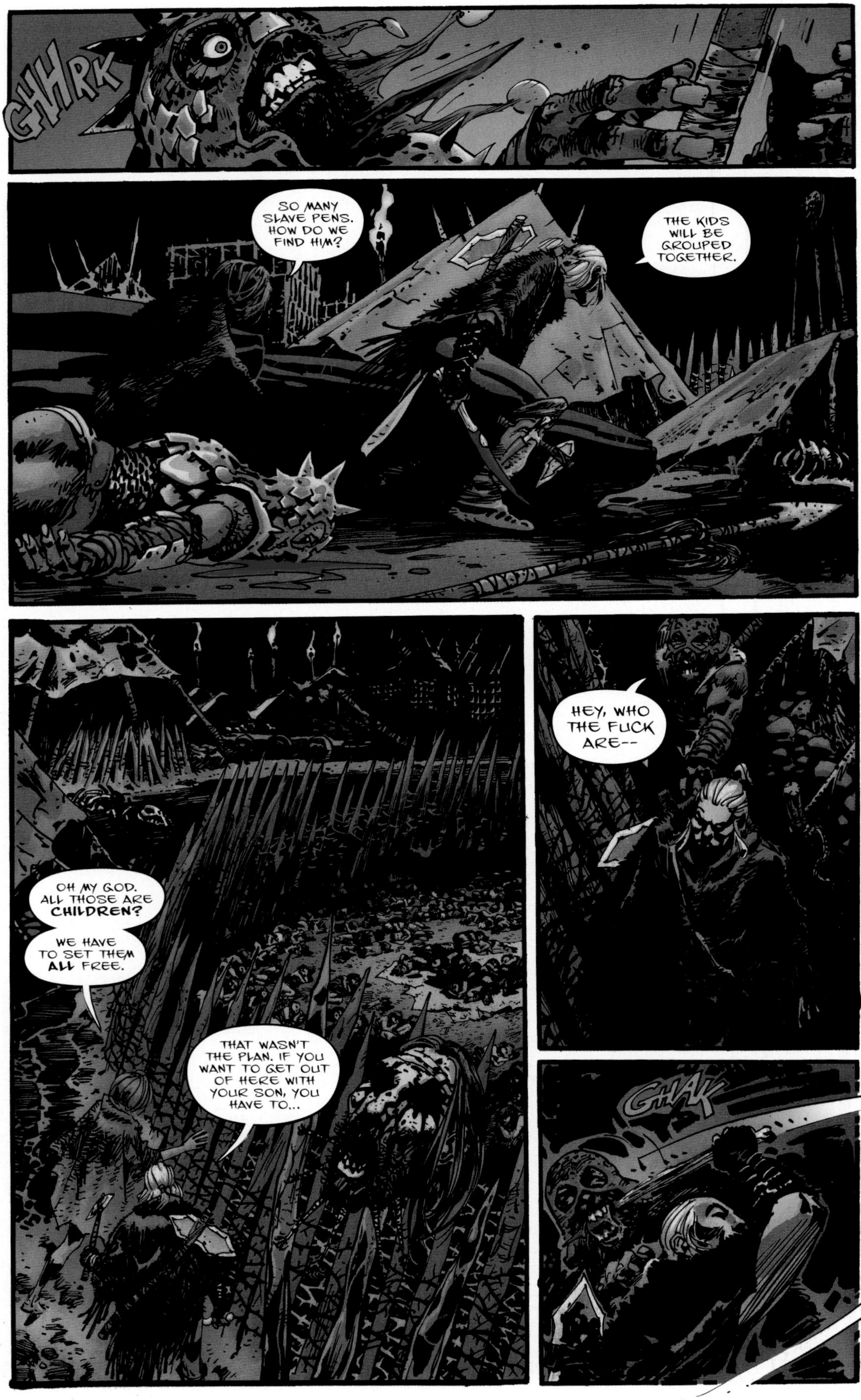
GHHRK
SO MANY SLAVE PENS. HOW DO WE FIND HIM?
THE KIDS WILL BE GROUPED TOGETHER.
OH MY GOD. ALL THOSE ARE **CHILDREN?**
WE HAVE TO SET THEM **ALL** FREE.
THAT WASN'T THE PLAN. IF YOU WANT TO GET OUT OF HERE WITH YOUR SON, YOU HAVE TO...
HEY, WHO THE FUCK ARE--
GHAK

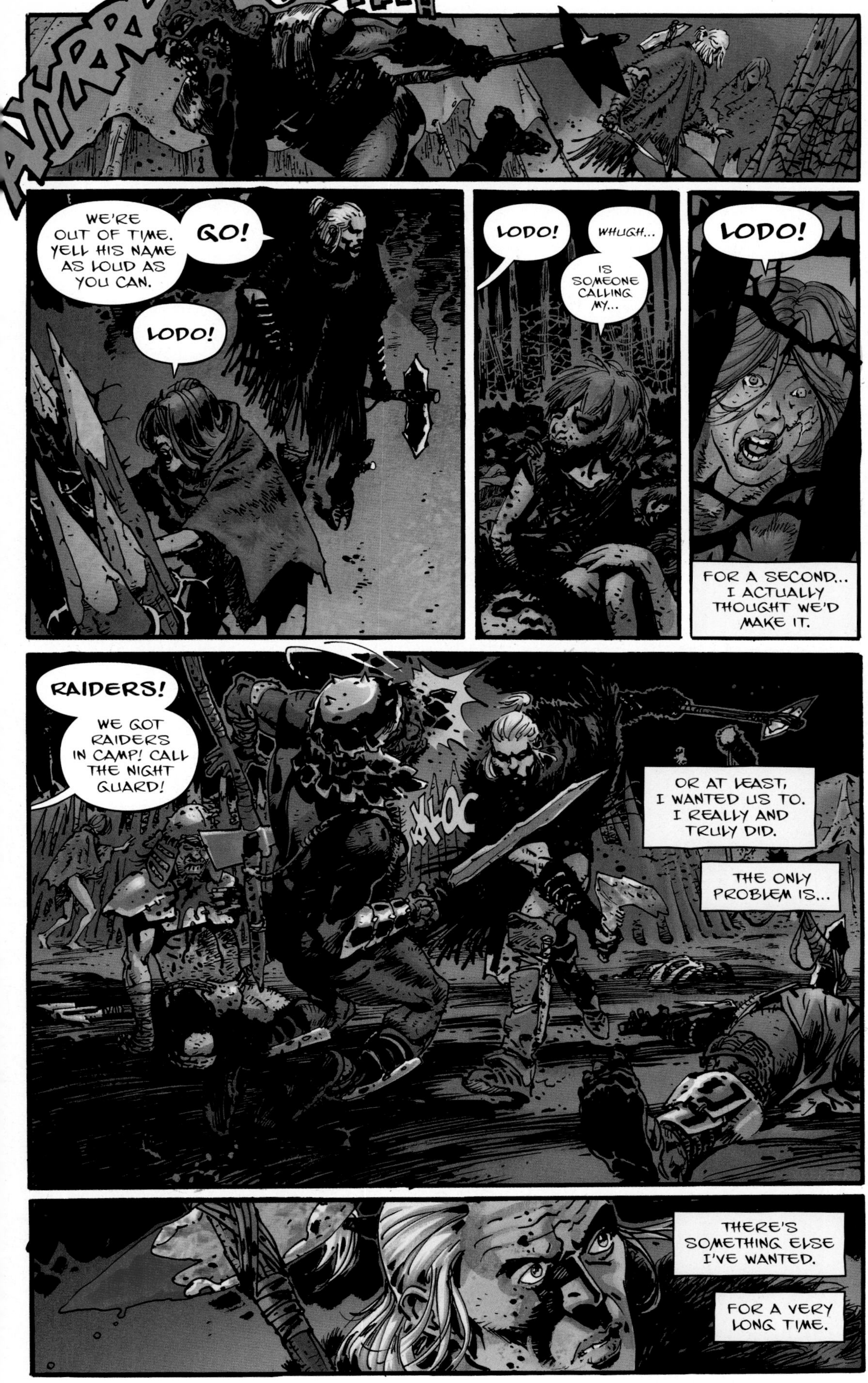
WE'RE OUT OF TIME. YELL HIS NAME AS LOUD AS YOU CAN.
GO!
LODO!
LODO!
WHUGH...
IS SOMEONE CALLING MY...
LODO!
FOR A SECOND... I ACTUALLY THOUGHT WE'D MAKE IT.
RAIDERS!
WE GOT RAIDERS IN CAMP! CALL THE NIGHT GUARD!
OR AT LEAST, I WANTED US TO. I REALLY AND TRULY DID.
THE ONLY PROBLEM IS...
THERE'S SOMETHING ELSE I'VE WANTED.
FOR A VERY LONG TIME.

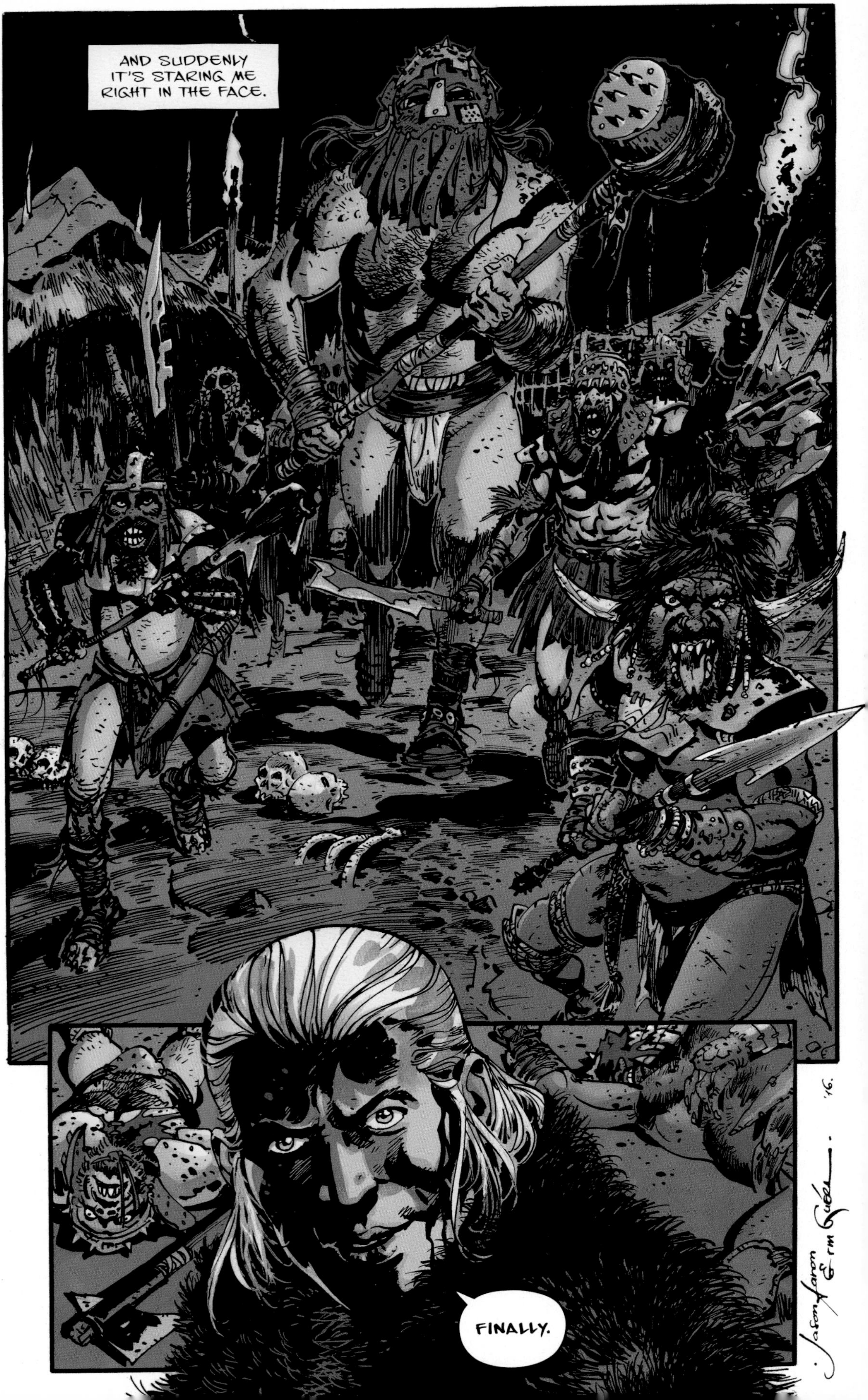
AND SUDDENLY IT'S STARING ME RIGHT IN THE FACE.
FINALLY.

chapter four

The Covenant of Noah

WOE UNTO THEM!
FOR THEY HAVE GONE
IN THE WAY OF CAIN.

JUDE 1:11

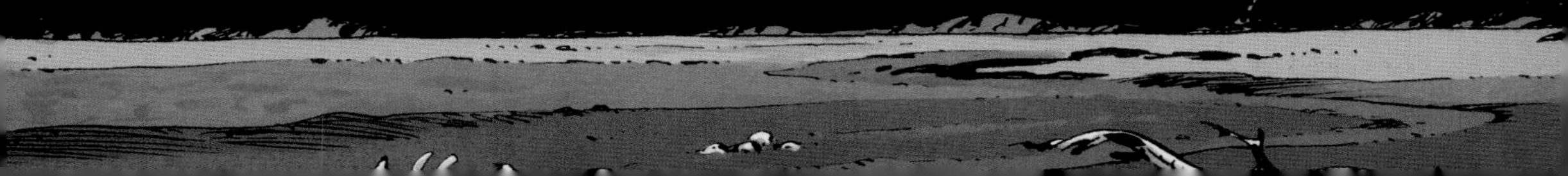

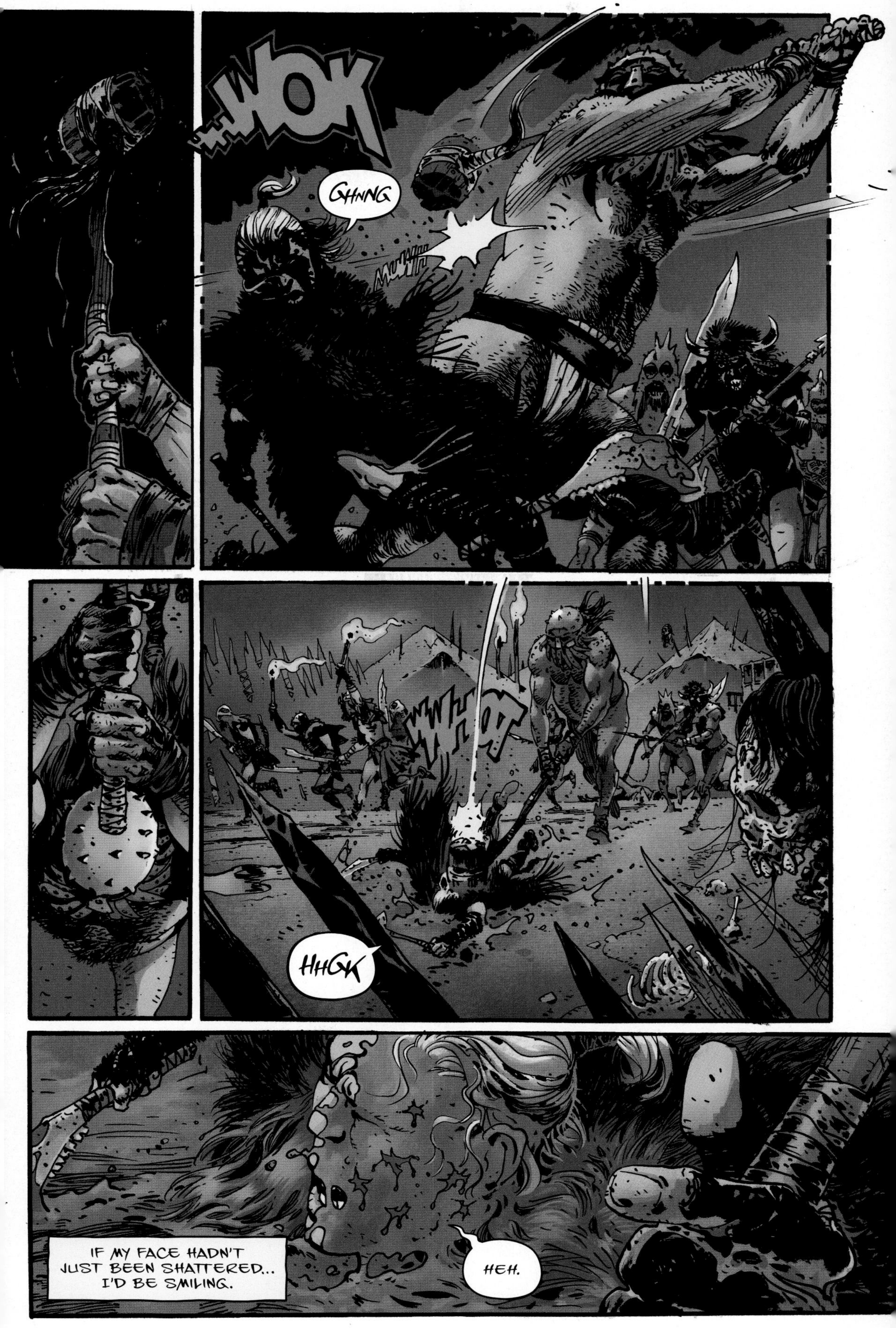
WOK
GHNNG
WWHOT
HHGK
IF MY FACE HADN'T JUST BEEN SHATTERED... I'D BE SMILING.
HEH.

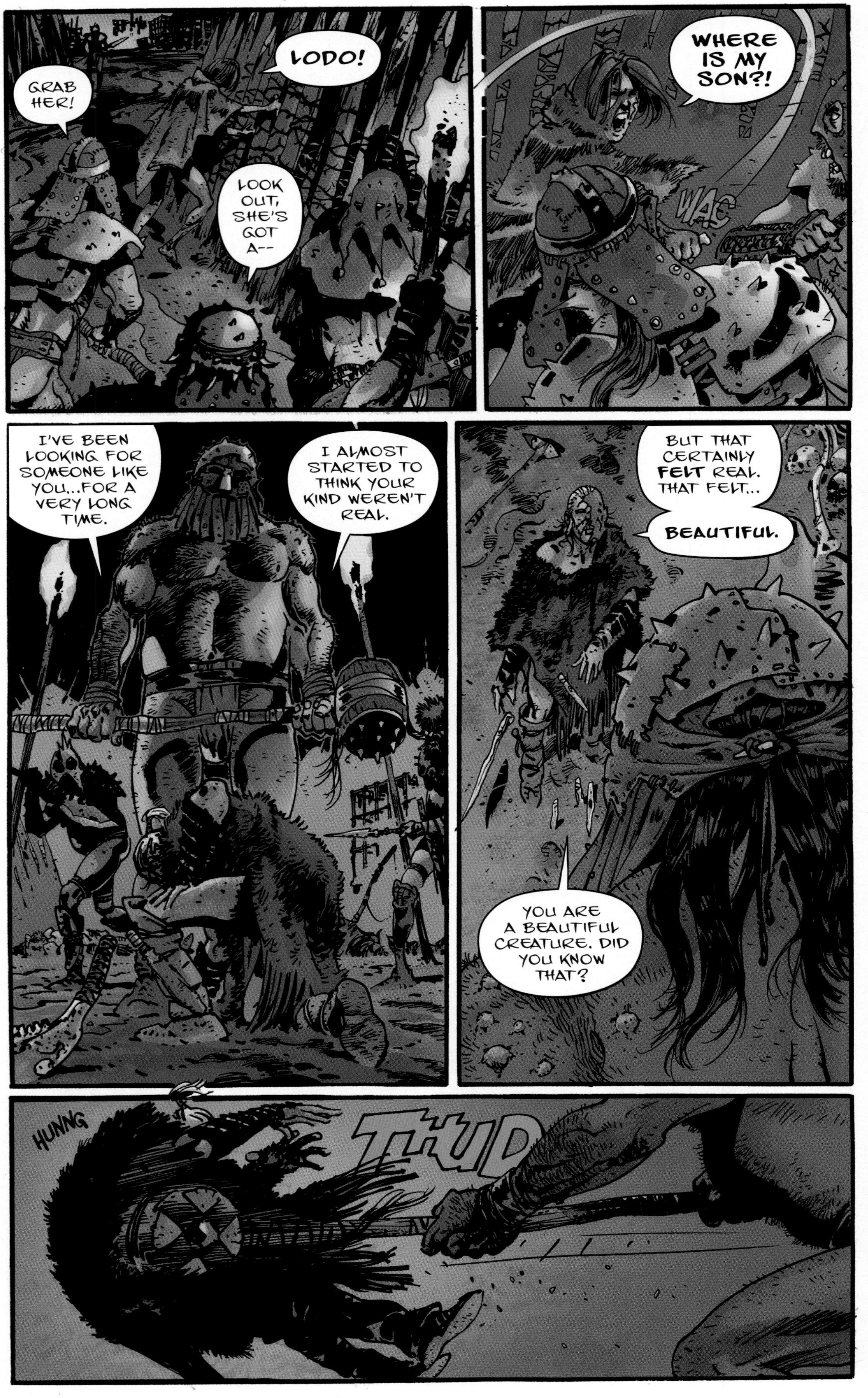
GRAB HER!
LODO!
LOOK OUT, SHE'S GOT A--
WHERE IS MY SON?!
WAC
I'VE BEEN LOOKING FOR SOMEONE LIKE YOU...FOR A VERY LONG TIME.
I ALMOST STARTED TO THINK YOUR KIND WEREN'T REAL.
BUT THAT CERTAINLY FELT REAL. THAT FELT...
BEAUTIFUL.
YOU ARE A BEAUTIFUL CREATURE. DID YOU KNOW THAT?
HUNNG
THUD

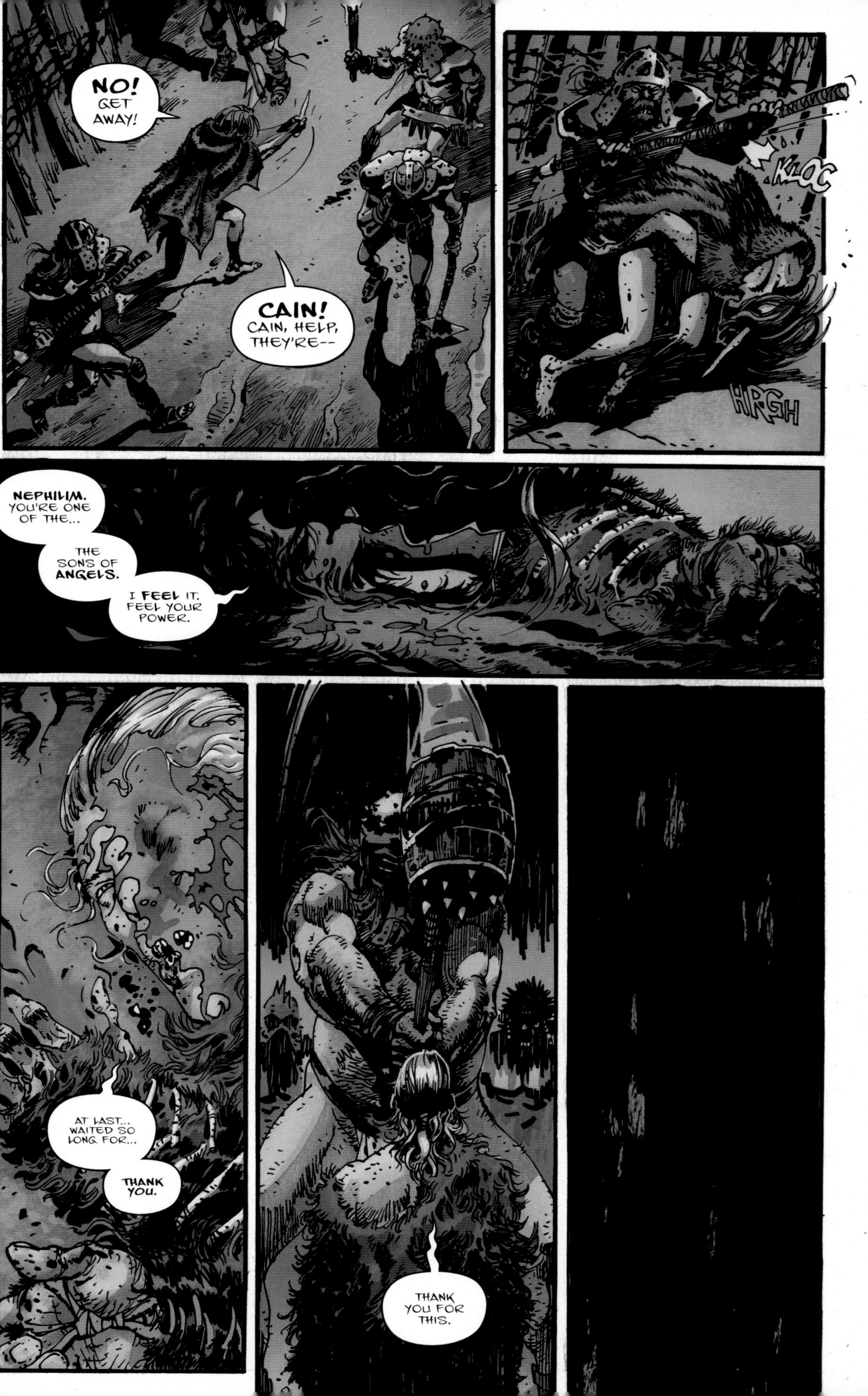
NO! GET AWAY!
CAIN! CAIN, HELP, THEY'RE--
KLOC
HRGH
NEPHILIM. YOU'RE ONE OF THE...
THE SONS OF ANGELS.
I FEEL IT. FEEL YOUR POWER.
AT LAST... WAITED SO LONG FOR...
THANK YOU.
THANK YOU FOR THIS.

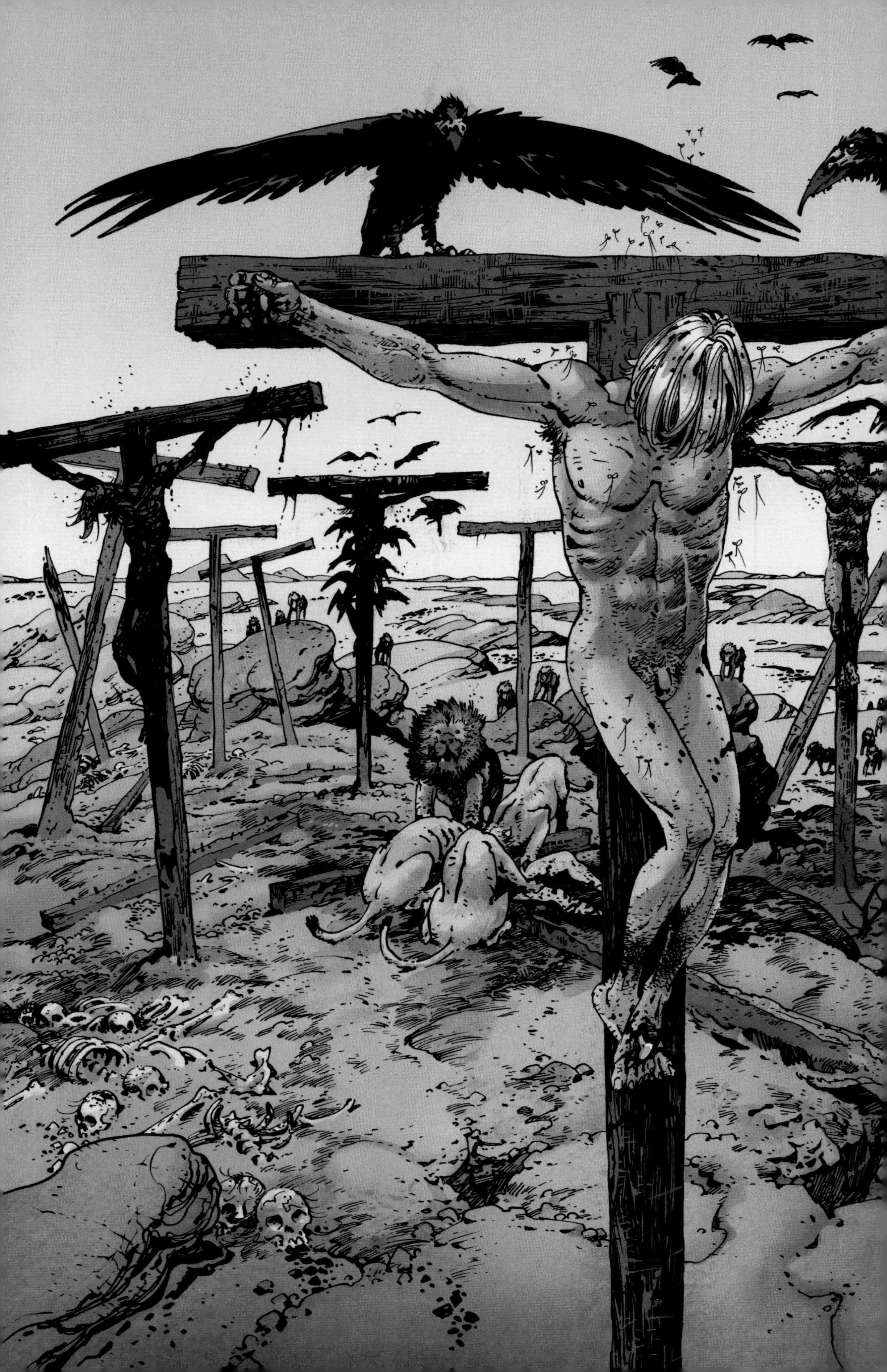

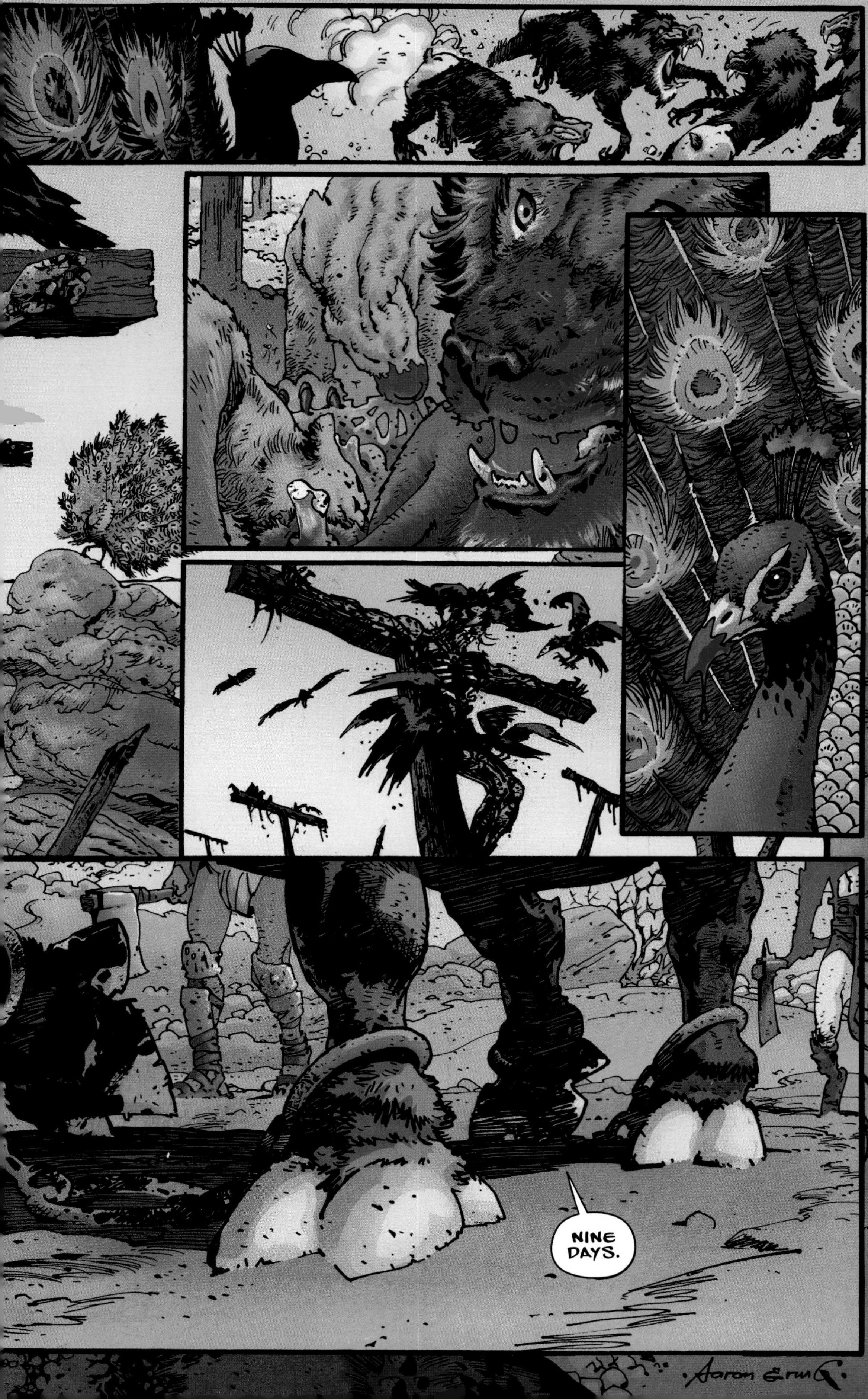
NINE DAYS.
Aaron Gruc

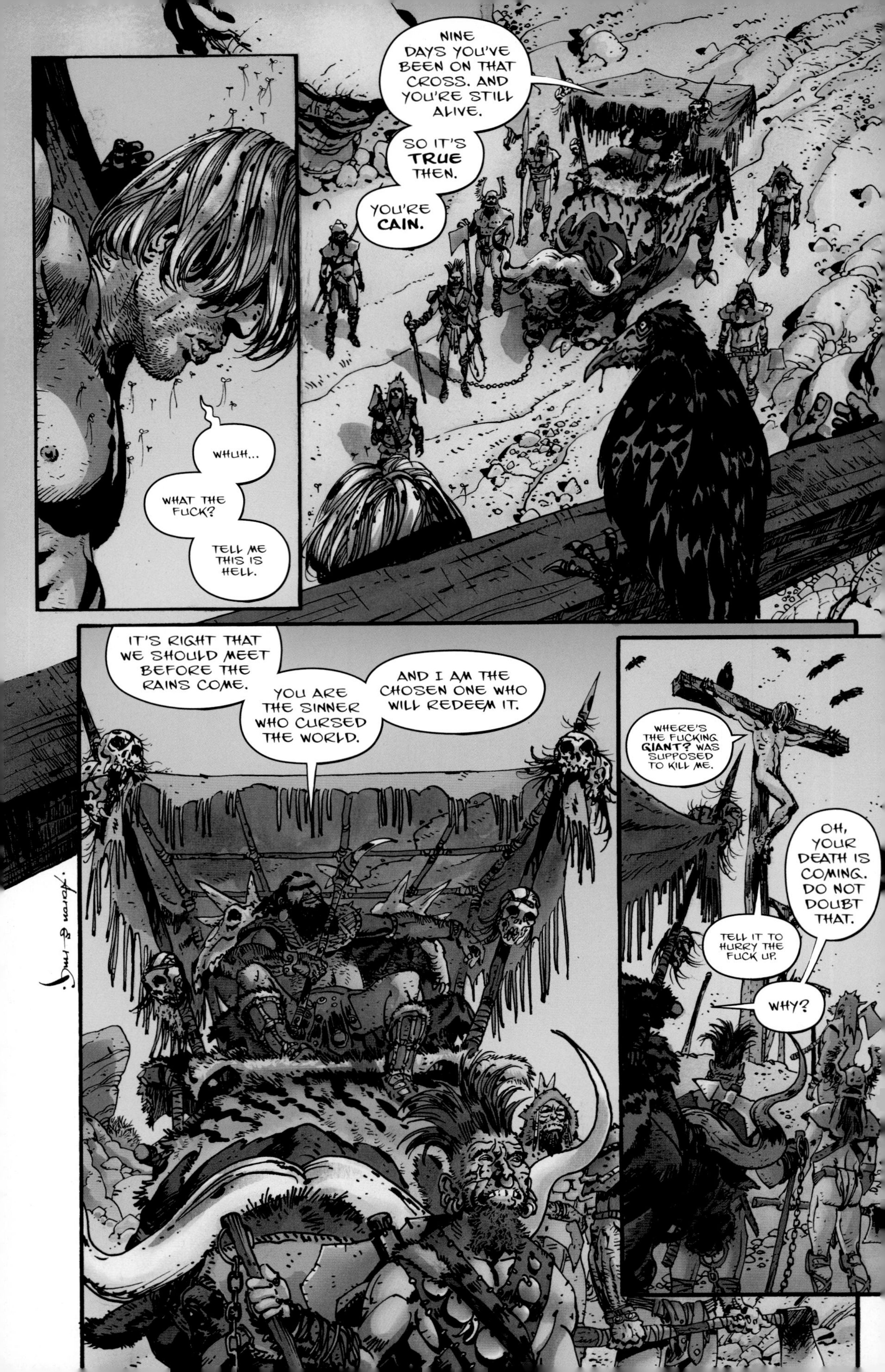
NINE DAYS YOU'VE BEEN ON THAT CROSS. AND YOU'RE STILL ALIVE.
SO IT'S TRUE THEN.
YOU'RE CAIN.
WHUH...
WHAT THE FUCK?
TELL ME THIS IS HELL.
IT'S RIGHT THAT WE SHOULD MEET BEFORE THE RAINS COME.
YOU ARE THE SINNER WHO CURSED THE WORLD.
AND I AM THE CHOSEN ONE WHO WILL REDEEM IT.
WHERE'S THE FUCKING GIANT? WAS SUPPOSED TO KILL ME.
OH, YOUR DEATH IS COMING. DO NOT DOUBT THAT.
TELL IT TO HURRY THE FUCK UP.
WHY?

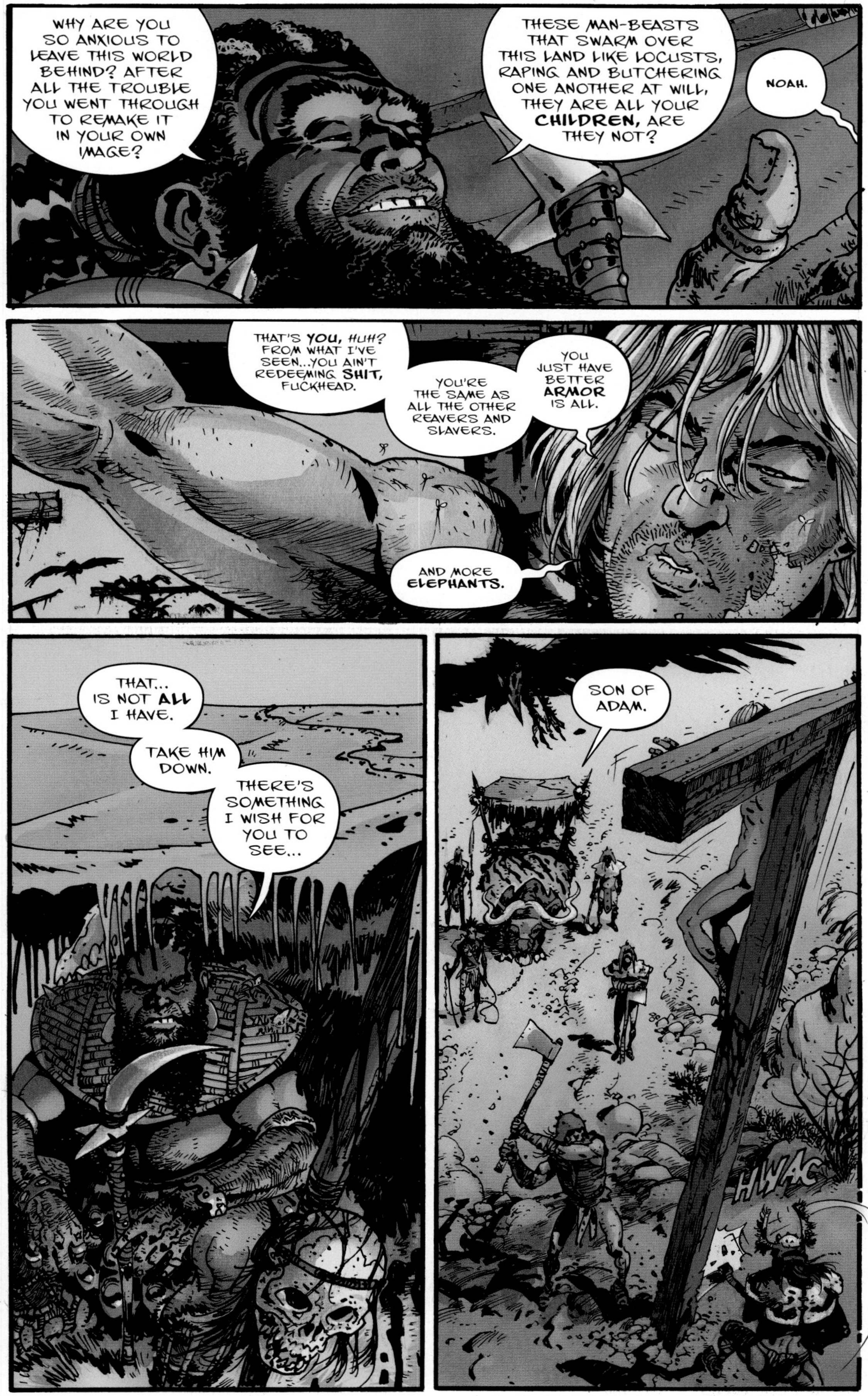
WHY ARE YOU SO ANXIOUS TO LEAVE THIS WORLD BEHIND? AFTER ALL THE TROUBLE YOU WENT THROUGH TO REMAKE IT IN YOUR OWN IMAGE?
THESE MAN-BEASTS THAT SWARM OVER THIS LAND LIKE LOCUSTS, RAPING AND BUTCHERING ONE ANOTHER AT WILL, THEY ARE ALL YOUR CHILDREN, ARE THEY NOT?
NOAH.
THAT'S YOU, HUH? FROM WHAT I'VE SEEN...YOU AIN'T REDEEMING SHIT, FUCKHEAD.
YOU'RE THE SAME AS ALL THE OTHER REAVERS AND SLAVERS.
YOU JUST HAVE BETTER ARMOR IS ALL.
AND MORE ELEPHANTS.
THAT... IS NOT ALL I HAVE.
TAKE HIM DOWN.
THERE'S SOMETHING I WISH FOR YOU TO SEE...
SON OF ADAM.
HWAC

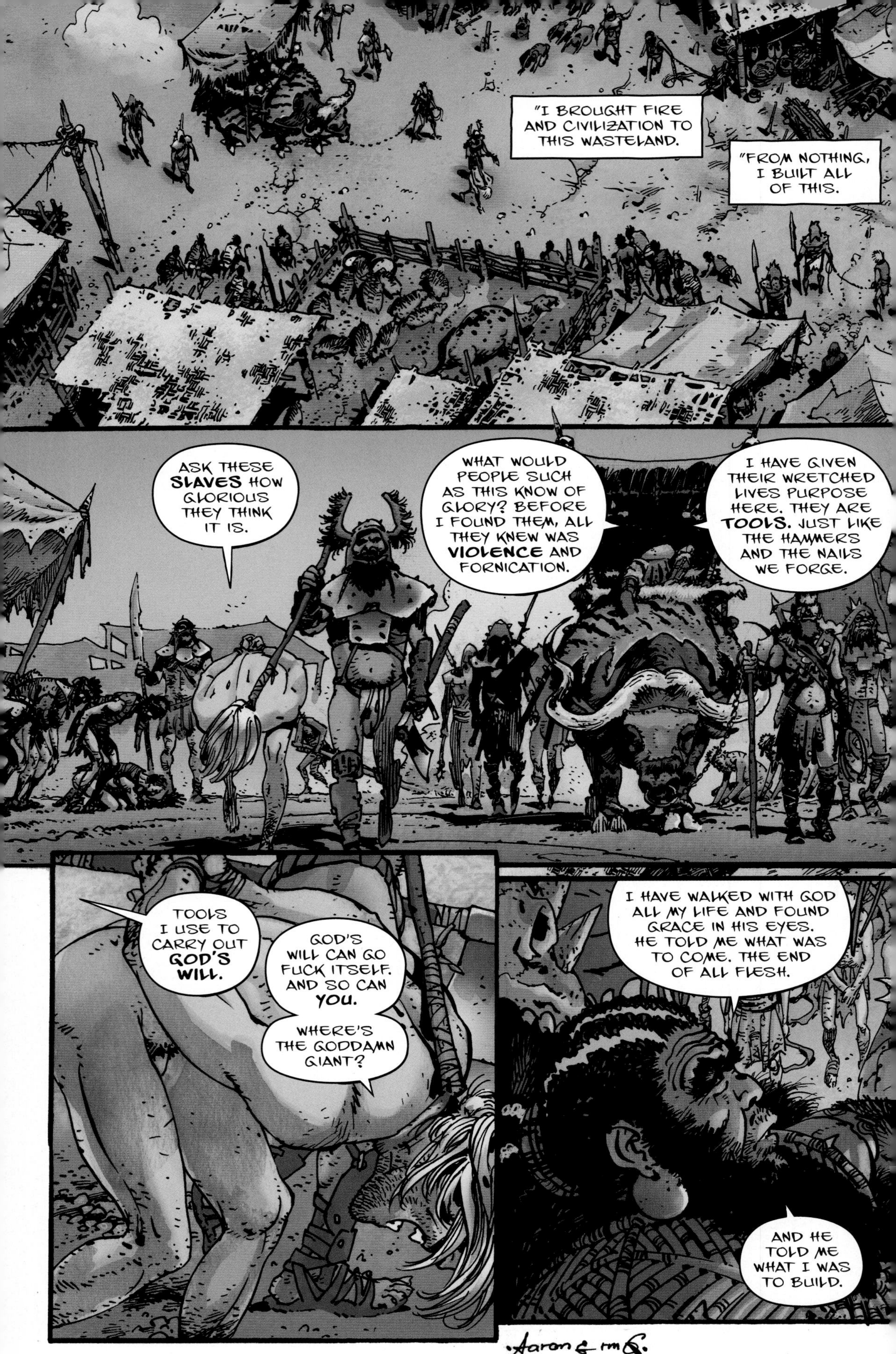
"I BROUGHT FIRE AND CIVILIZATION TO THIS WASTELAND.
"FROM NOTHING, I BUILT ALL OF THIS.
ASK THESE **SLAVES** HOW GLORIOUS THEY THINK IT IS.
WHAT WOULD PEOPLE SUCH AS THIS KNOW OF GLORY? BEFORE I FOUND THEM, ALL THEY KNEW WAS **VIOLENCE** AND FORNICATION.
I HAVE GIVEN THEIR WRETCHED LIVES PURPOSE HERE. THEY ARE **TOOLS.** JUST LIKE THE HAMMERS AND THE NAILS WE FORGE.
TOOLS I USE TO CARRY OUT **GOD'S WILL.**
GOD'S WILL CAN GO FUCK ITSELF. AND SO CAN **YOU.**
WHERE'S THE GODDAMN GIANT?
I HAVE WALKED WITH GOD ALL MY LIFE AND FOUND GRACE IN HIS EYES. HE TOLD ME WHAT WAS TO COME. THE END OF ALL FLESH.
AND HE TOLD ME WHAT I WAS TO BUILD.
·Aaron & rm G·

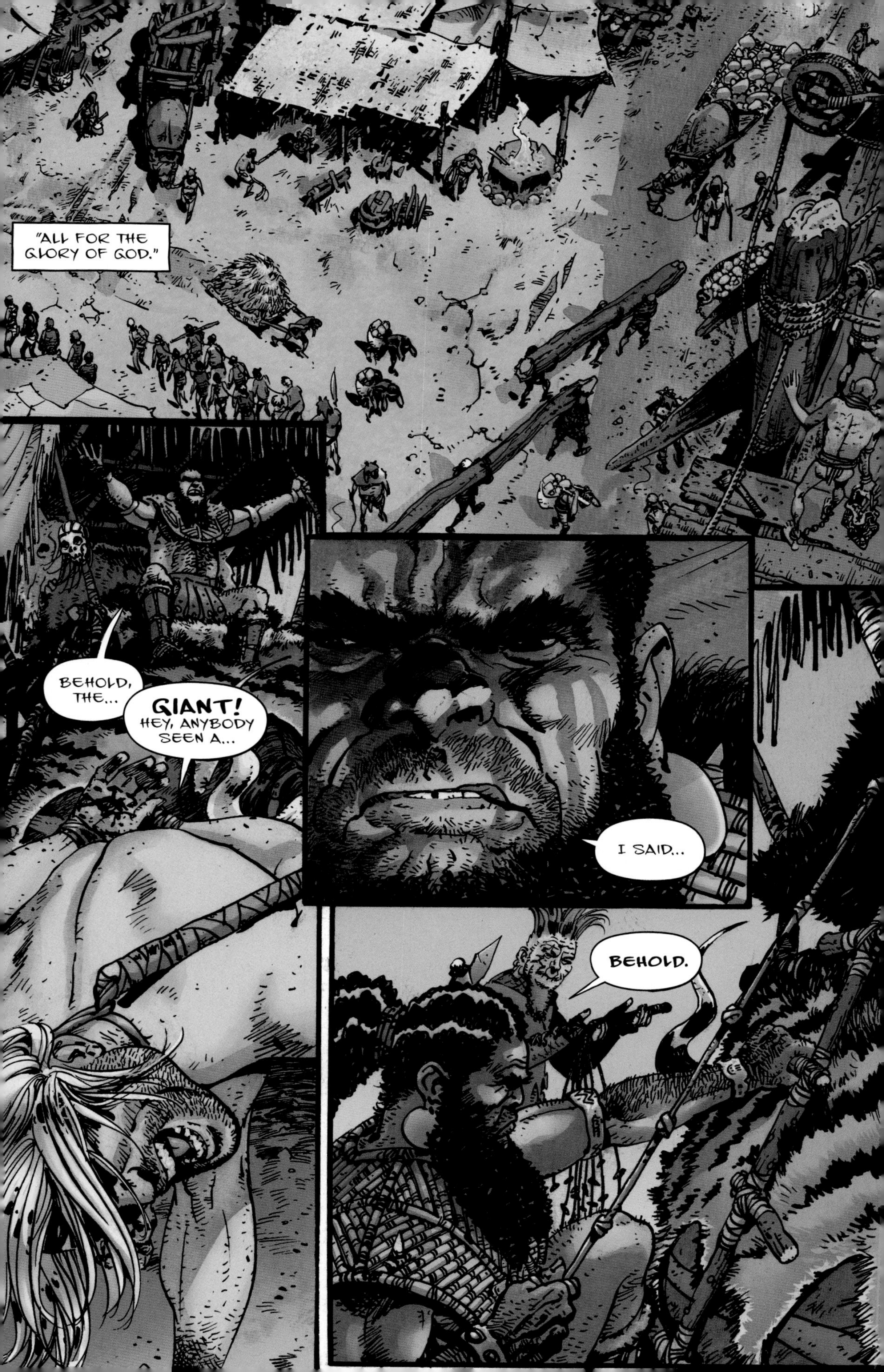
"ALL FOR THE GLORY OF GOD."
BEHOLD, THE...
GIANT! HEY, ANYBODY SEEN A...
I SAID...
BEHOLD.

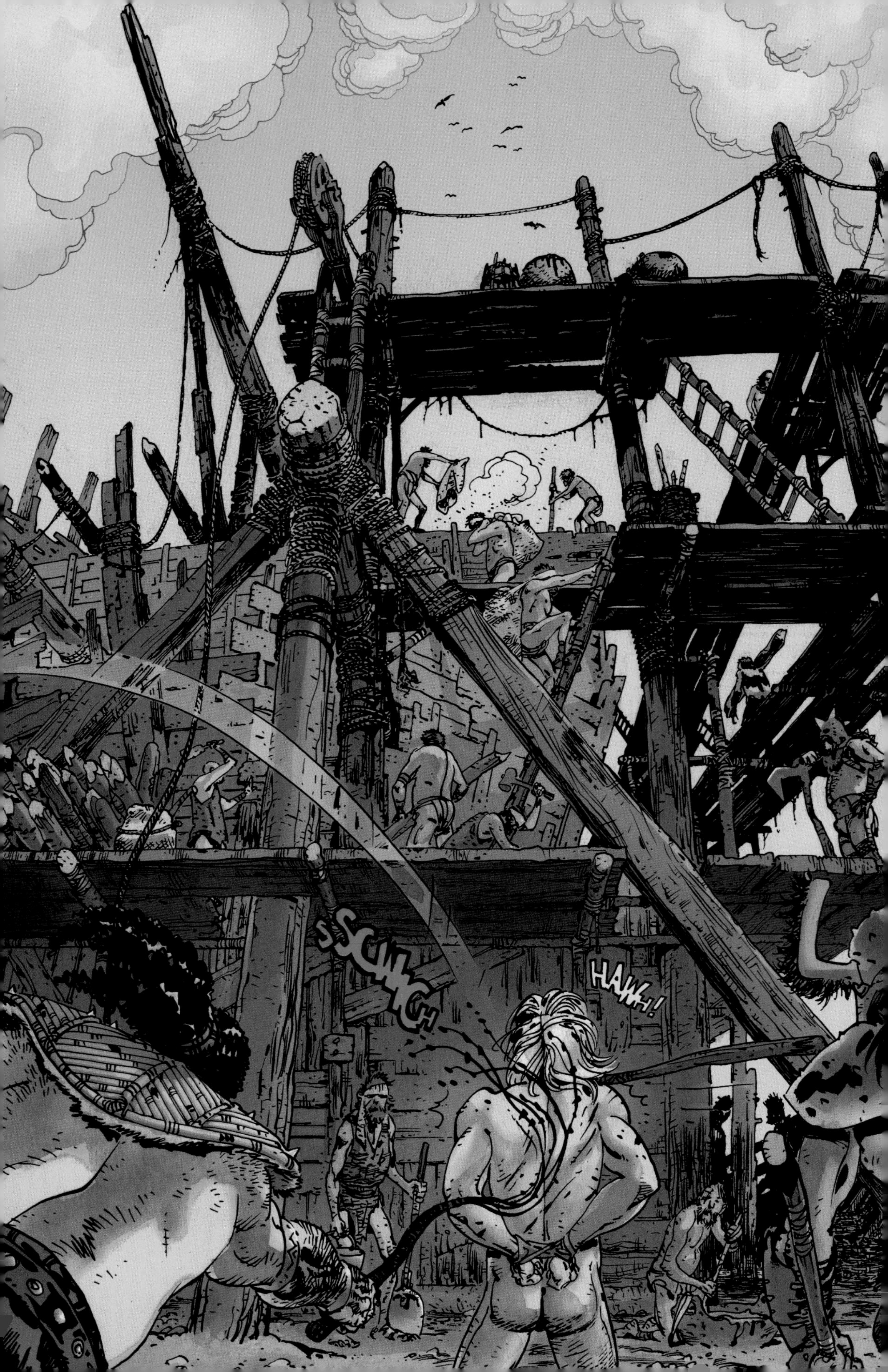

SSCWNCH
HAWK!

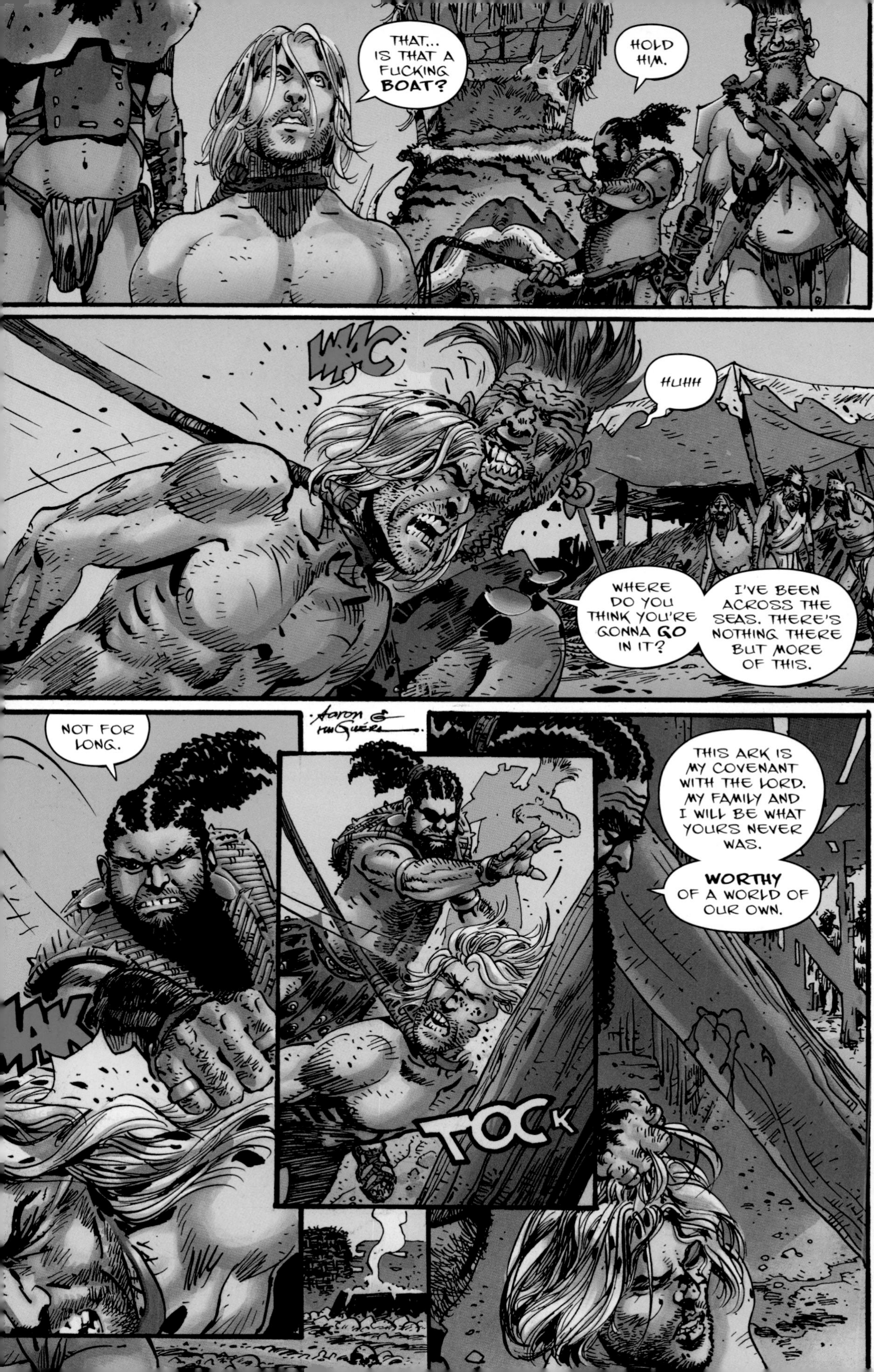

THAT... IS THAT A FUCKING **BOAT?**
HOLD HIM.
WHAC
HUHH
WHERE DO YOU THINK YOU'RE GONNA **GO** IN IT?
I'VE BEEN ACROSS THE SEAS. THERE'S NOTHING THERE BUT MORE OF THIS.
NOT FOR LONG.
THIS ARK IS MY COVENANT WITH THE LORD. MY FAMILY AND I WILL BE WHAT YOURS NEVER WAS.
WORTHY OF A WORLD OF OUR OWN.
TOCK

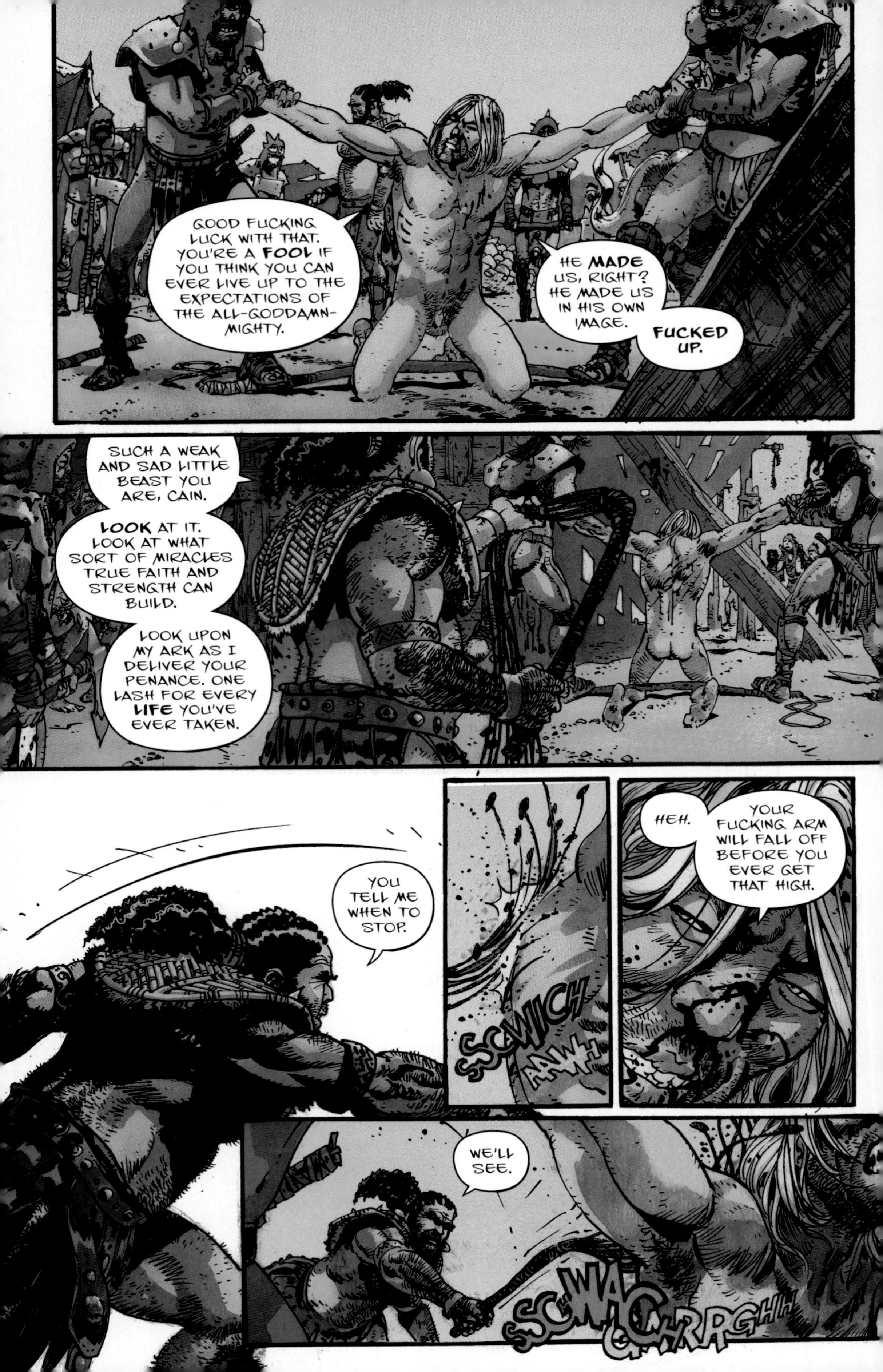

GOOD FUCKING LUCK WITH THAT. YOU'RE A FOOL IF YOU THINK YOU CAN EVER LIVE UP TO THE EXPECTATIONS OF THE ALL-GODDAMN-MIGHTY.
HE MADE US, RIGHT? HE MADE US IN HIS OWN IMAGE.
FUCKED UP.
SUCH A WEAK AND SAD LITTLE BEAST YOU ARE, CAIN.
LOOK AT IT. LOOK AT WHAT SORT OF MIRACLES TRUE FAITH AND STRENGTH CAN BUILD.
LOOK UPON MY ARK AS I DELIVER YOUR PENANCE. ONE LASH FOR EVERY LIFE YOU'VE EVER TAKEN.
YOU TELL ME WHEN TO STOP.
SCWICH
AAWH
HEH.
YOUR FUCKING ARM WILL FALL OFF BEFORE YOU EVER GET THAT HIGH.
WE'LL SEE.
SCHWACK
GHRRAGHH

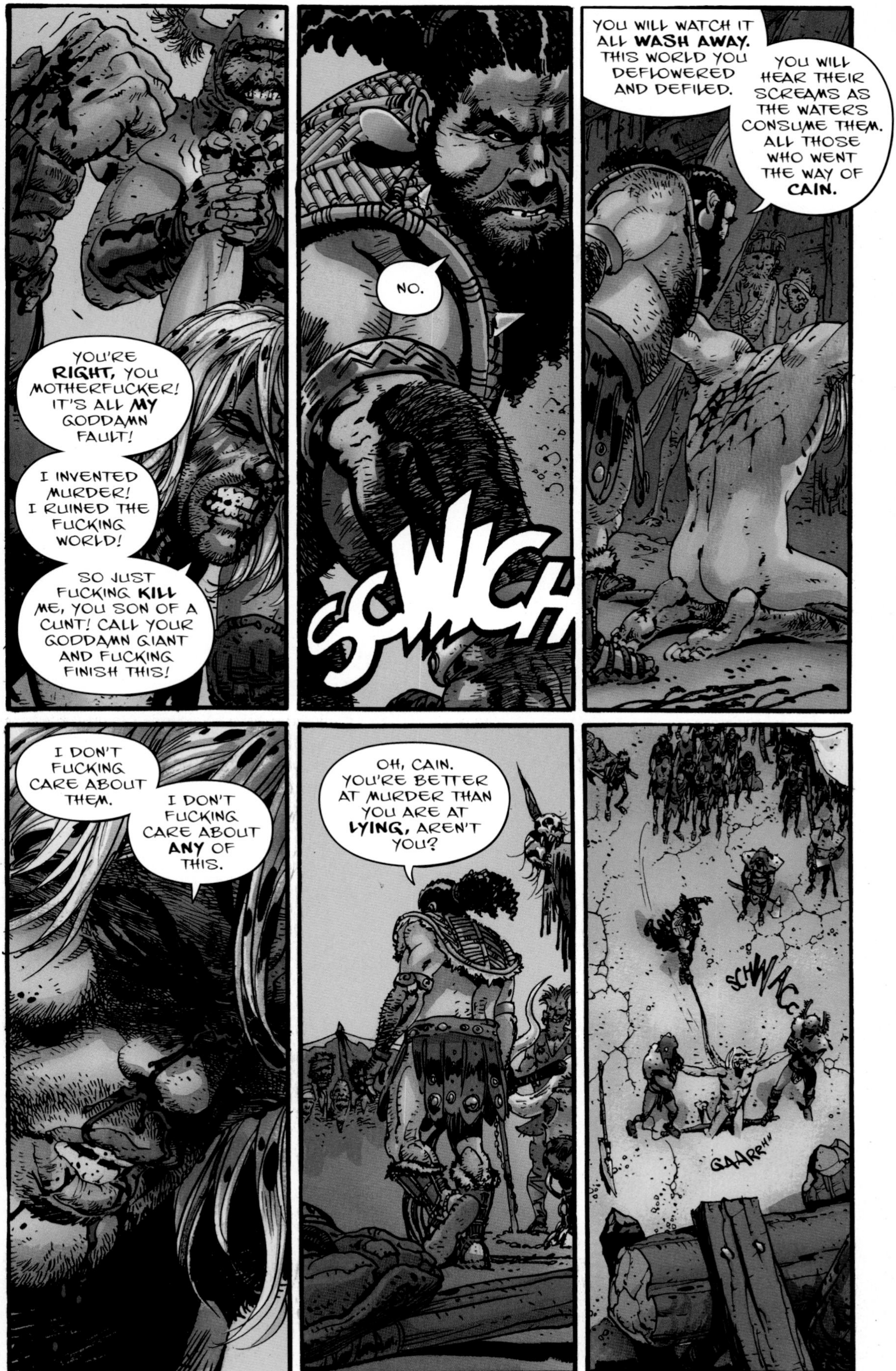
YOU'RE RIGHT, YOU MOTHERFUCKER! IT'S ALL MY GODDAMN FAULT!
I INVENTED MURDER! I RUINED THE FUCKING WORLD!
SO JUST FUCKING KILL ME, YOU SON OF A CUNT! CALL YOUR GODDAMN GIANT AND FUCKING FINISH THIS!
NO.
YOU WILL WATCH IT ALL WASH AWAY. THIS WORLD YOU DEFLOWERED AND DEFILED.
YOU WILL HEAR THEIR SCREAMS AS THE WATERS CONSUME THEM. ALL THOSE WHO WENT THE WAY OF CAIN.
I DON'T FUCKING CARE ABOUT THEM.
I DON'T FUCKING CARE ABOUT ANY OF THIS.
OH, CAIN. YOU'RE BETTER AT MURDER THAN YOU ARE AT LYING, AREN'T YOU?
SCHWACC
GAARRHN

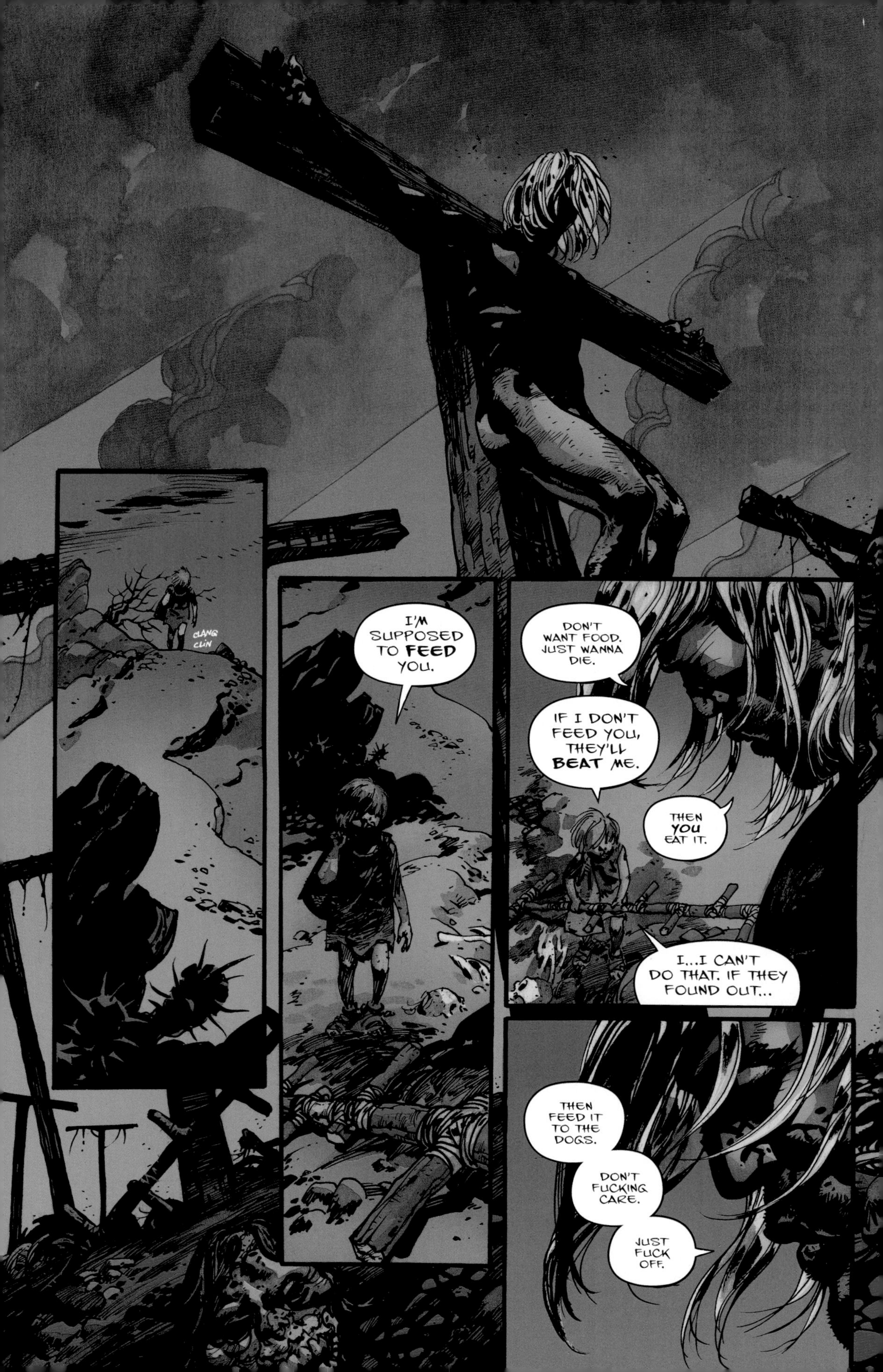

CLANG
CLIN
I'M SUPPOSED TO FEED YOU.
DON'T WANT FOOD. JUST WANNA DIE.
IF I DON'T FEED YOU, THEY'LL BEAT ME.
THEN YOU EAT IT.
I...I CAN'T DO THAT. IF THEY FOUND OUT...
THEN FEED IT TO THE DOGS.
DON'T FUCKING CARE.
JUST FUCK OFF.

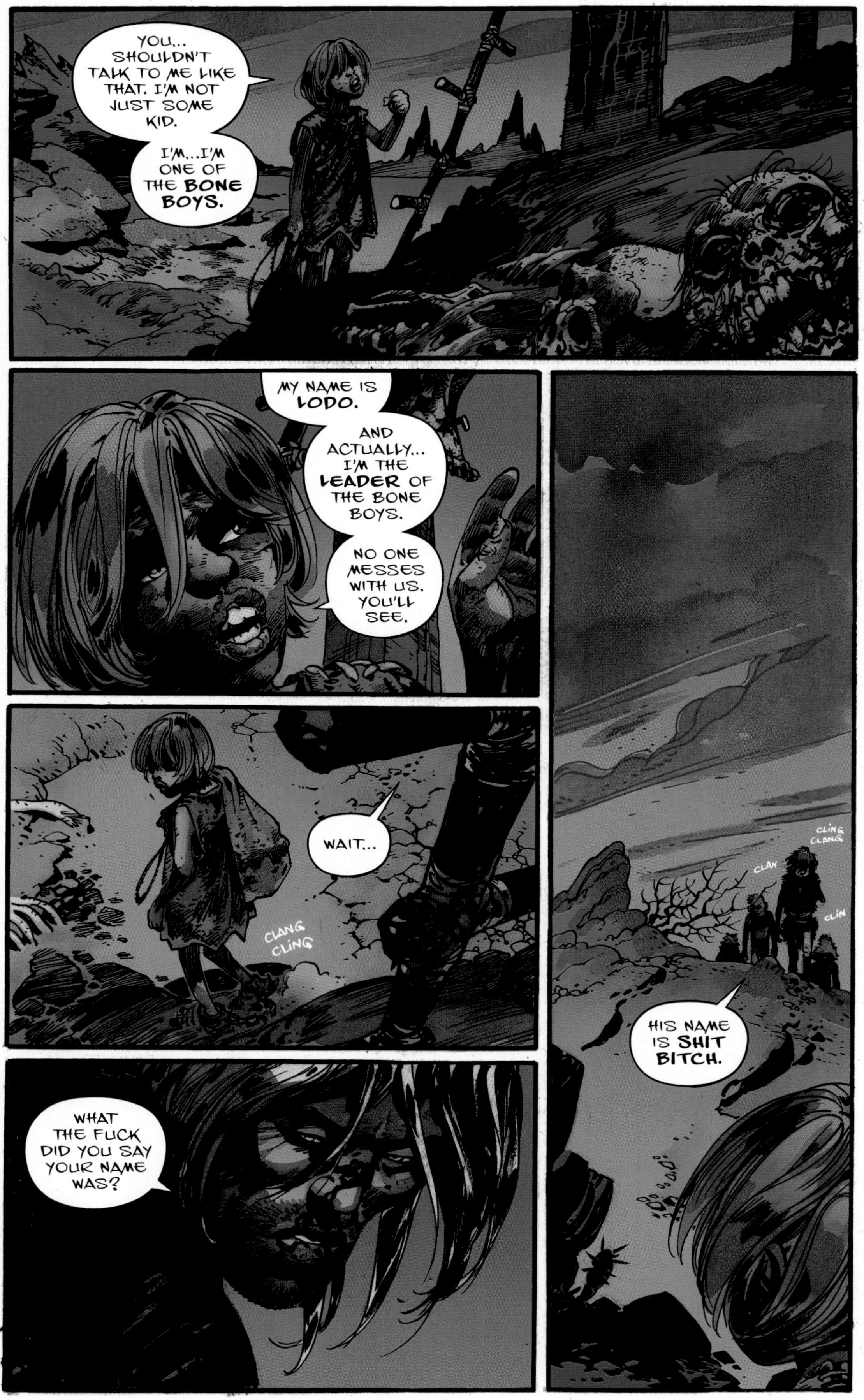
YOU... SHOULDN'T TALK TO ME LIKE THAT. I'M NOT JUST SOME KID.
I'M...I'M ONE OF THE BONE BOYS.
MY NAME IS LODO.
AND ACTUALLY... I'M THE LEADER OF THE BONE BOYS.
NO ONE MESSES WITH US. YOU'LL SEE.
WAIT...
CLANG
CLING
WHAT THE FUCK DID YOU SAY YOUR NAME WAS?
CLING
CLANG
CLAN
CLIN
HIS NAME IS SHIT BITCH.

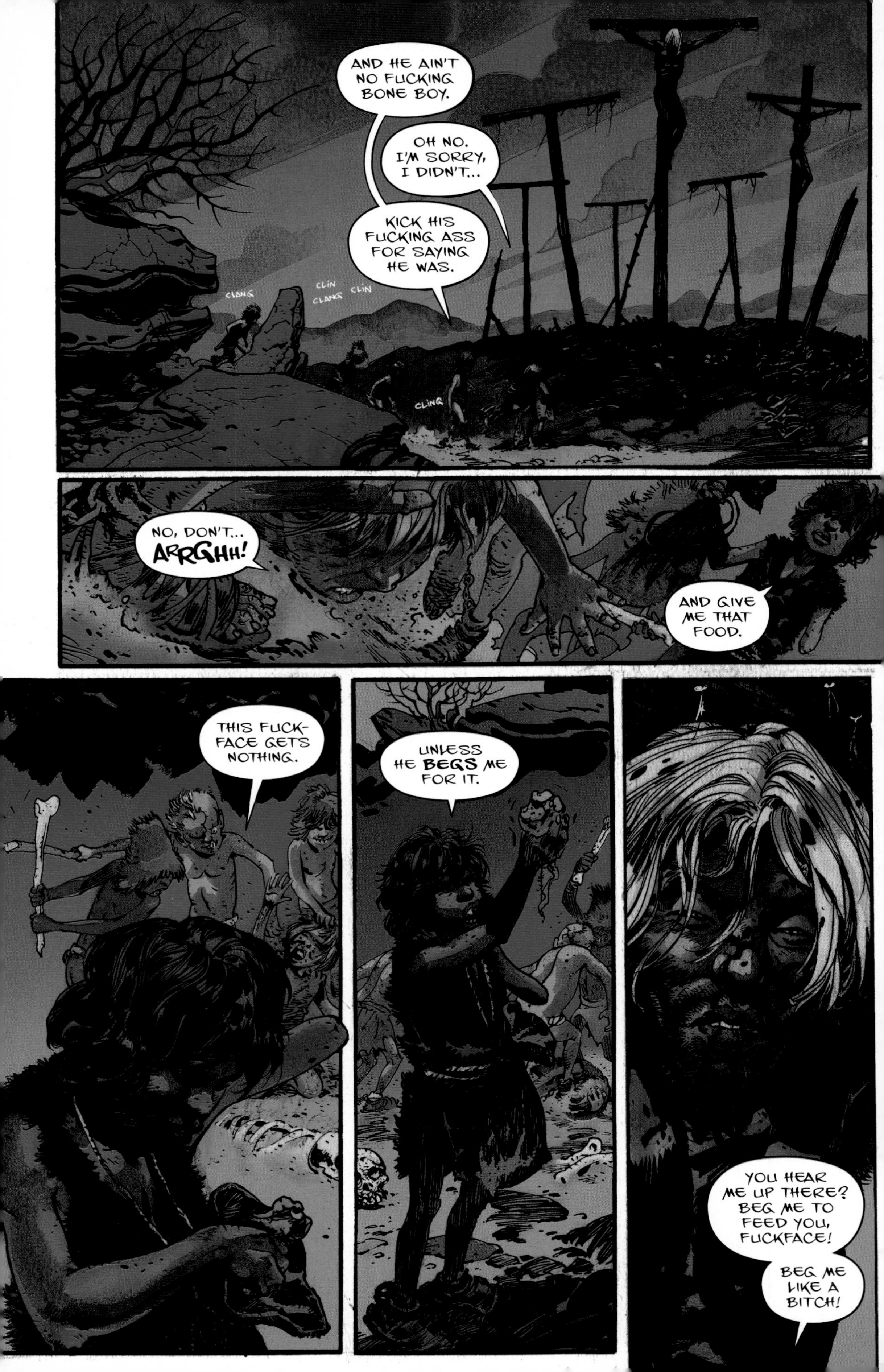
AND HE AIN'T NO FUCKING BONE BOY.
OH NO. I'M SORRY, I DIDN'T...
KICK HIS FUCKING ASS FOR SAYING HE WAS.
CLANG
CLIN
CLANG
CLIN
CLING
NO, DON'T... ARRGHH!
AND GIVE ME THAT FOOD.
THIS FUCK-FACE GETS NOTHING.
UNLESS HE BEGS ME FOR IT.
YOU HEAR ME UP THERE? BEG ME TO FEED YOU, FUCKFACE!
BEG ME LIKE A BITCH!

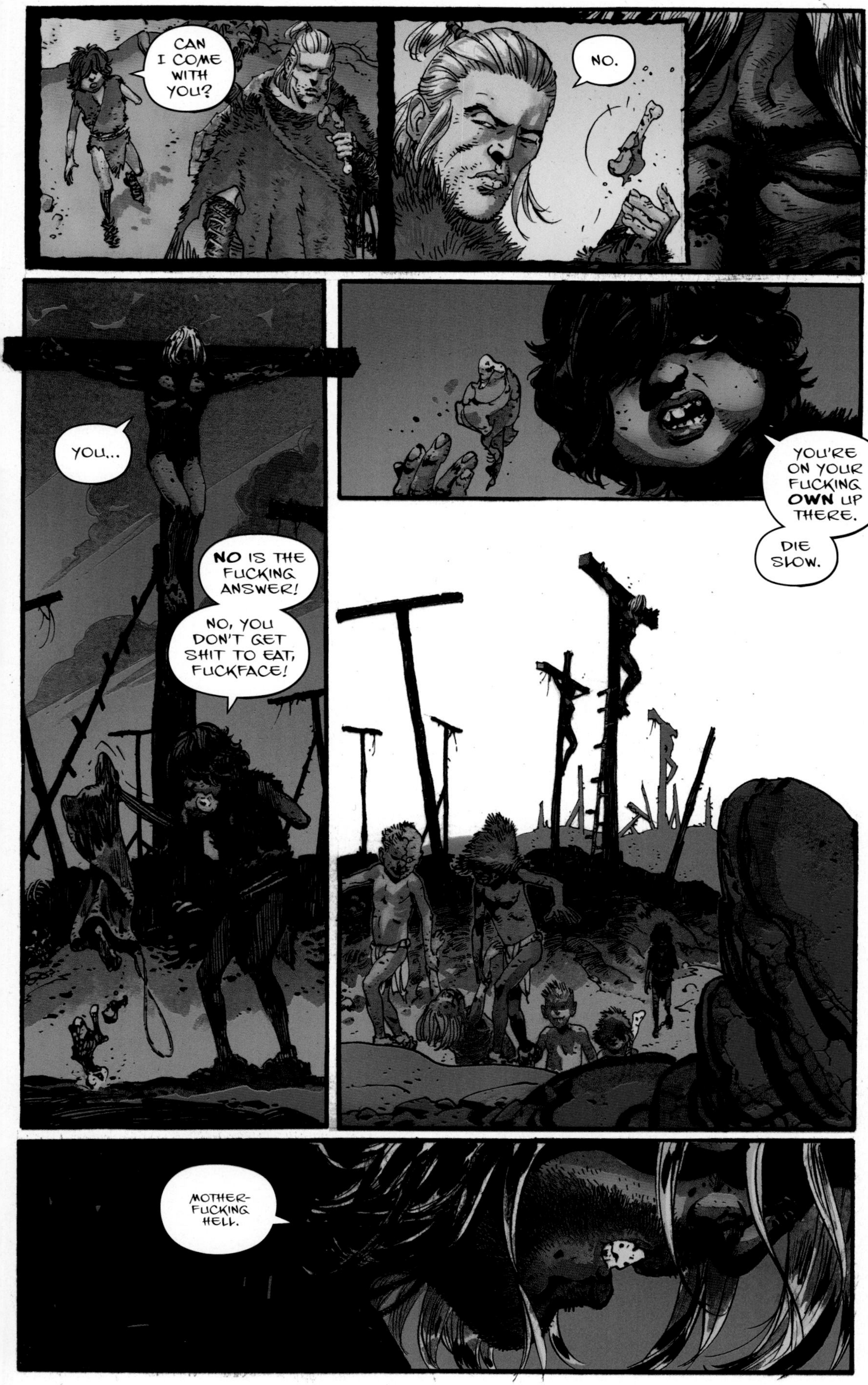
CAN I COME WITH YOU?
NO.
YOU...
YOU'RE ON YOUR FUCKING OWN UP THERE.
DIE SLOW.
NO IS THE FUCKING ANSWER!
NO, YOU DON'T GET SHIT TO EAT, FUCKFACE!
MOTHER-FUCKING HELL.

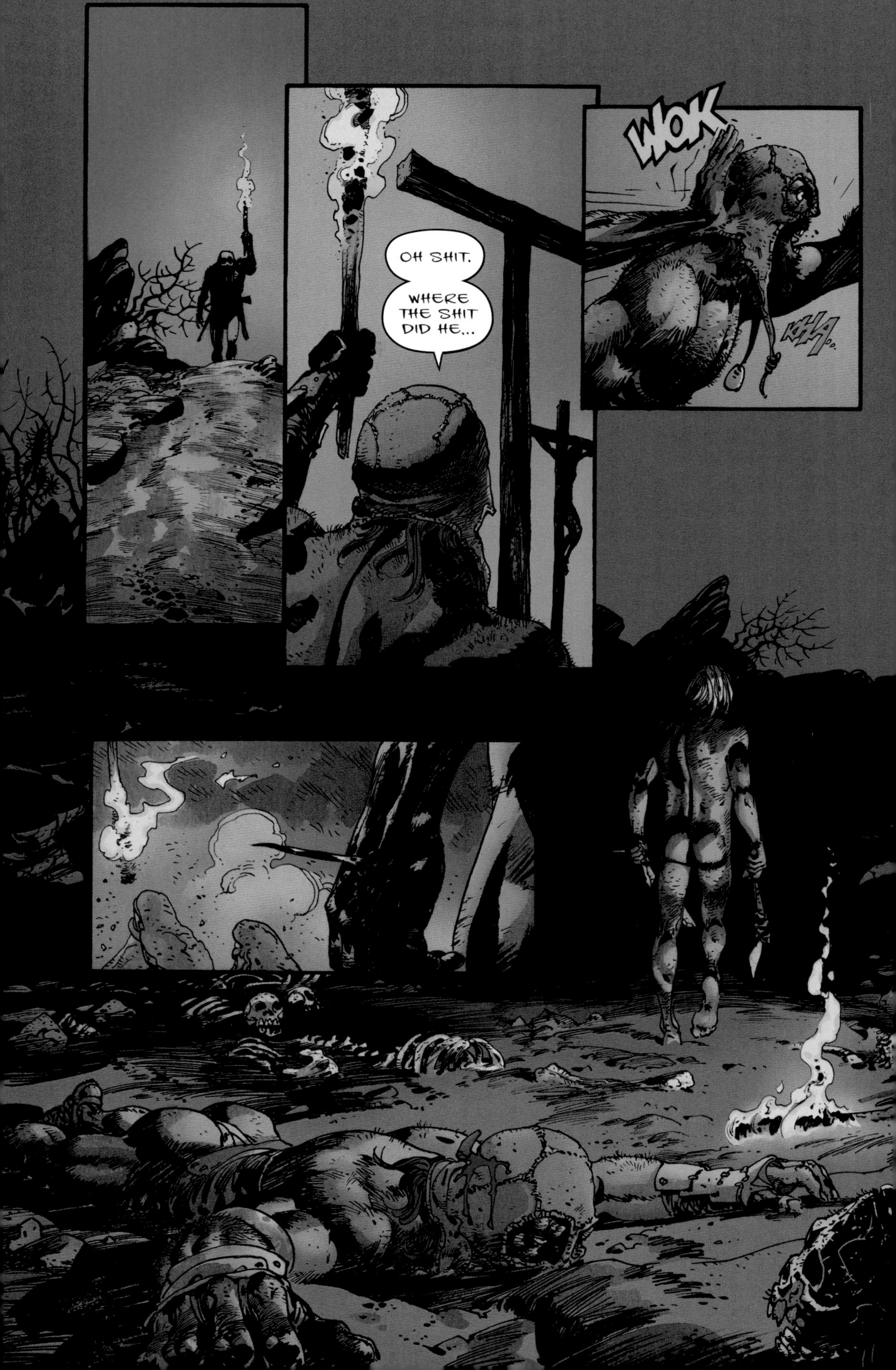
OH SHIT.
WHERE THE SHIT DID HE...
WOK

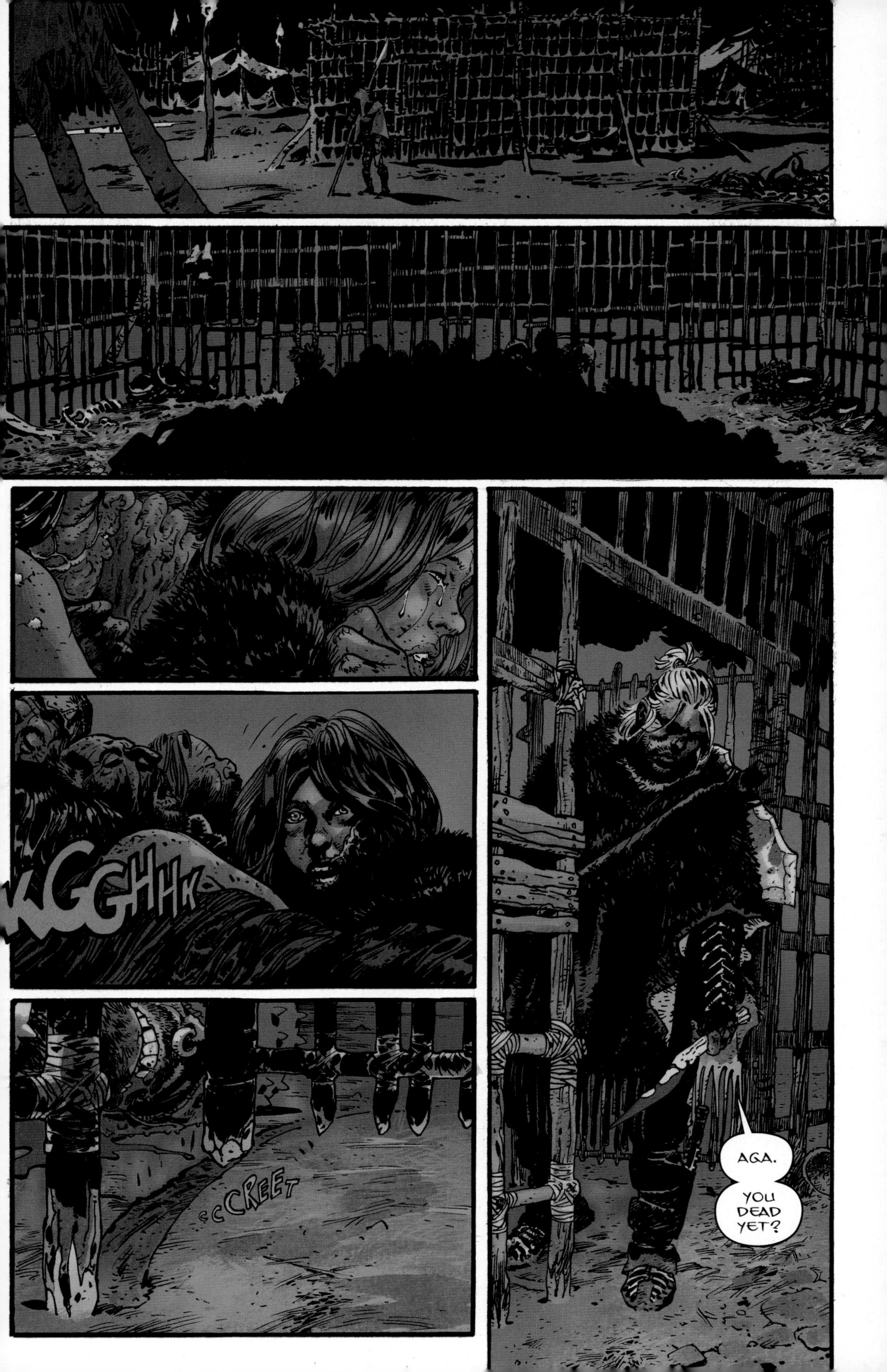

KGGHHK
CCCREET
AGA.
YOU DEAD YET?

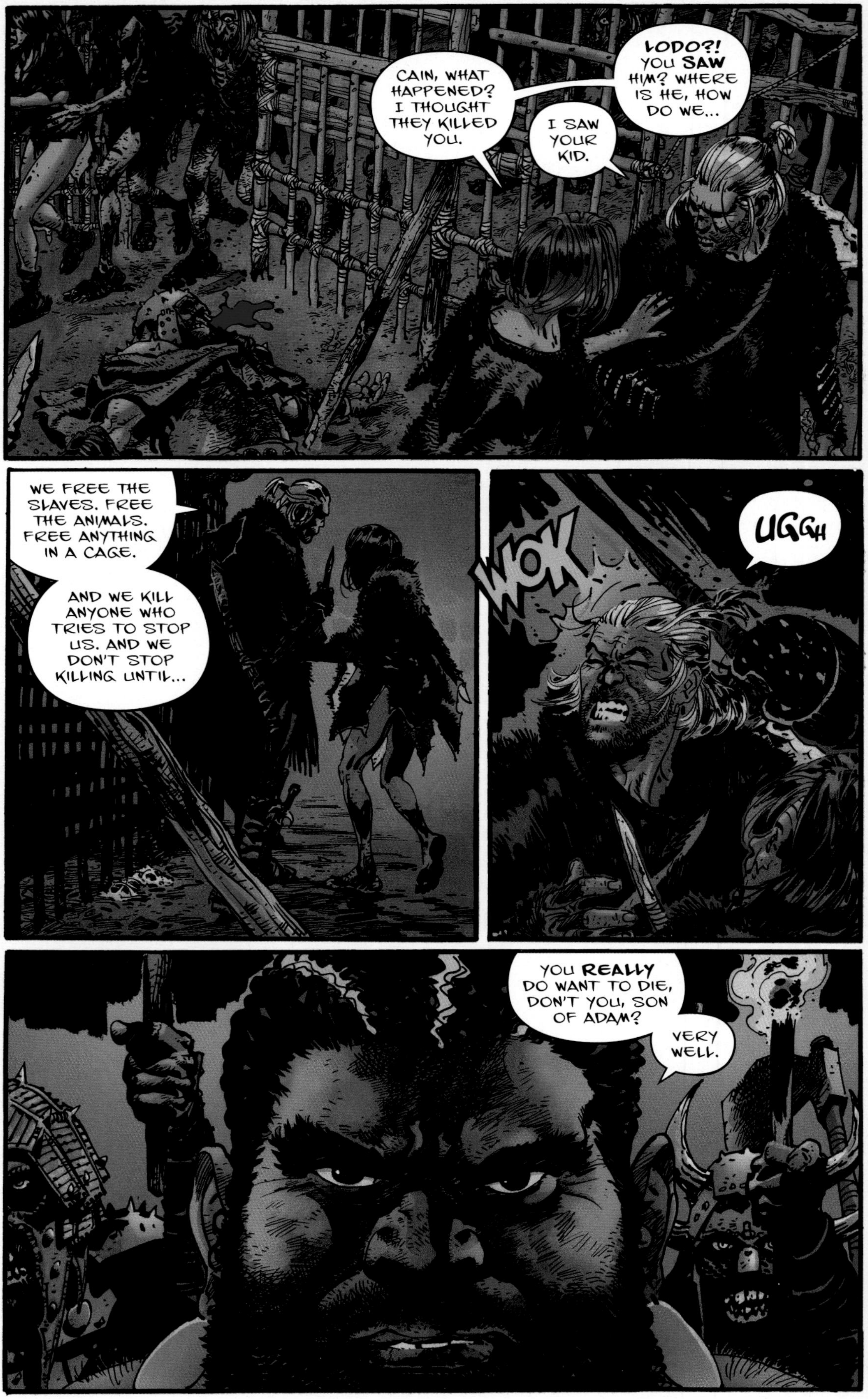
CAIN, WHAT HAPPENED? I THOUGHT THEY KILLED YOU.
I SAW YOUR KID.
LODO?! YOU SAW HIM? WHERE IS HE, HOW DO WE...
WE FREE THE SLAVES. FREE THE ANIMALS. FREE ANYTHING IN A CAGE.
AND WE KILL ANYONE WHO TRIES TO STOP US. AND WE DON'T STOP KILLING UNTIL...
WOK
UGGH
YOU REALLY DO WANT TO DIE, DON'T YOU, SON OF ADAM?
VERY WELL.

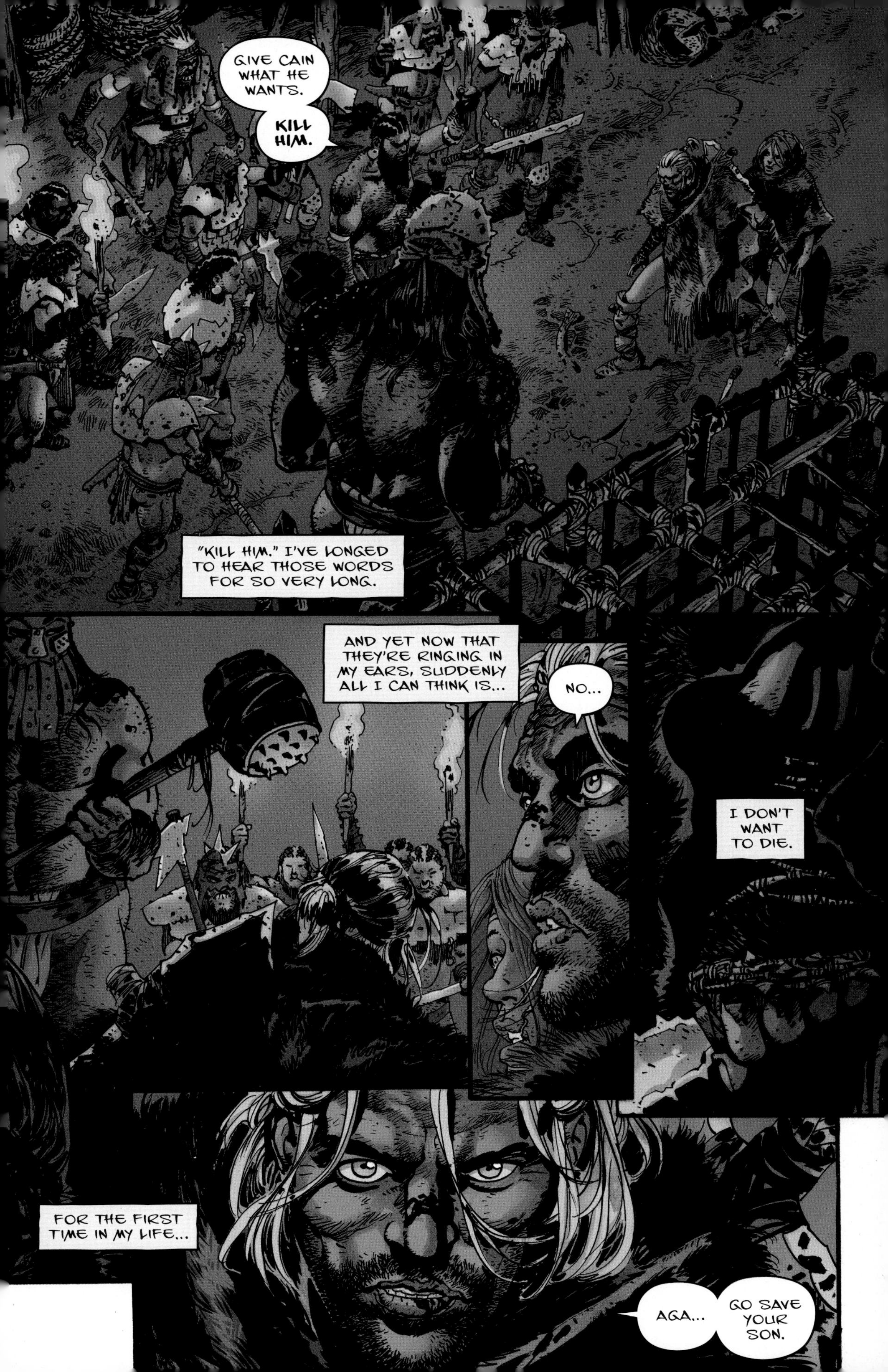

GIVE CAIN WHAT HE WANTS.
KILL HIM.
"KILL HIM." I'VE LONGED TO HEAR THOSE WORDS FOR SO VERY LONG.
AND YET NOW THAT THEY'RE RINGING IN MY EARS, SUDDENLY ALL I CAN THINK IS...
NO...
I DON'T WANT TO DIE.
FOR THE FIRST TIME IN MY LIFE...
AGA...
GO SAVE YOUR SON.

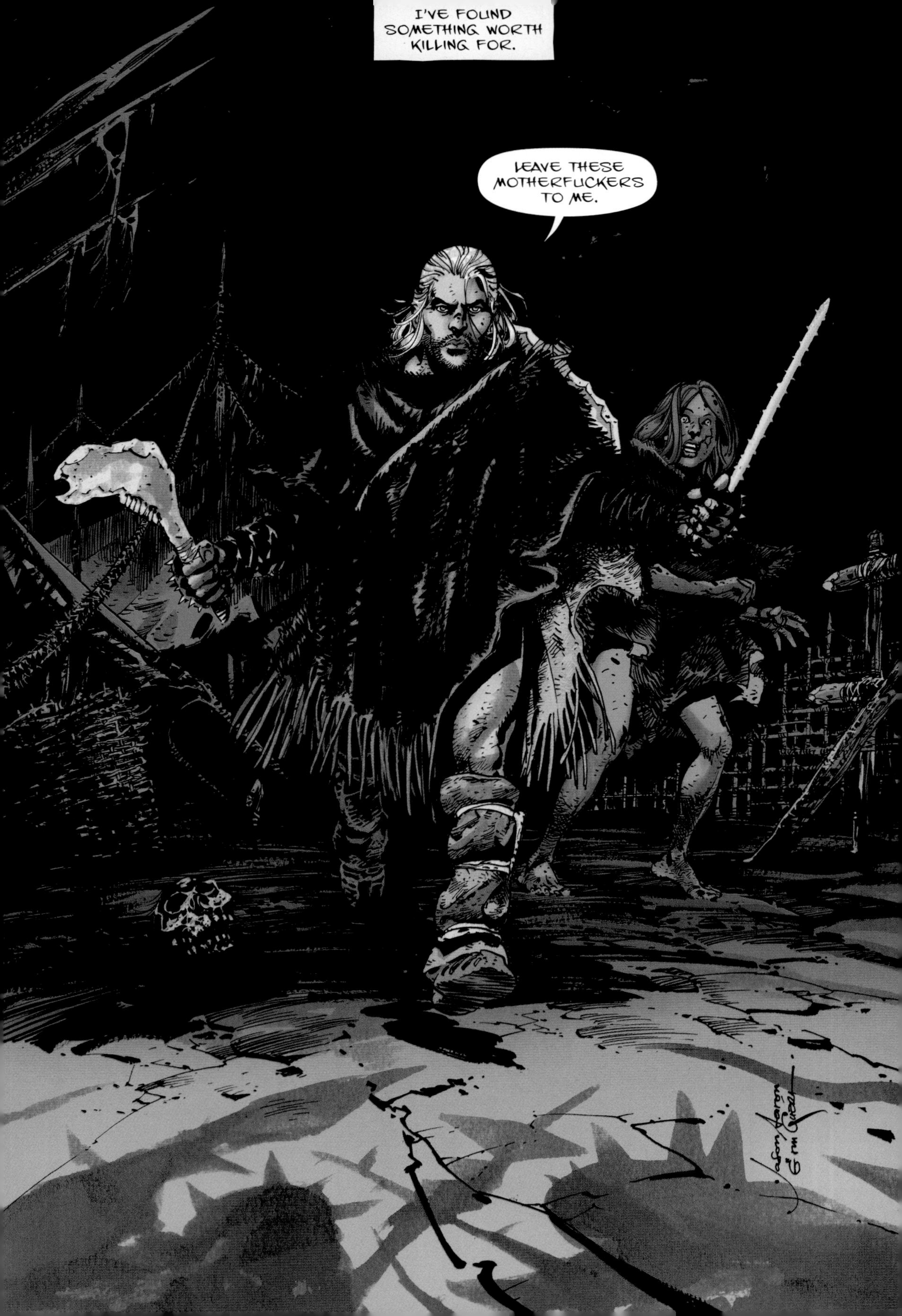
I'VE FOUND SOMETHING WORTH KILLING FOR.
LEAVE THESE MOTHERFUCKERS TO ME.

chapter five

God's Monsters

AND THE LORD SAID, I WILL DESTROY MAN WHOM I HAVE CREATED FROM THE FACE OF THE EARTH.

BOTH MAN, AND BEAST, AND THE CREEPING THING, AND THE FOWLS OF THE AIR.

FOR IT REPENTETH ME THAT I HAVE MADE THEM.

GENESIS 6:7

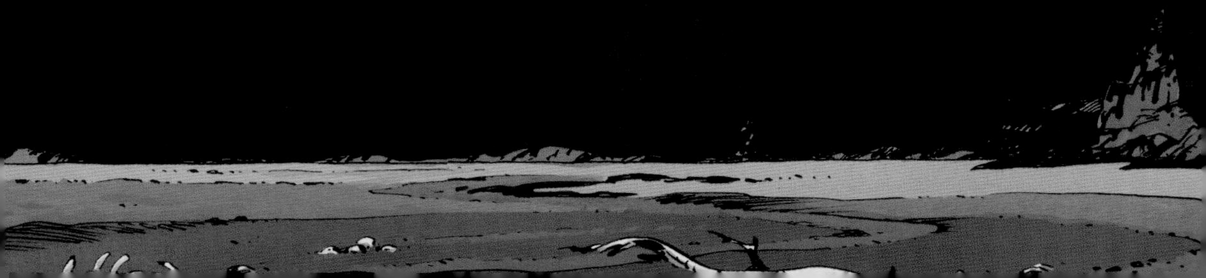

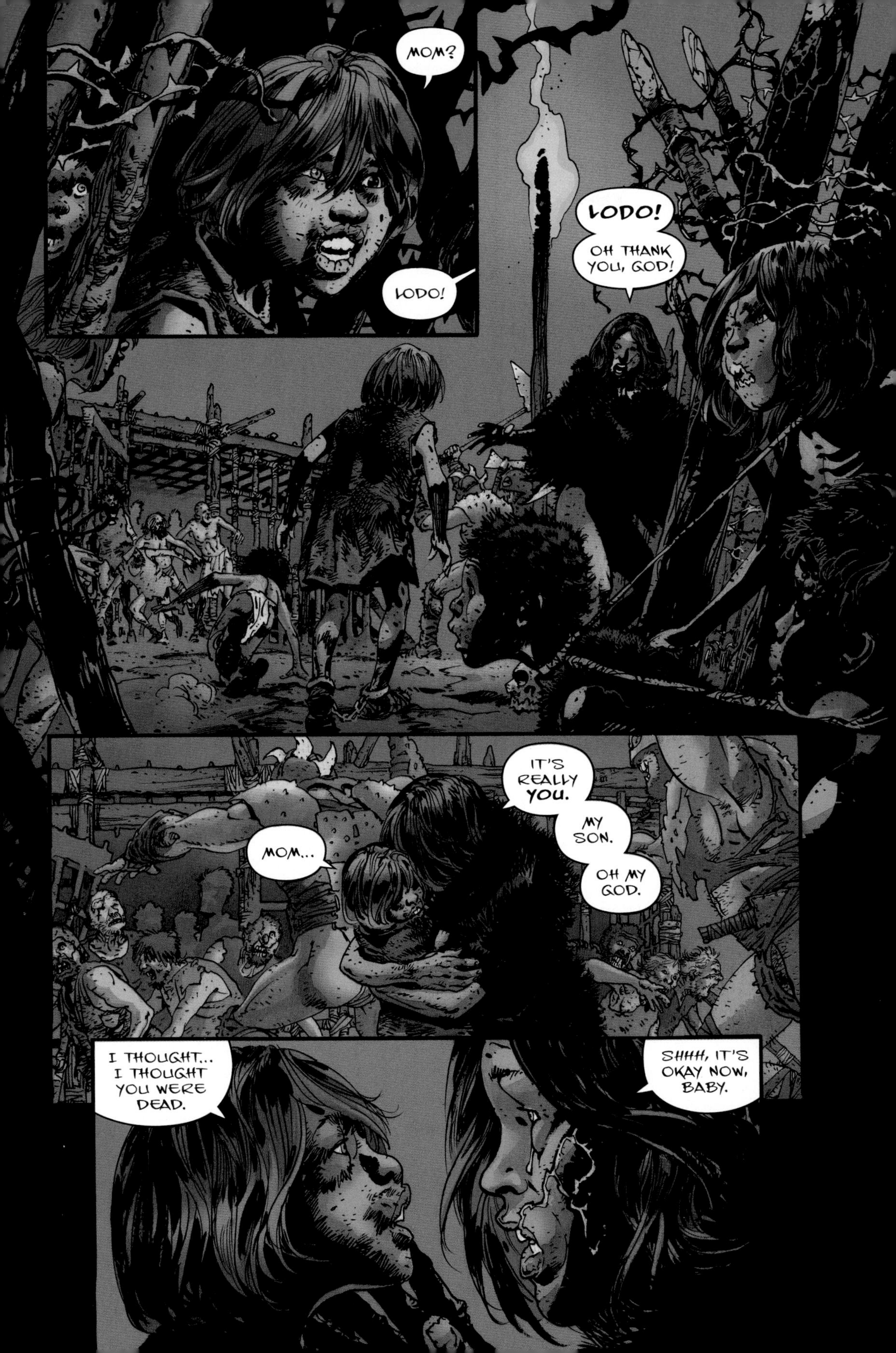
MOM?
LODO!
LODO!
OH THANK YOU, GOD!
IT'S REALLY YOU.
MOM...
MY SON.
OH MY GOD.
I THOUGHT... I THOUGHT YOU WERE DEAD.
SHHH, IT'S OKAY NOW, BABY.

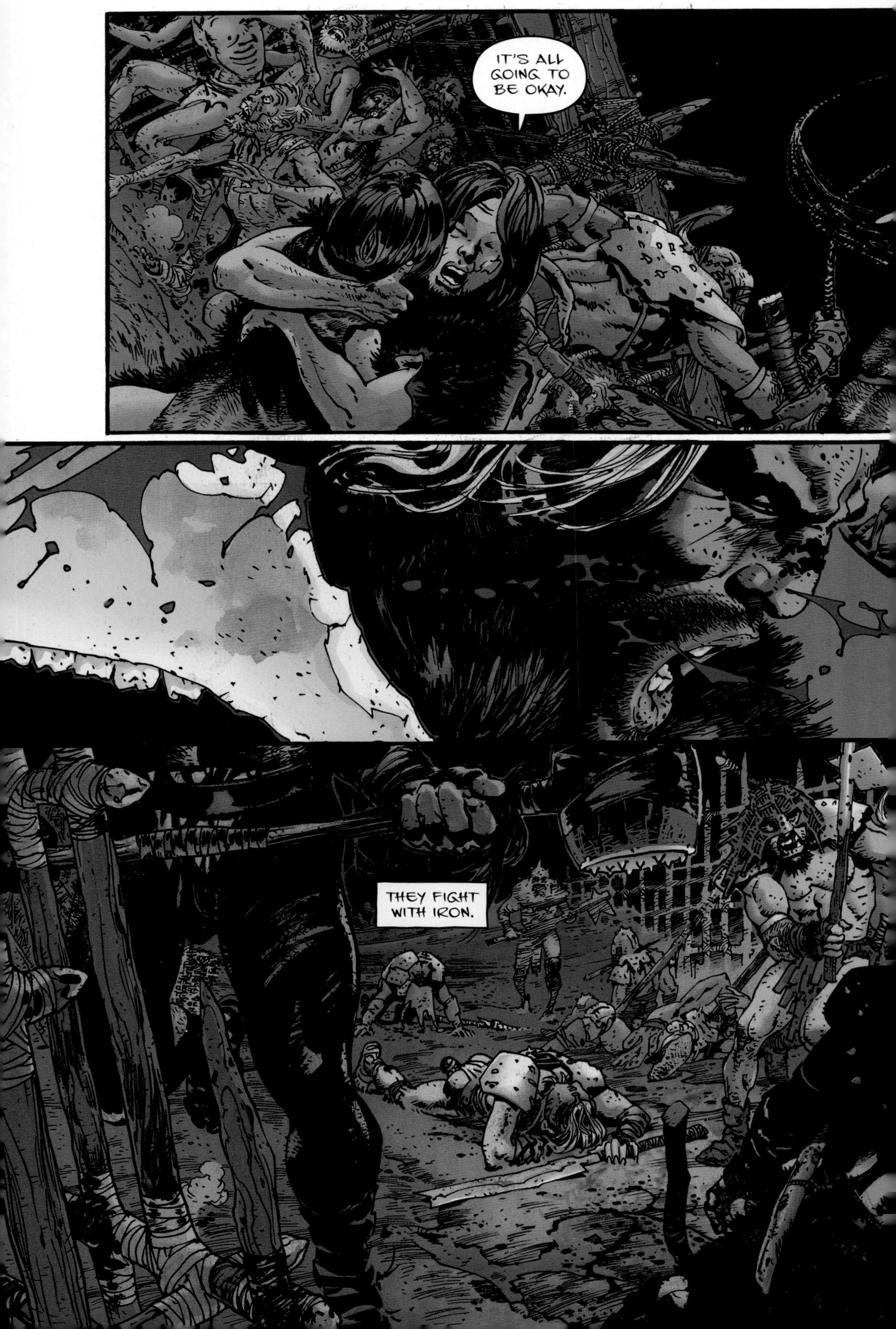
IT'S ALL GOING TO BE OKAY.
THEY FIGHT WITH IRON.

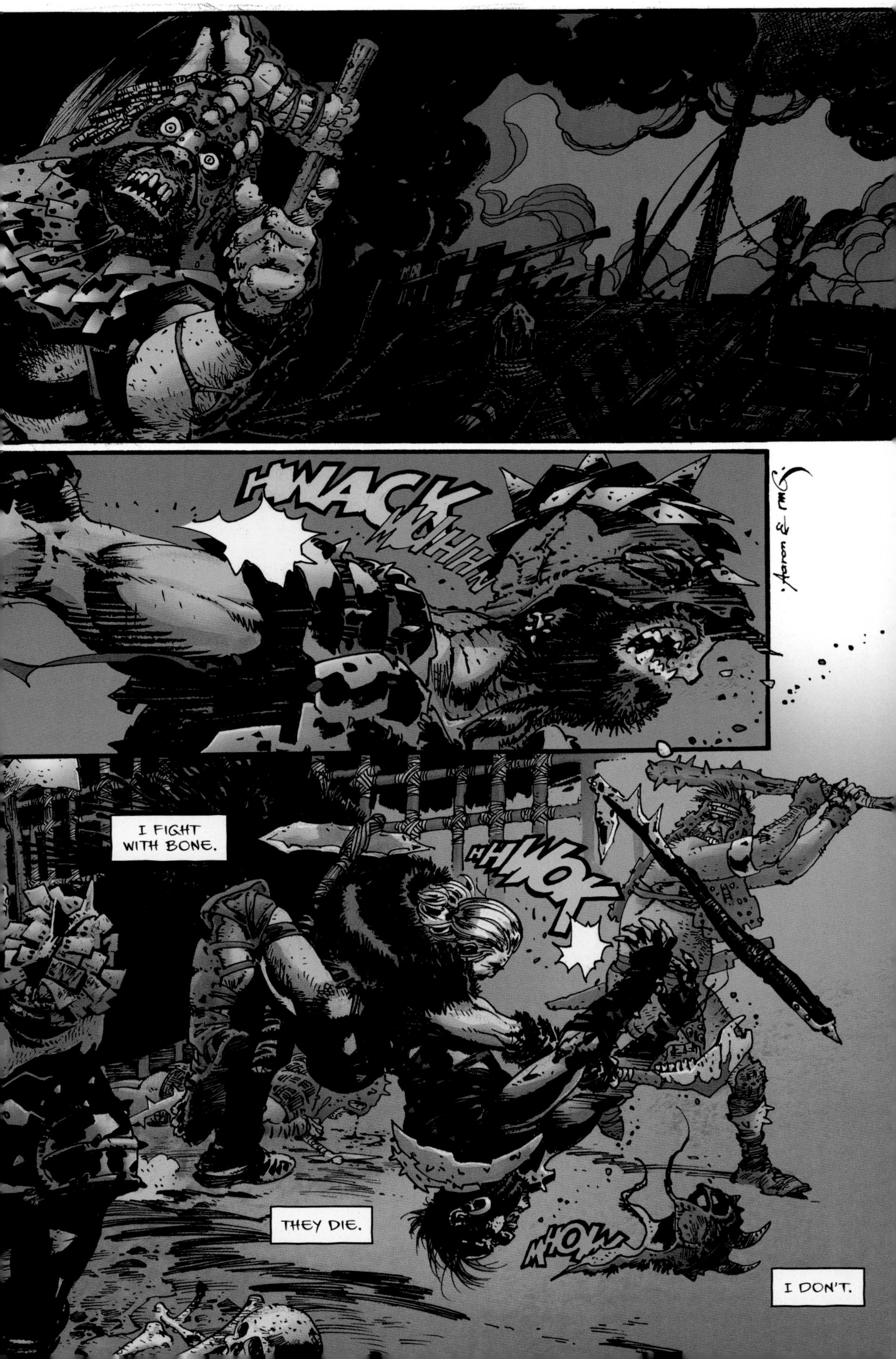
HWACK
I FIGHT WITH BONE.
HWOK
THEY DIE.
WHOW
I DON'T.

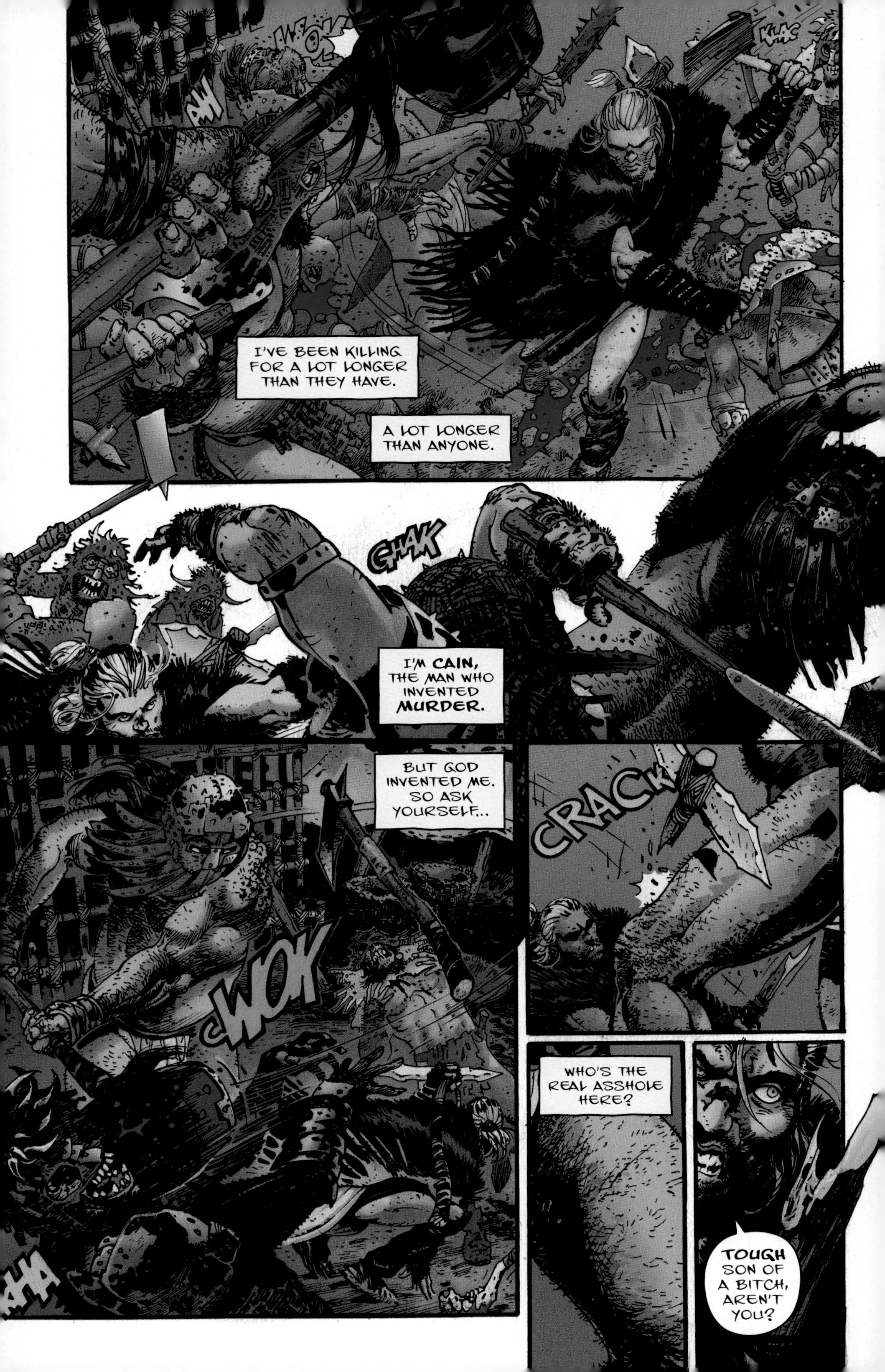
WOK
I'VE BEEN KILLING FOR A LOT LONGER THAN THEY HAVE.
A LOT LONGER THAN ANYONE.
GHAK
I'M CAIN, THE MAN WHO INVENTED MURDER.
BUT GOD INVENTED ME. SO ASK YOURSELF...
CWOK
CRACK
WHO'S THE REAL ASSHOLE HERE?
TOUGH SON OF A BITCH, AREN'T YOU?

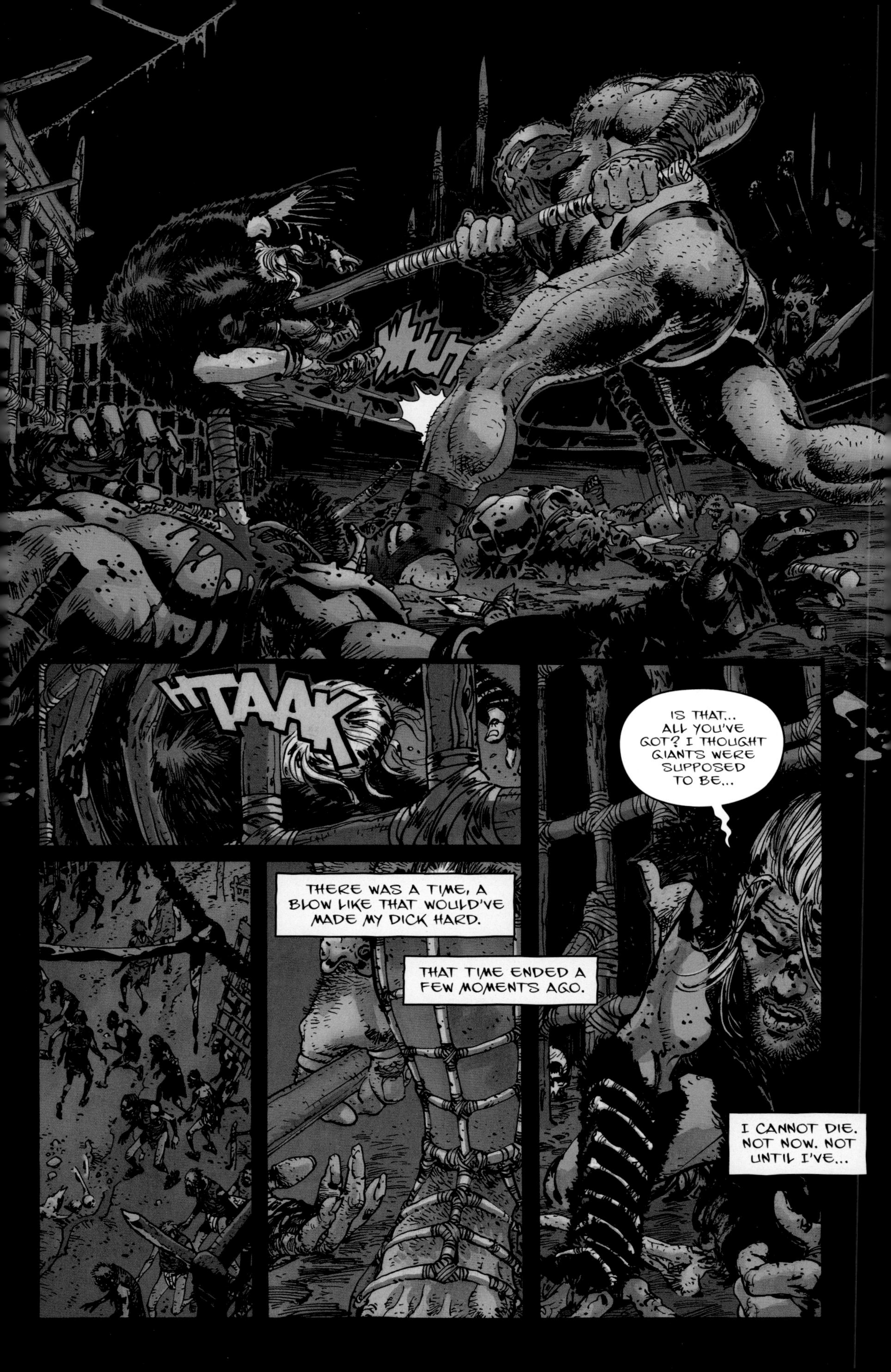
WHUT
HTAAK
IS THAT... ALL YOU'VE GOT? I THOUGHT GIANTS WERE SUPPOSED TO BE...
THERE WAS A TIME, A BLOW LIKE THAT WOULD'VE MADE MY DICK HARD.
THAT TIME ENDED A FEW MOMENTS AGO.
I CANNOT DIE. NOT NOW. NOT UNTIL I'VE...

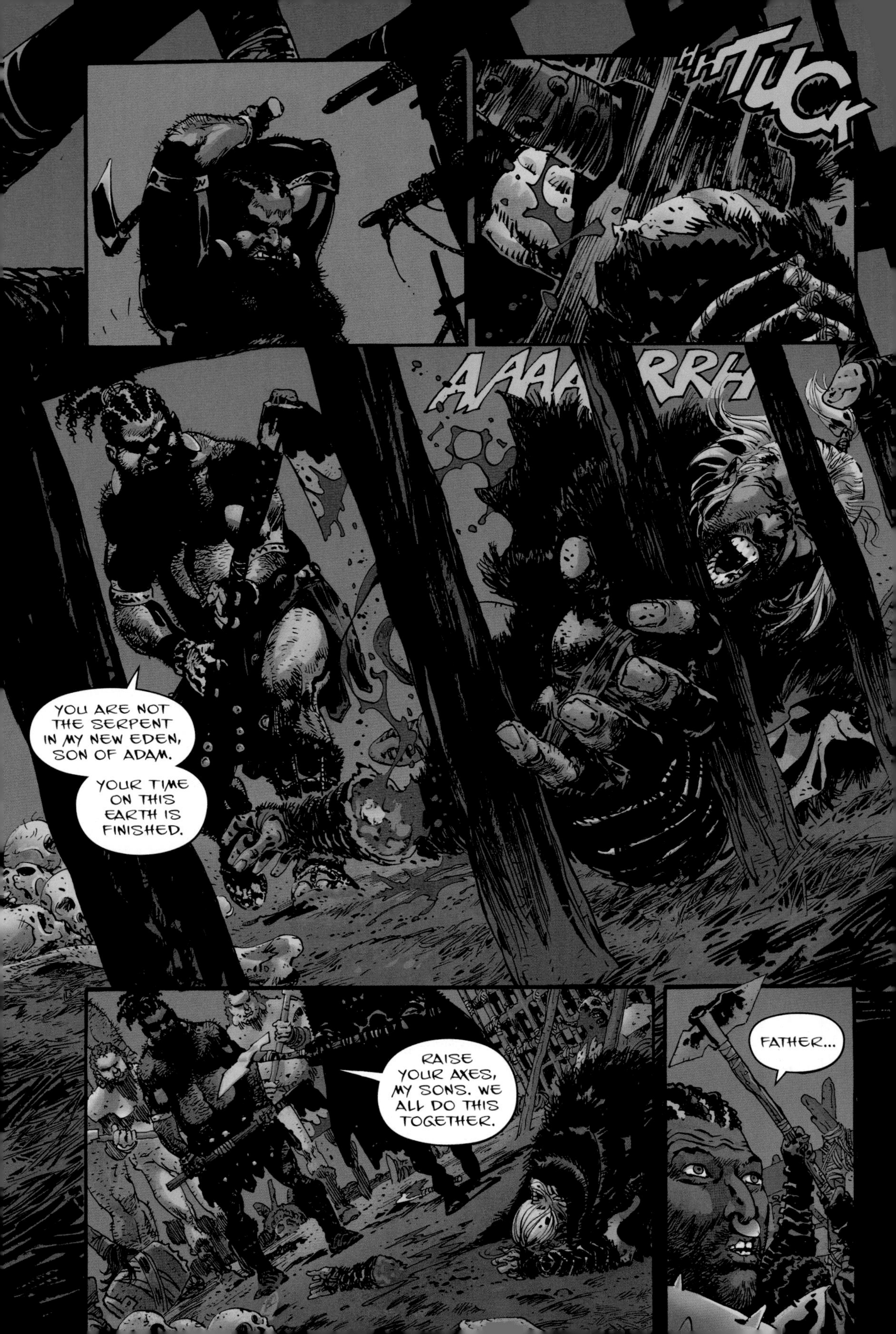
THTUCK
AAAARRH
YOU ARE NOT THE SERPENT IN MY NEW EDEN, SON OF ADAM.
YOUR TIME ON THIS EARTH IS FINISHED.
RAISE YOUR AXES, MY SONS. WE ALL DO THIS TOGETHER.
FATHER...

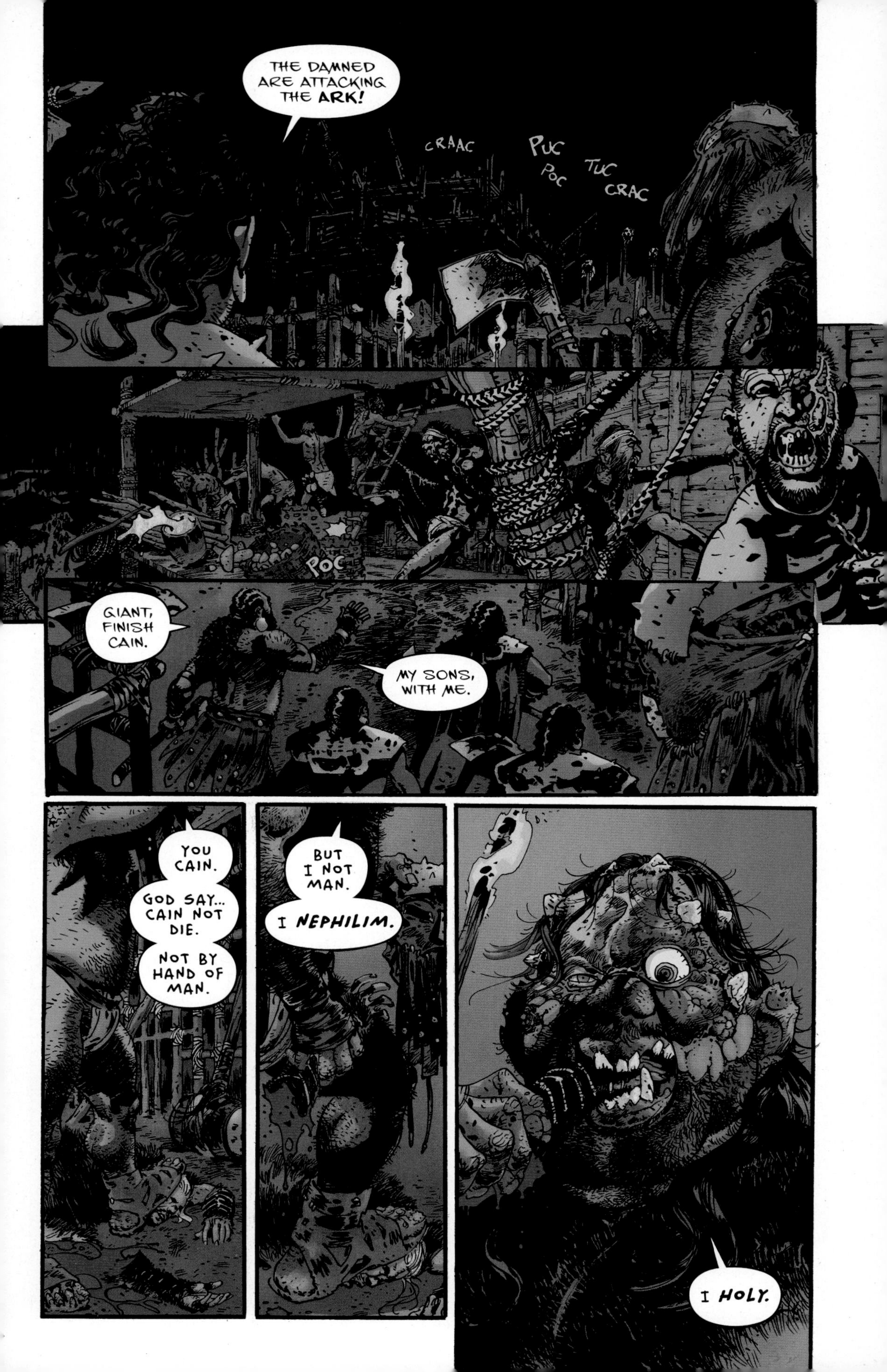
THE DAMNED ARE ATTACKING THE ARK!
CRAAC
PUC
POC
TUC
CRAC
POC
GIANT, FINISH CAIN.
MY SONS, WITH ME.
YOU CAIN.
GOD SAY... CAIN NOT DIE.
NOT BY HAND OF MAN.
BUT I NOT MAN.
I NEPHILIM.
I HOLY.

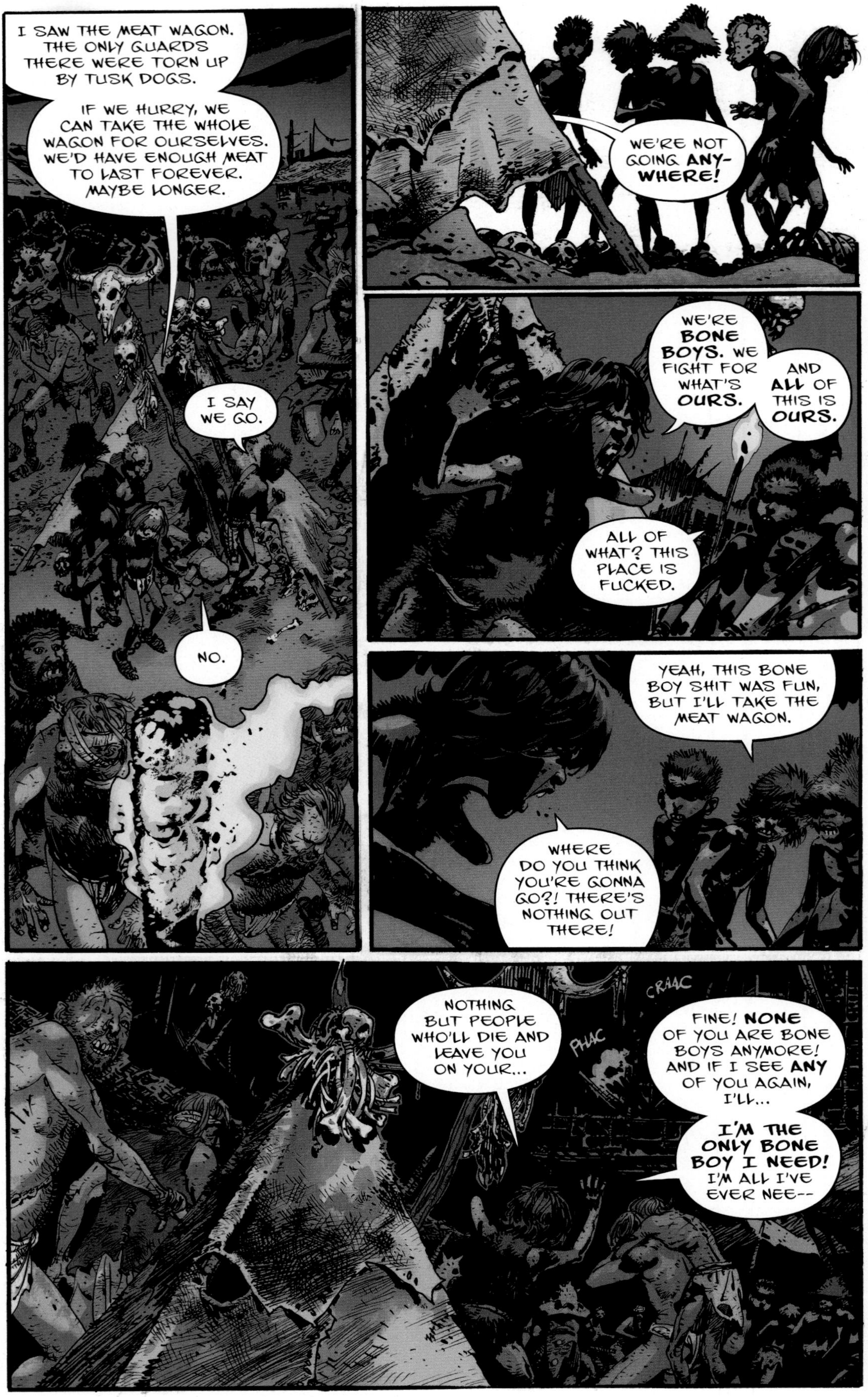
I SAW THE MEAT WAGON. THE ONLY GUARDS THERE WERE TORN UP BY TUSK DOGS.
IF WE HURRY, WE CAN TAKE THE WHOLE WAGON FOR OURSELVES. WE'D HAVE ENOUGH MEAT TO LAST FOREVER. MAYBE LONGER.
I SAY WE GO.
NO.
WE'RE NOT GOING **ANY-WHERE!**
WE'RE **BONE BOYS.** WE FIGHT FOR WHAT'S **OURS.**
AND **ALL** OF THIS IS **OURS.**
ALL OF WHAT? THIS PLACE IS FUCKED.
YEAH, THIS BONE BOY SHIT WAS FUN, BUT I'LL TAKE THE MEAT WAGON.
WHERE DO YOU THINK YOU'RE GONNA GO?! THERE'S NOTHING OUT THERE!
NOTHING BUT PEOPLE WHO'LL DIE AND LEAVE YOU ON YOUR...
PHAC
CRAAC
FINE! **NONE** OF YOU ARE BONE BOYS ANYMORE! AND IF I SEE **ANY** OF YOU AGAIN, I'LL...
I'M THE ONLY BONE BOY I NEED! I'M ALL I'VE EVER NEE--

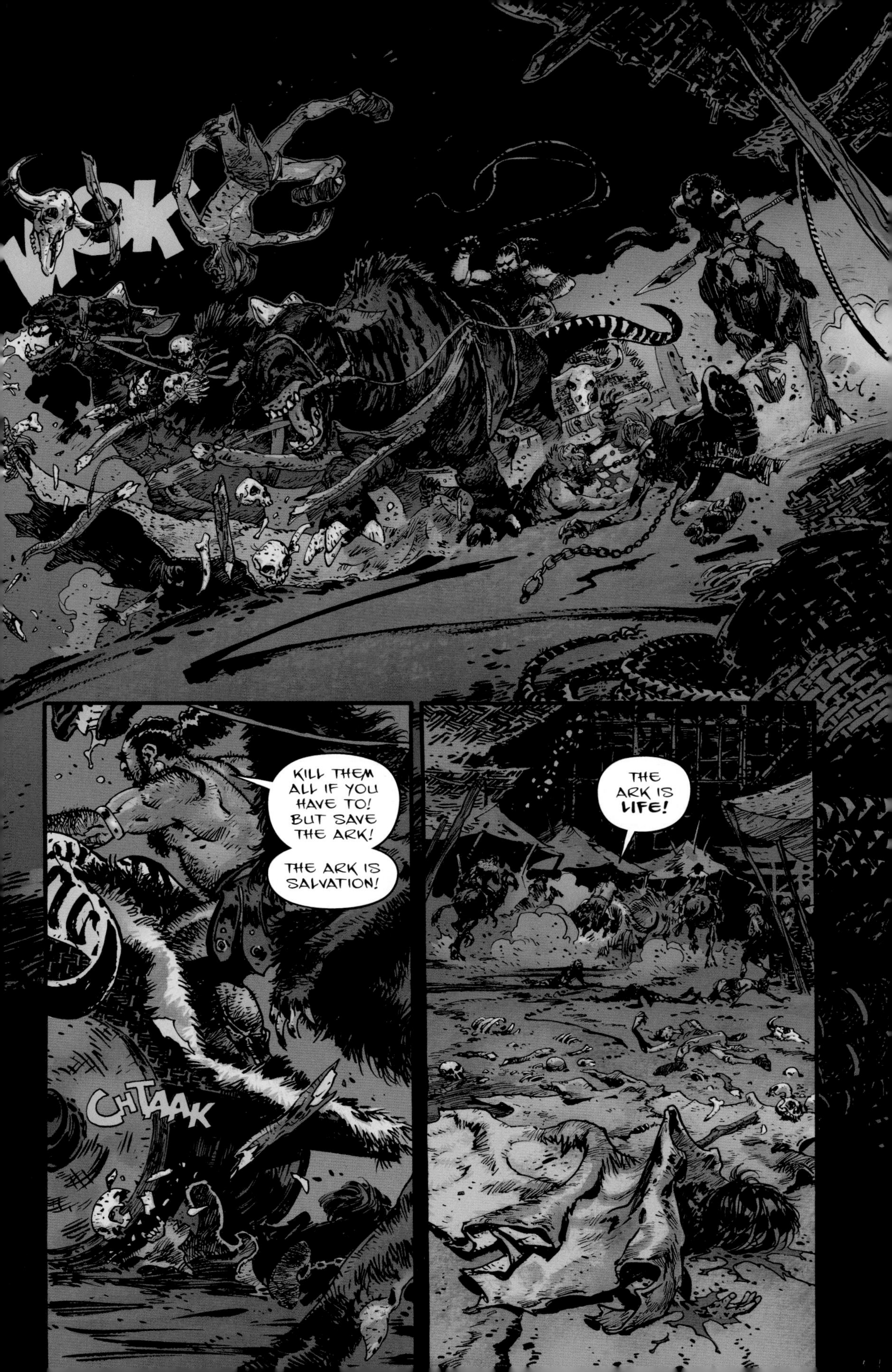
WOK
KILL THEM ALL IF YOU HAVE TO! BUT SAVE THE ARK!
THE ARK IS SALVATION!
CHTAAK
THE ARK IS LIFE!

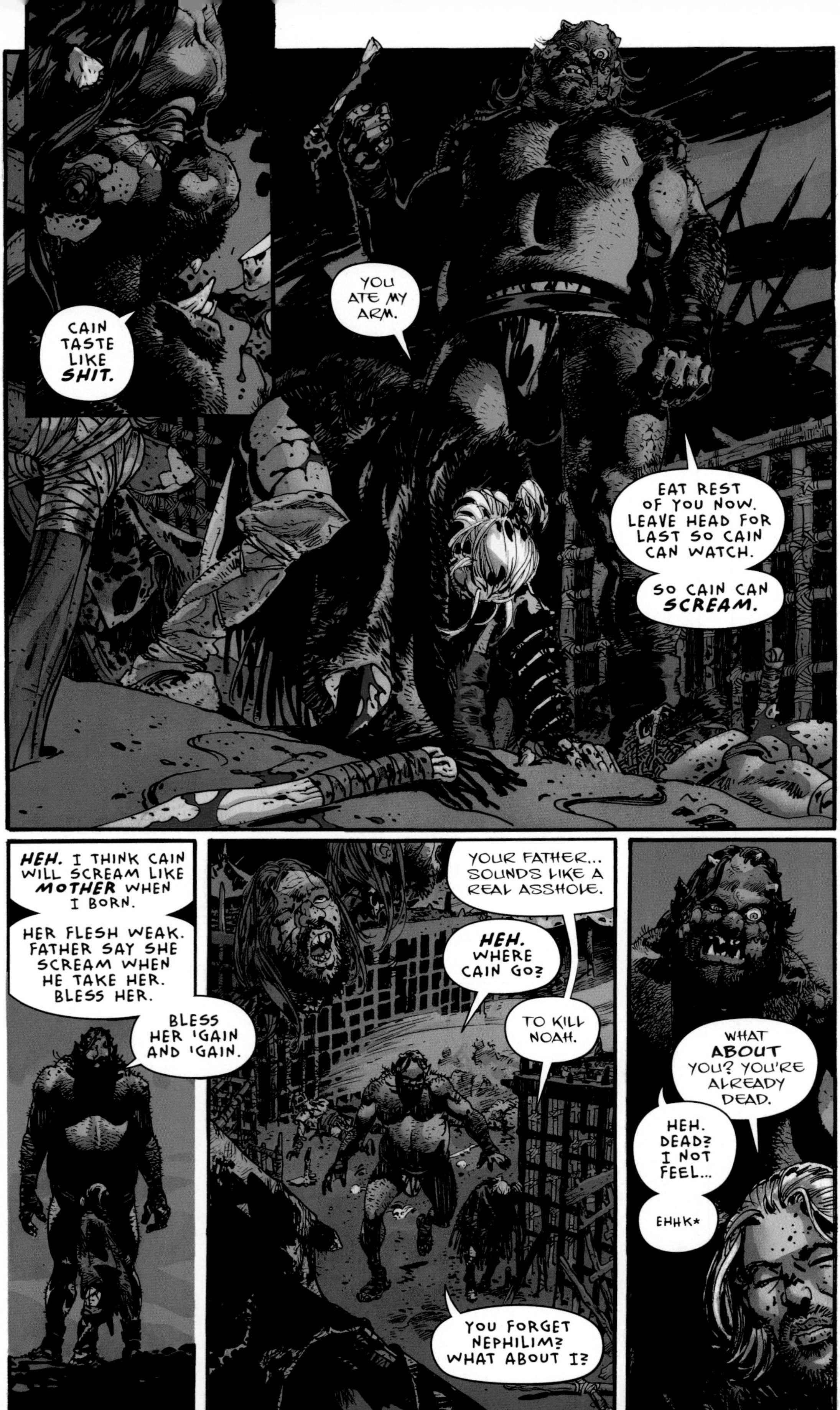
CAIN TASTE LIKE **SHIT.**
YOU ATE MY ARM.
EAT REST OF YOU NOW. LEAVE HEAD FOR LAST SO CAIN CAN WATCH.
SO CAIN CAN **SCREAM.**
HEH. I THINK CAIN WILL SCREAM LIKE **MOTHER** WHEN I BORN.
HER FLESH WEAK. FATHER SAY SHE SCREAM WHEN HE TAKE HER. BLESS HER.
BLESS HER 'GAIN AND 'GAIN.
YOUR FATHER... SOUNDS LIKE A REAL ASSHOLE.
HEH. WHERE CAIN GO?
TO KILL NOAH.
YOU FORGET NEPHILIM? WHAT ABOUT I?
WHAT **ABOUT** YOU? YOU'RE ALREADY DEAD.
HEH. DEAD? I NOT FEEL...
EHHK*

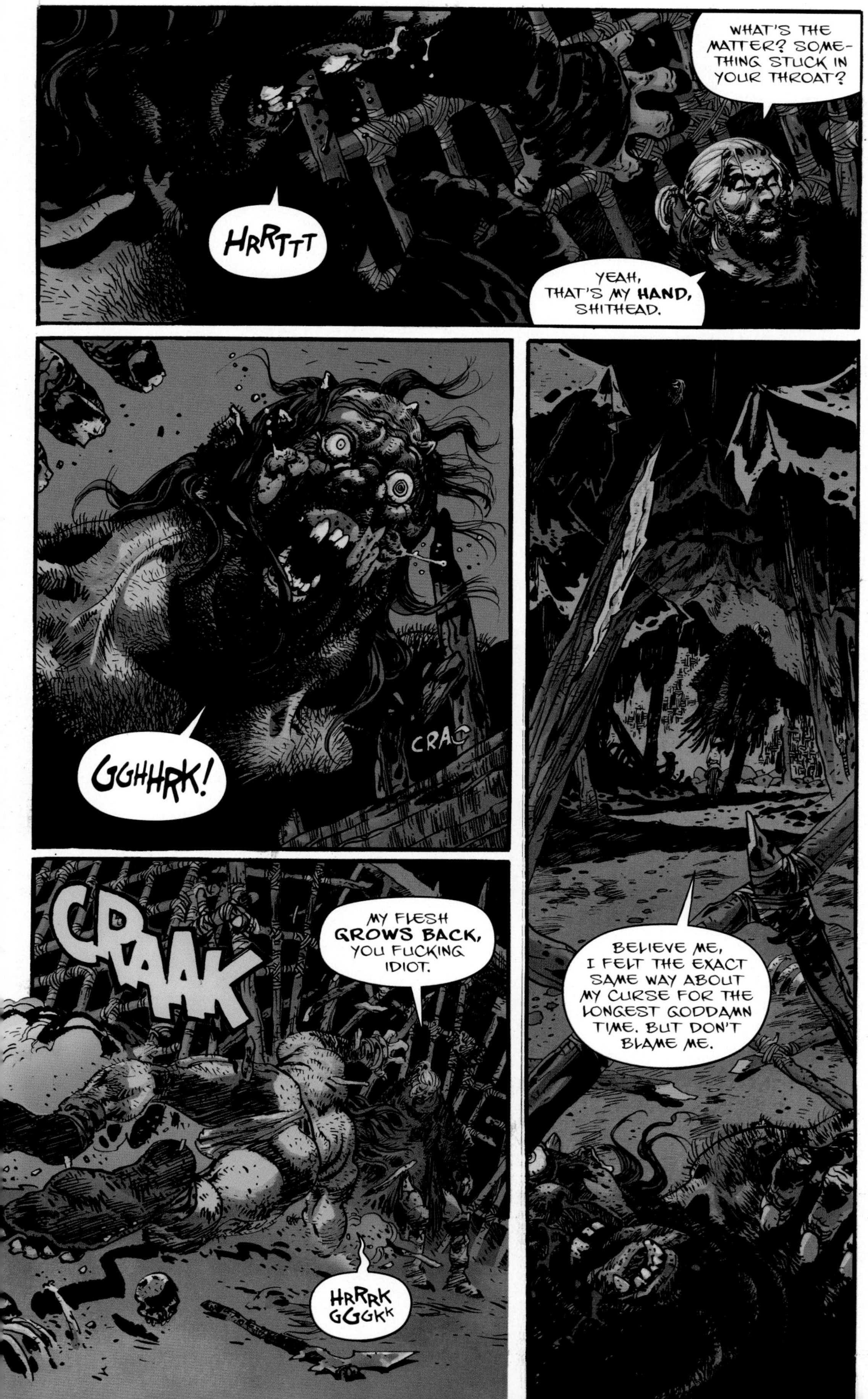
WHAT'S THE MATTER? SOME-THING STUCK IN YOUR THROAT?
HRRTTT
YEAH, THAT'S MY **HAND,** SHITHEAD.
GGHHRK!
CRAC
CRAAK
MY FLESH **GROWS BACK,** YOU FUCKING IDIOT.
HRRRK GGGKK
BELIEVE ME, I FELT THE EXACT SAME WAY ABOUT MY CURSE FOR THE LONGEST GODDAMN TIME. BUT DON'T BLAME ME.

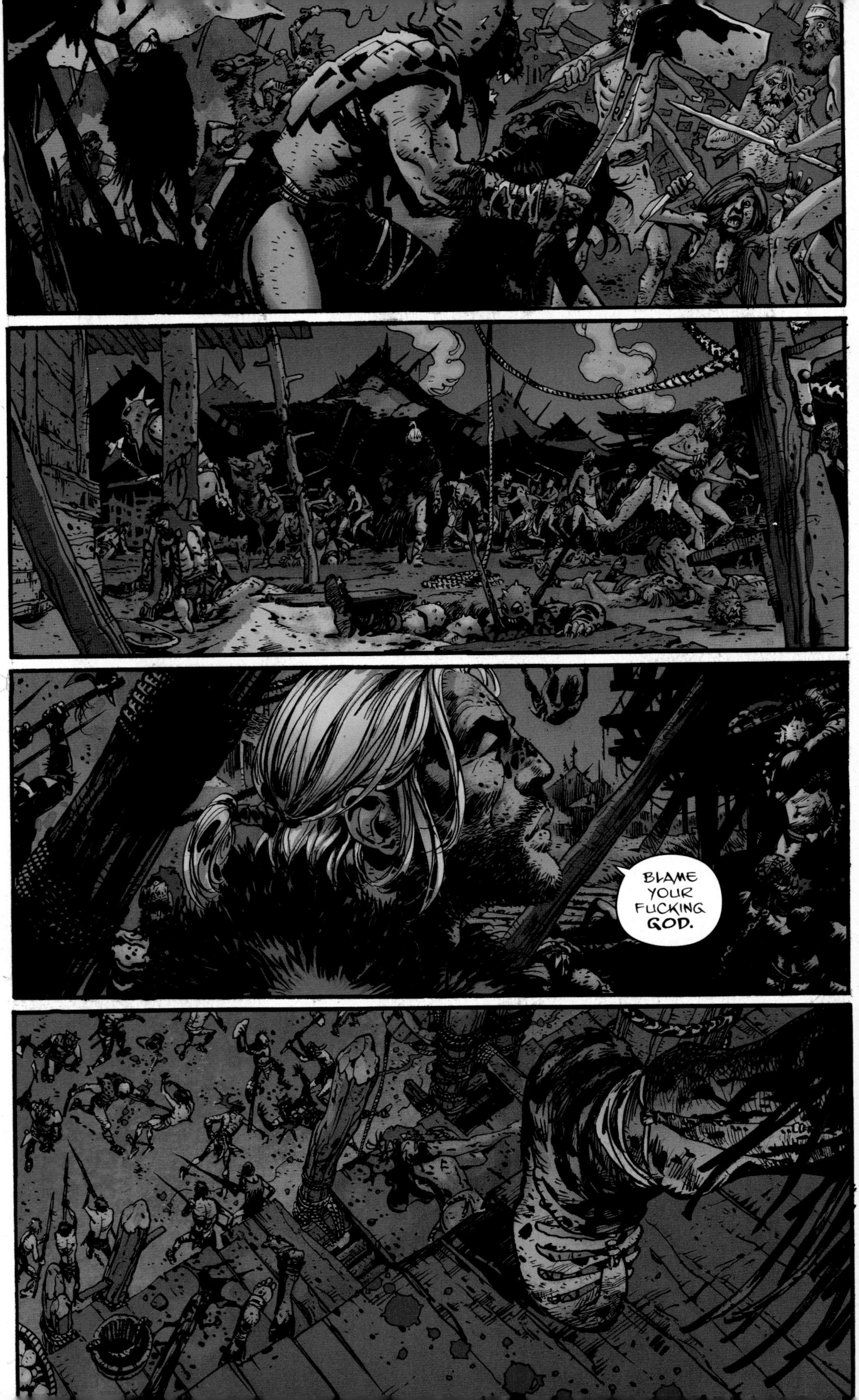
BLAME YOUR FUCKING GOD.

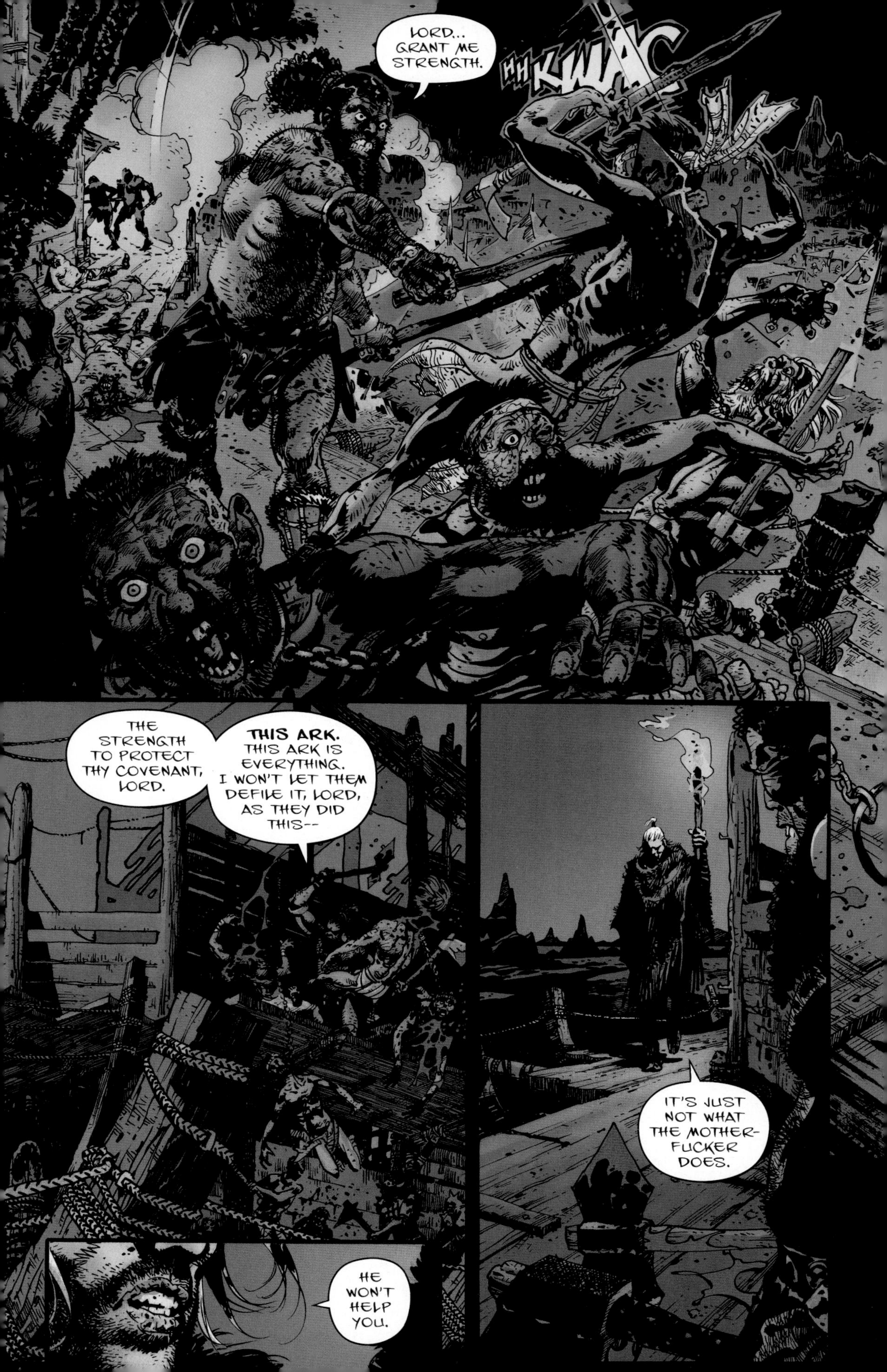
LORD... GRANT ME STRENGTH.
HHKWAC
THE STRENGTH TO PROTECT THY COVENANT, LORD.
THIS ARK. THIS ARK IS EVERYTHING. I WON'T LET THEM DEFILE IT, LORD, AS THEY DID THIS--
IT'S JUST NOT WHAT THE MOTHER-FUCKER DOES.
HE WON'T HELP YOU.

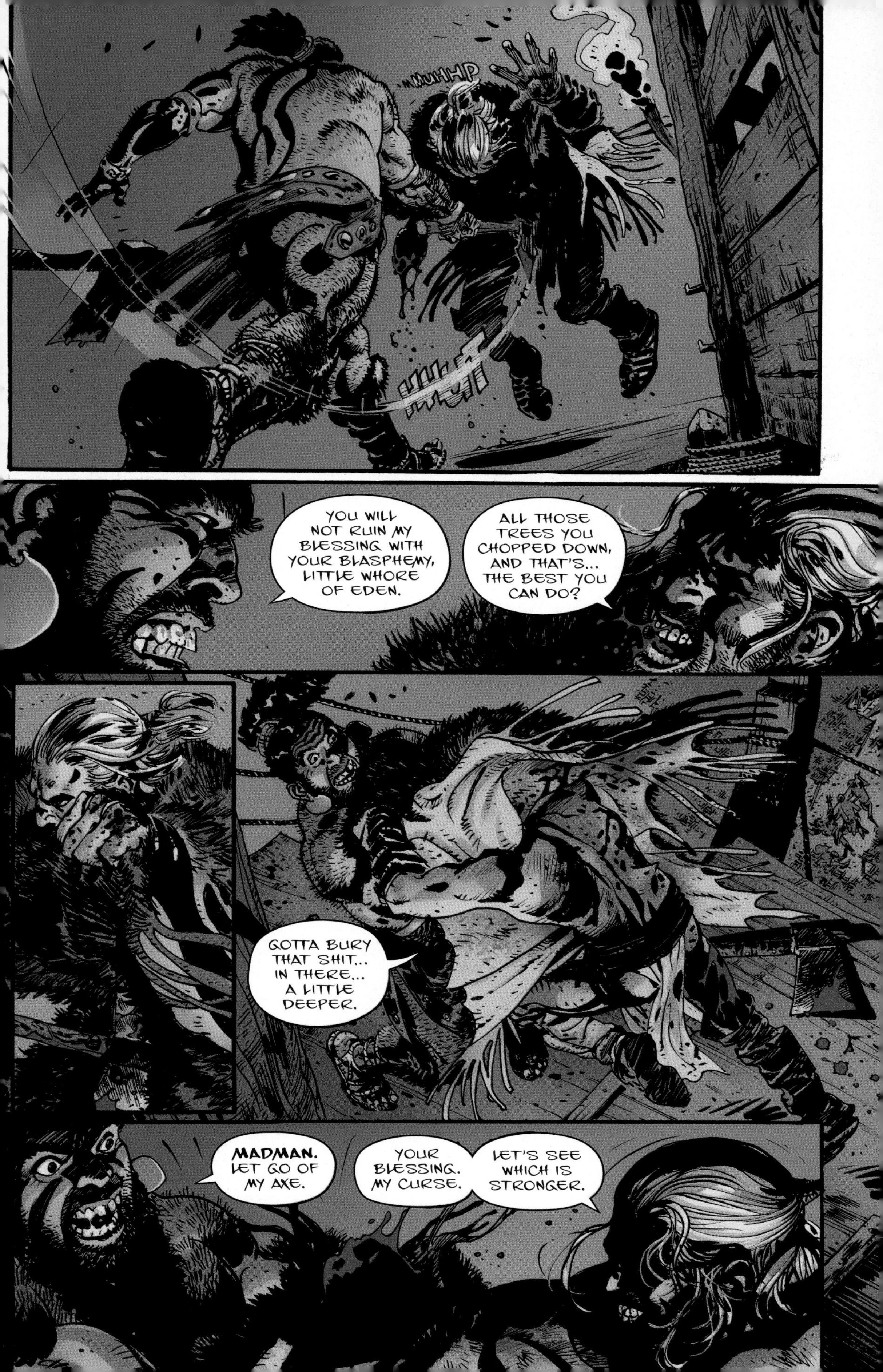
MMUHHP
YOU WILL NOT RUIN MY BLESSING WITH YOUR BLASPHEMY, LITTLE WHORE OF EDEN.
ALL THOSE TREES YOU CHOPPED DOWN, AND THAT'S... THE BEST YOU CAN DO?
GOTTA BURY THAT SHIT... IN THERE... A LITTLE DEEPER.
MADMAN. LET GO OF MY AXE.
YOUR BLESSING. MY CURSE.
LET'S SEE WHICH IS STRONGER.

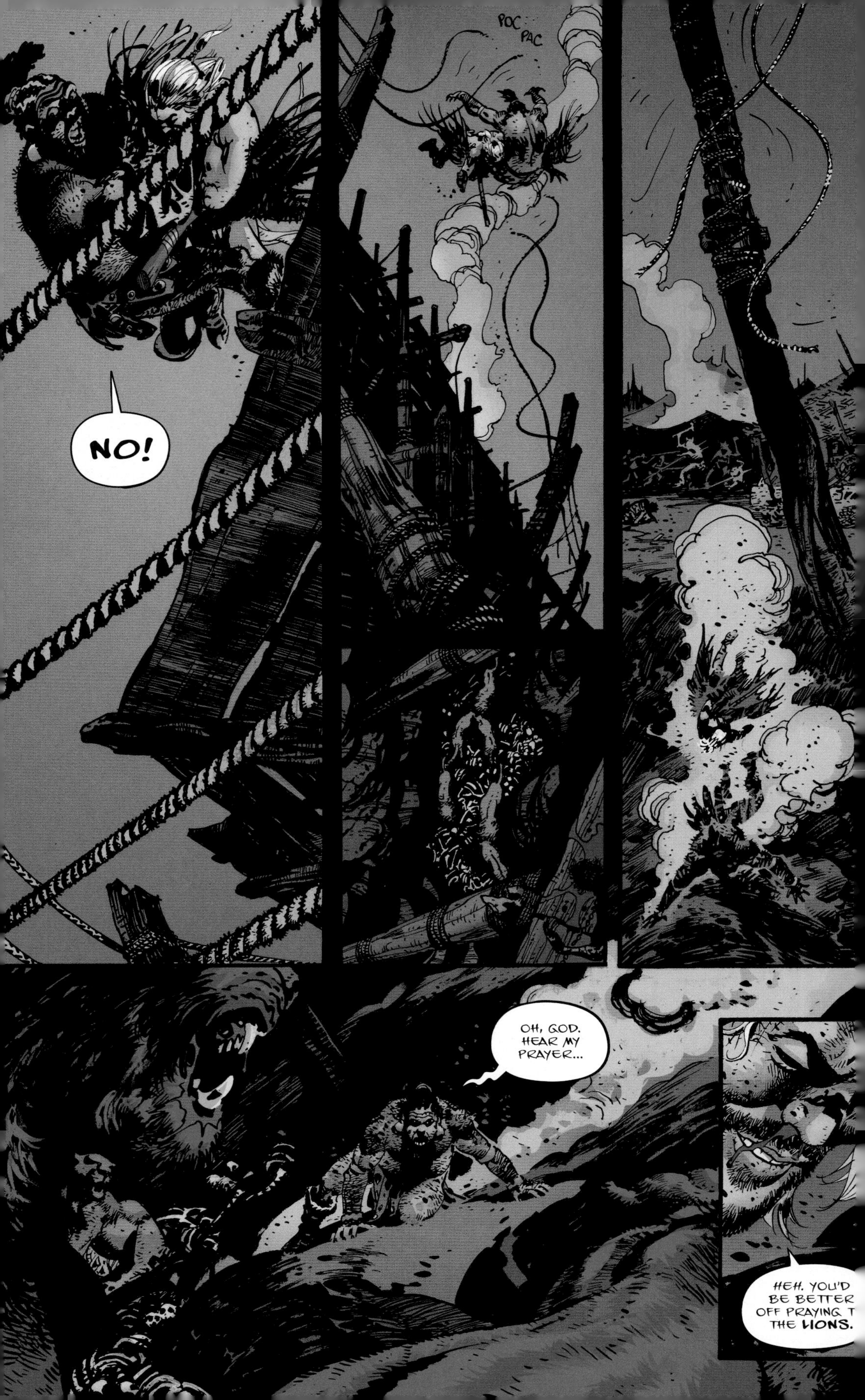
NO!
POC
PAC
OH, GOD. HEAR MY PRAYER...
HEH. YOU'D BE BETTER OFF PRAYING T THE LIONS.

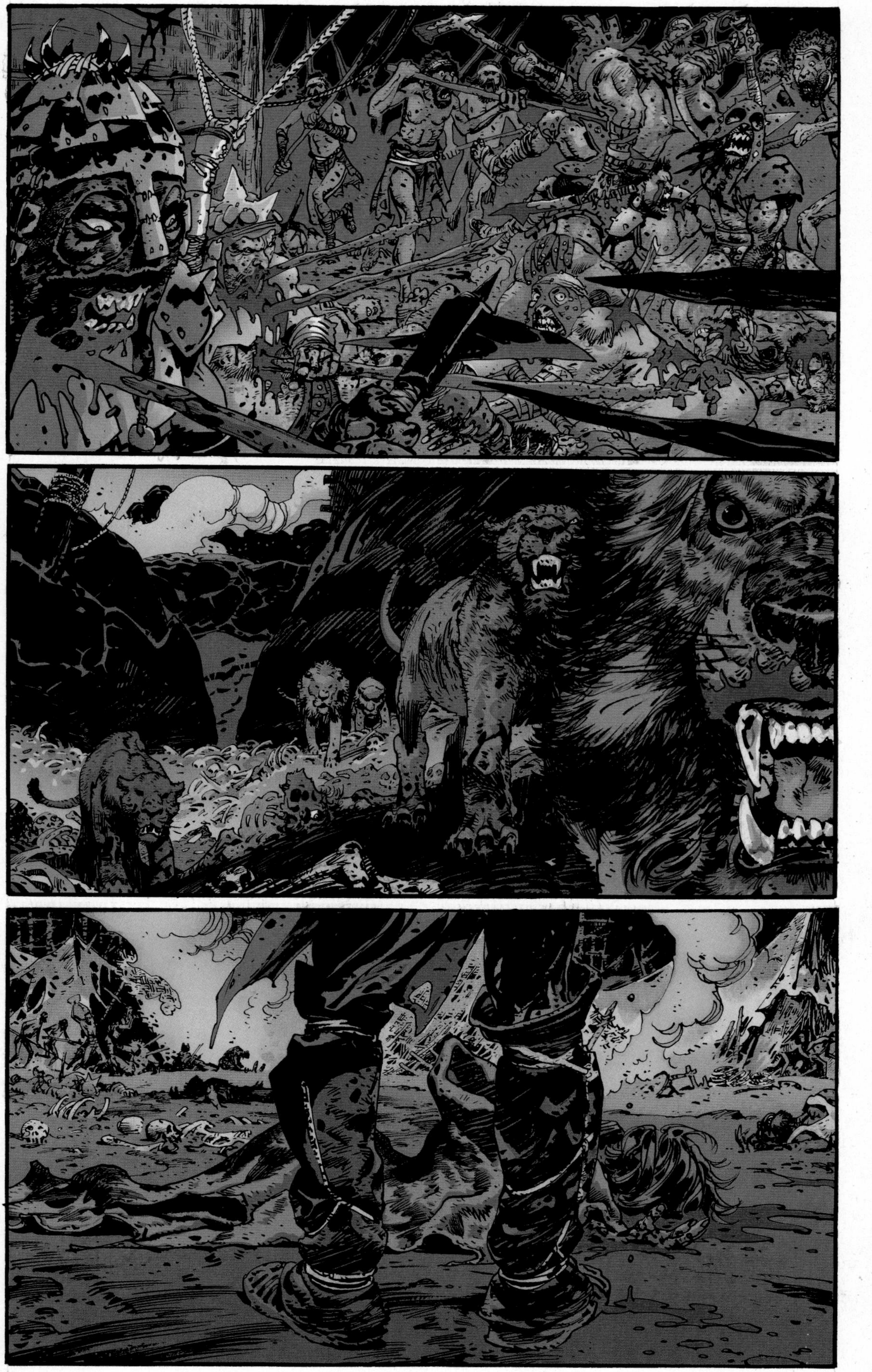

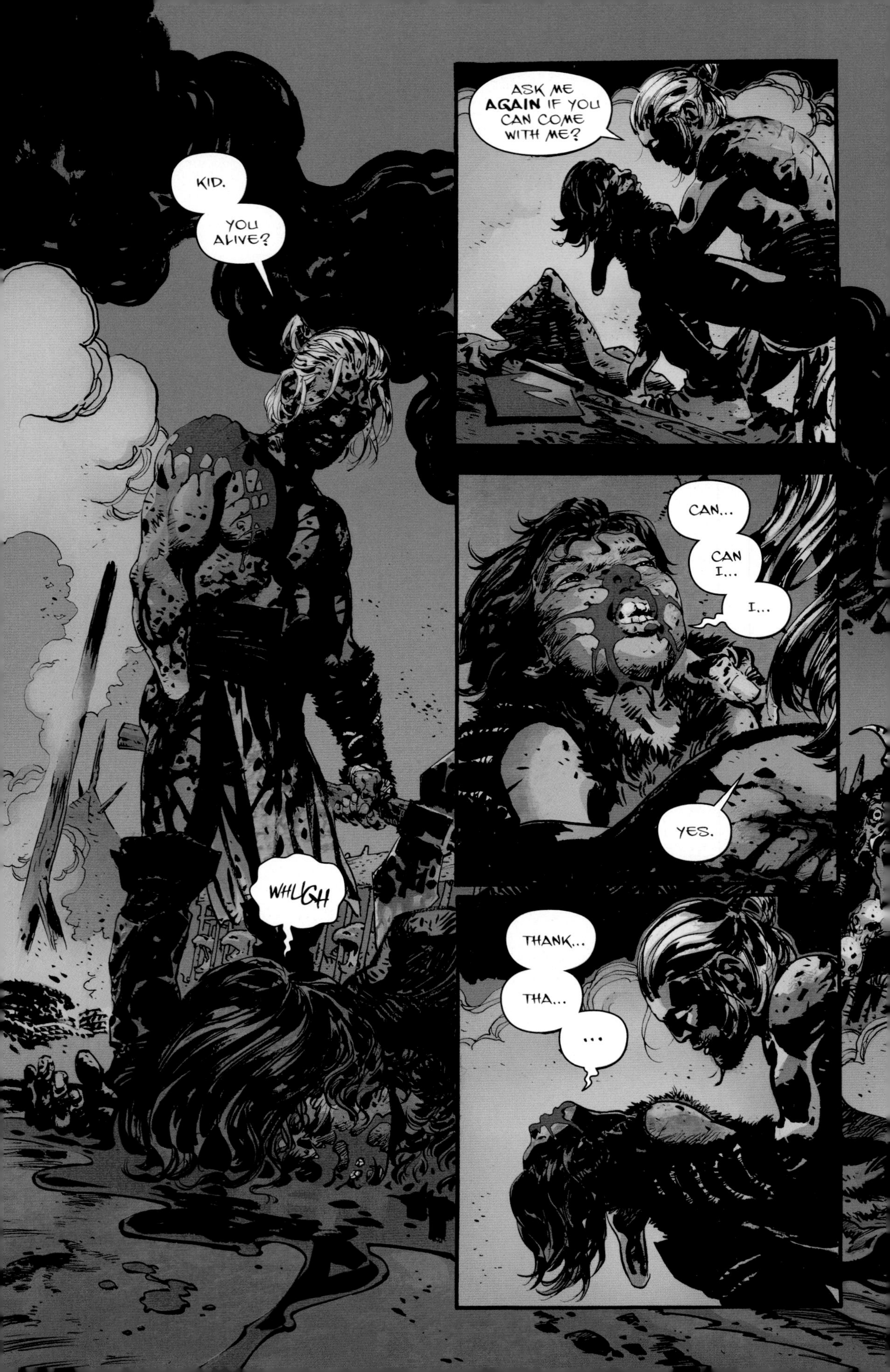
KID.
YOU ALIVE?
WHUGH
ASK ME AGAIN IF YOU CAN COME WITH ME?
CAN...
CAN I...
I...
YES.
THANK...
THA...
...

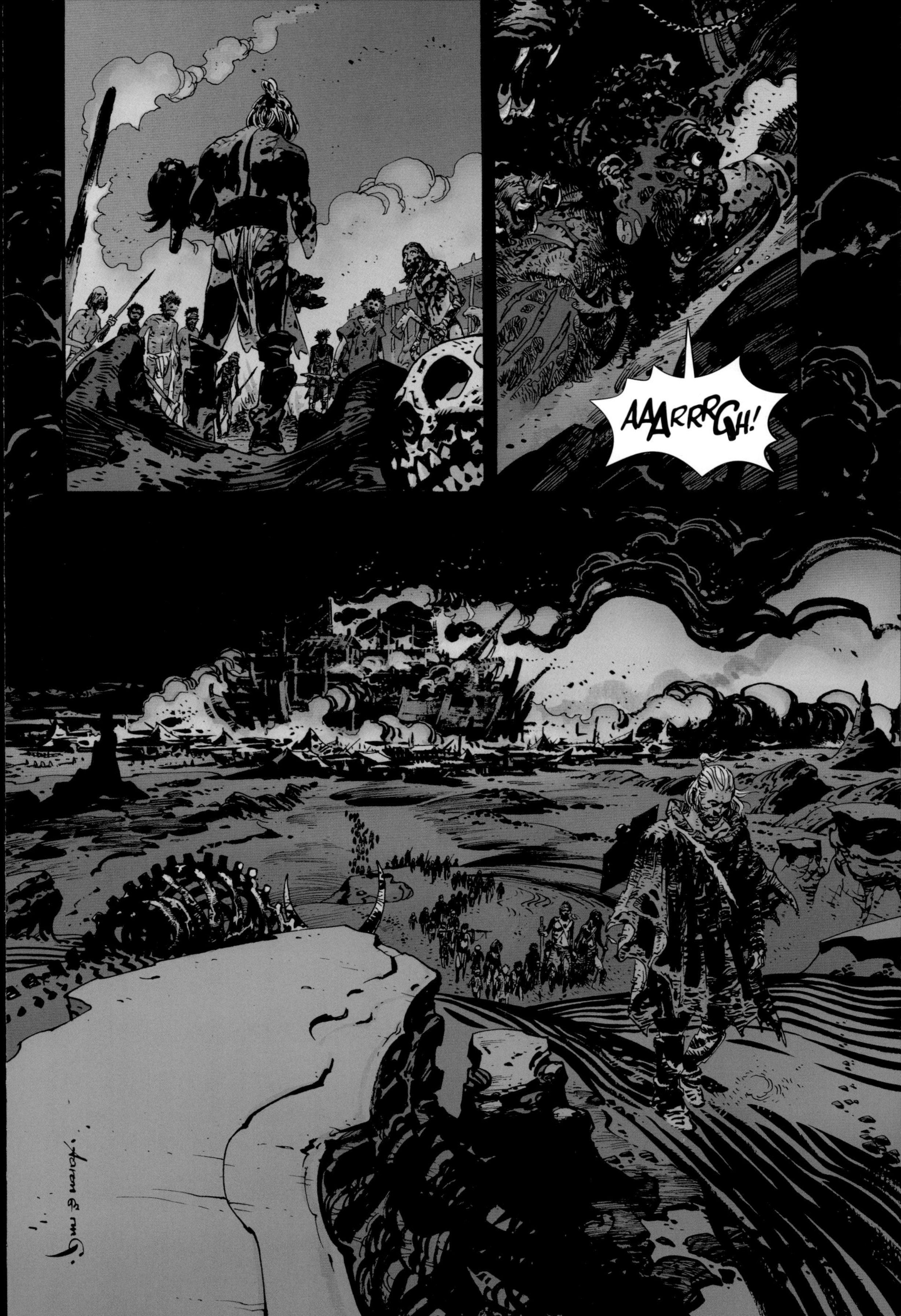
AAARRRGH!

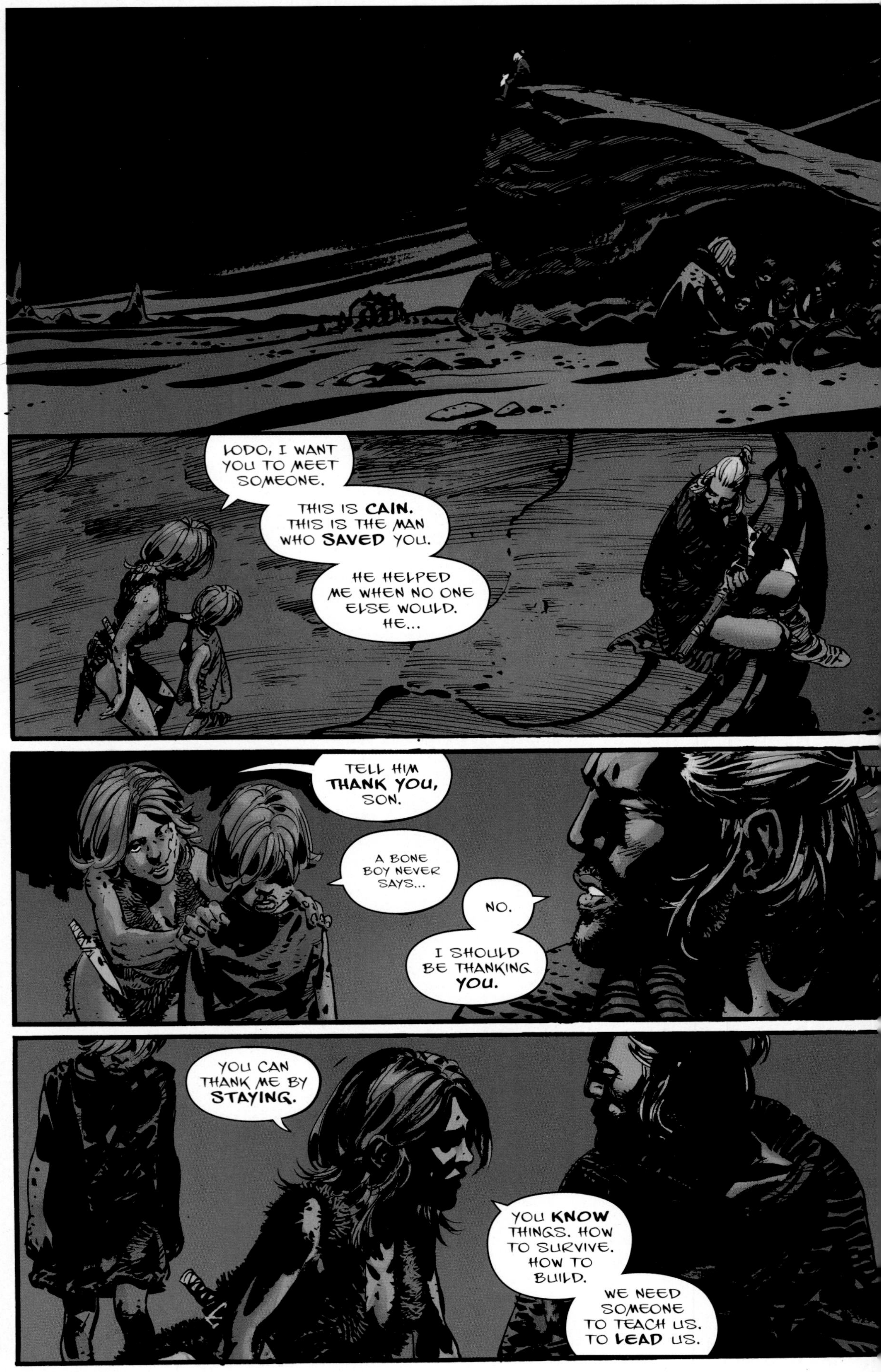

LODO, I WANT YOU TO MEET SOMEONE.
THIS IS CAIN. THIS IS THE MAN WHO SAVED YOU.
HE HELPED ME WHEN NO ONE ELSE WOULD. HE...
TELL HIM THANK YOU, SON.
A BONE BOY NEVER SAYS...
NO.
I SHOULD BE THANKING YOU.
YOU CAN THANK ME BY STAYING.
YOU KNOW THINGS. HOW TO SURVIVE. HOW TO BUILD.
WE NEED SOMEONE TO TEACH US. TO LEAD US.

AND I KNOW...
YOU MISS
YOUR FAMILY.

WE CAN BE
THAT FAMILY.
ALL OF US.

IF YOU
LET US.

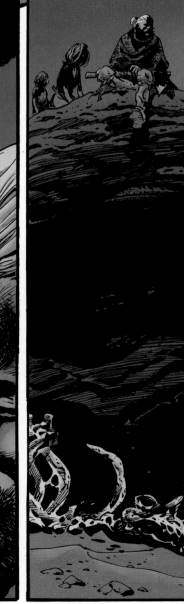

OKAY,
I'LL...

SHUNK

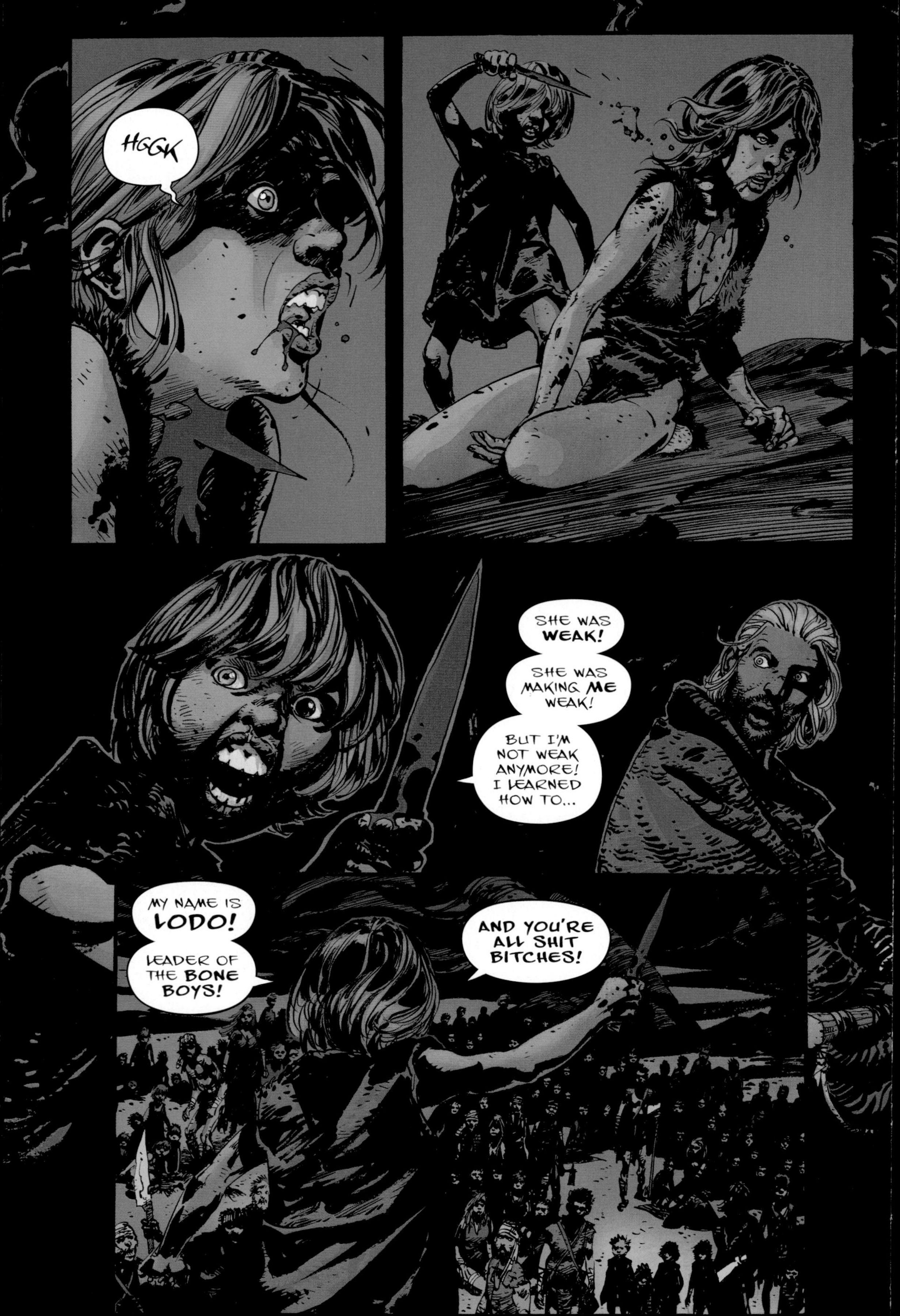
HGGK
SHE WAS WEAK!
SHE WAS MAKING ME WEAK!
BUT I'M NOT WEAK ANYMORE! I LEARNED HOW TO...
MY NAME IS LODO!
LEADER OF THE BONE BOYS!
AND YOU'RE ALL SHIT BITCHES!

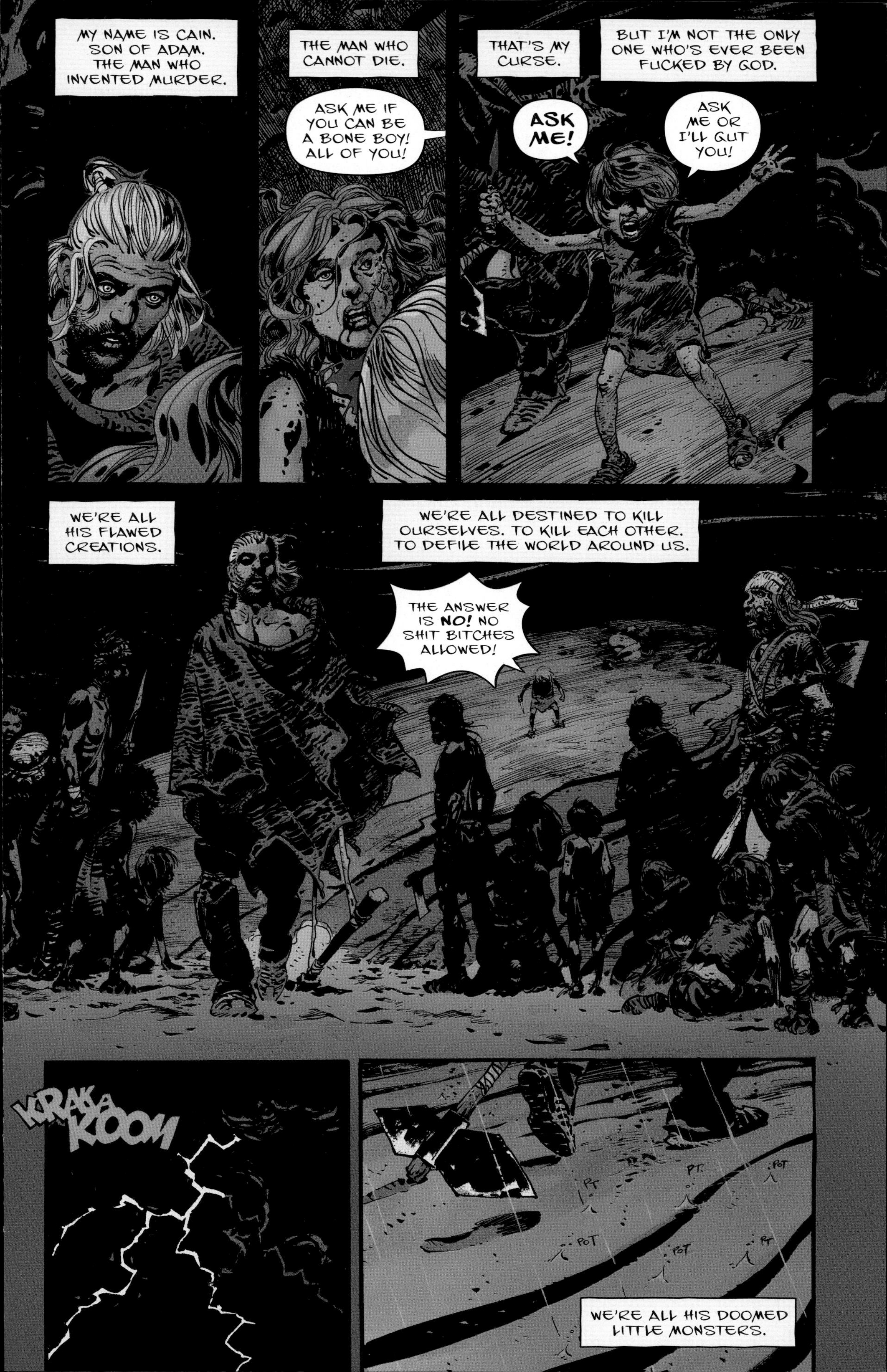
MY NAME IS CAIN. SON OF ADAM. THE MAN WHO INVENTED MURDER.
THE MAN WHO CANNOT DIE.
ASK ME IF YOU CAN BE A BONE BOY! ALL OF YOU!
THAT'S MY CURSE.
BUT I'M NOT THE ONLY ONE WHO'S EVER BEEN FUCKED BY GOD.
ASK ME!
ASK ME OR I'LL GUT YOU!
WE'RE ALL HIS FLAWED CREATIONS.
WE'RE ALL DESTINED TO KILL OURSELVES. TO KILL EACH OTHER. TO DEFILE THE WORLD AROUND US.
THE ANSWER IS NO! NO SHIT BITCHES ALLOWED!
KRAKA KOOM
WE'RE ALL HIS DOOMED LITTLE MONSTERS.

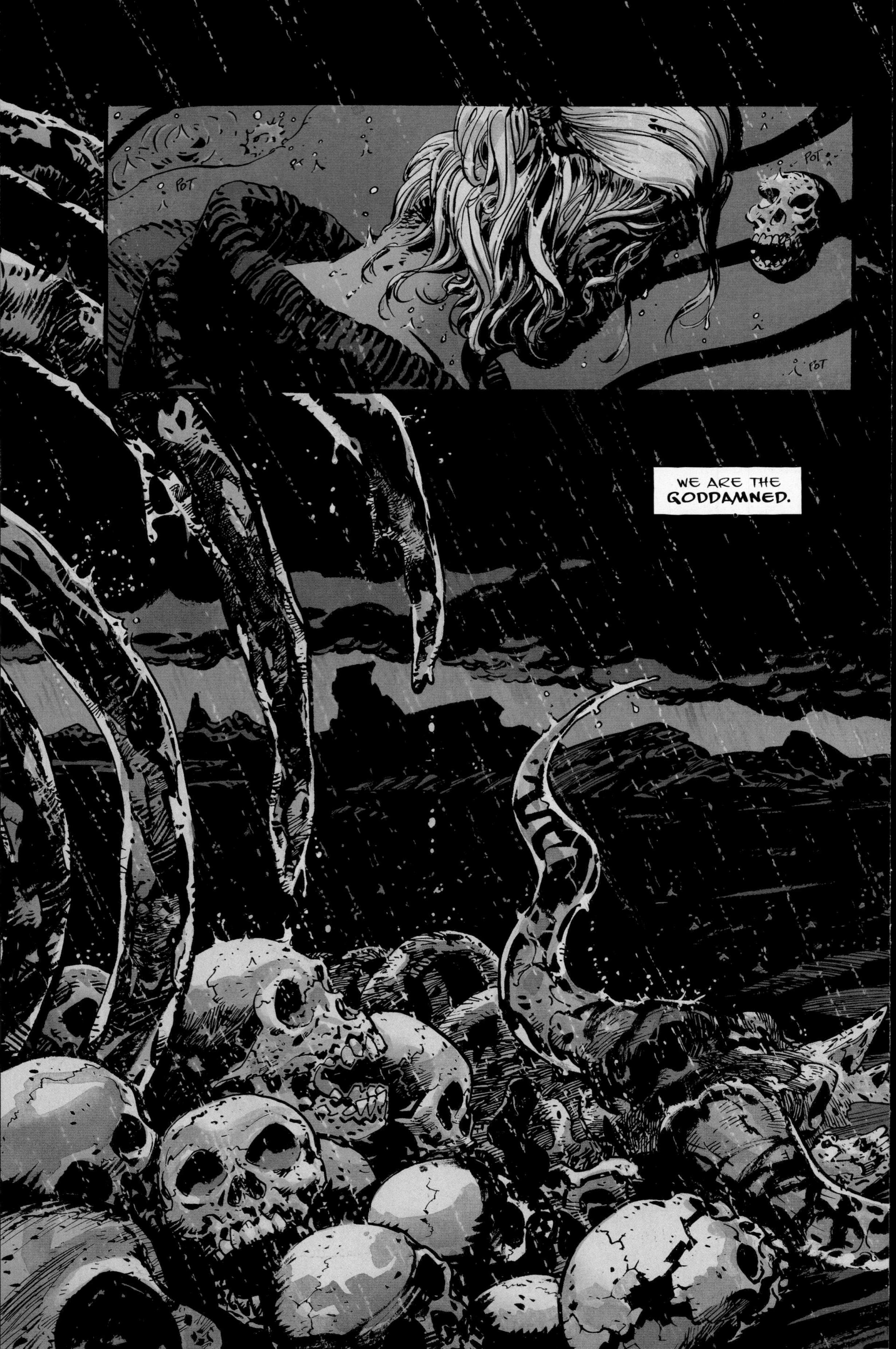
POT
POT
POT
WE ARE THE GODDAMNED.

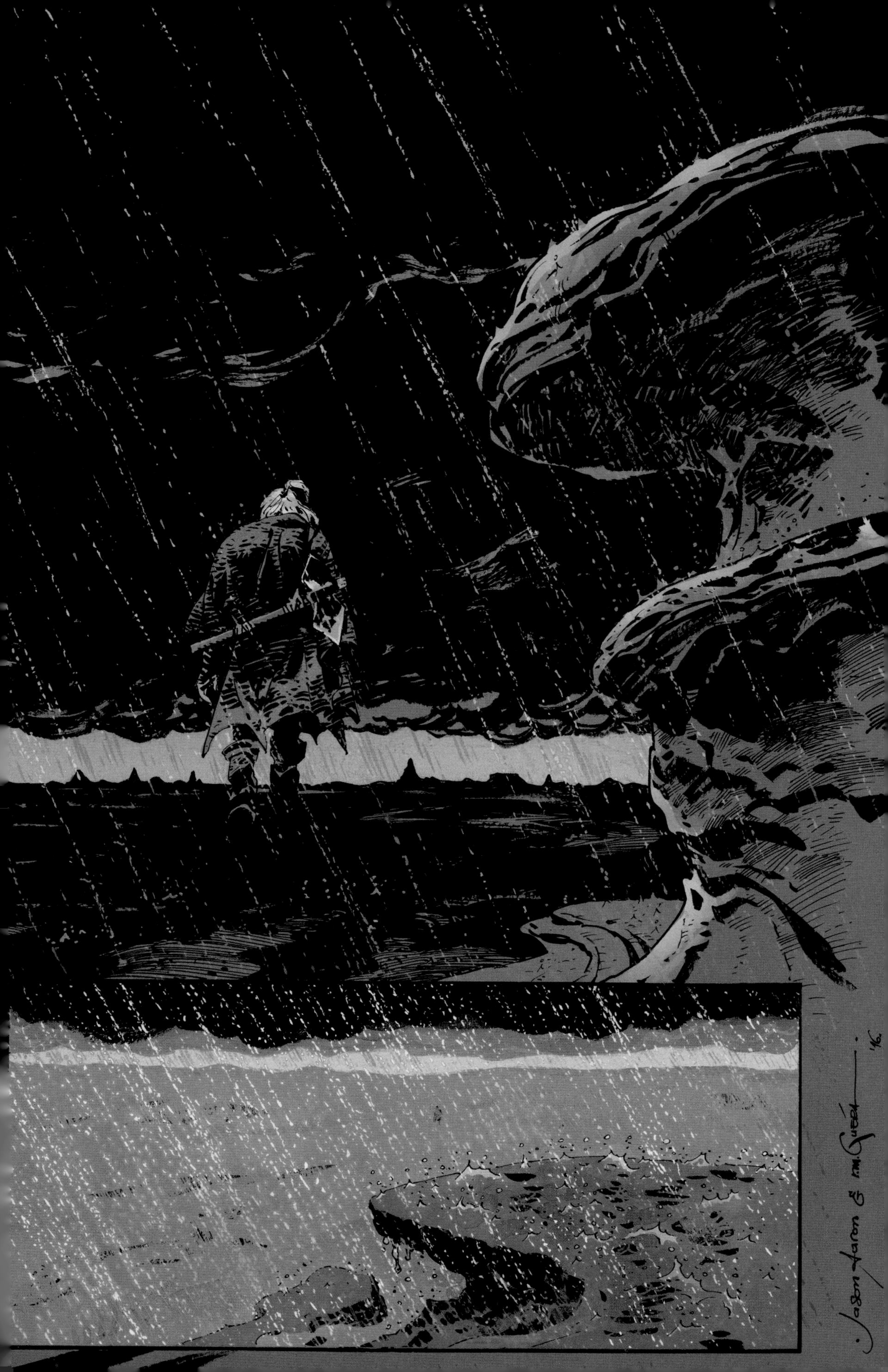

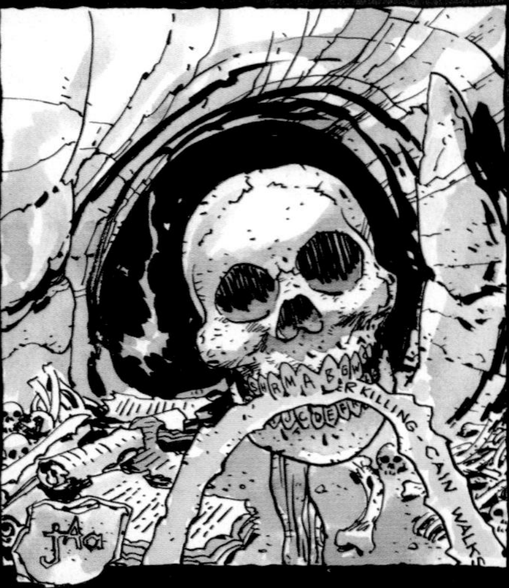
jAa

Jason Aaron is a comic book writer best known for his work on the *New York Times* best-selling crime series SCALPED for Vertigo Comics and the Eisner Award-winning SOUTHERN BASTARDS from Image Comics, as well as for various projects with Marvel Comics. Aaron's current work for Marvel includes the creation of the headline-grabbing female version of THOR and the launch of an all-new STAR WARS series, the first issue of which sold over one million copies to become the best-selling American comic book in more than 20 years. Aaron was born in Alabama but currently resides in Kansas City.

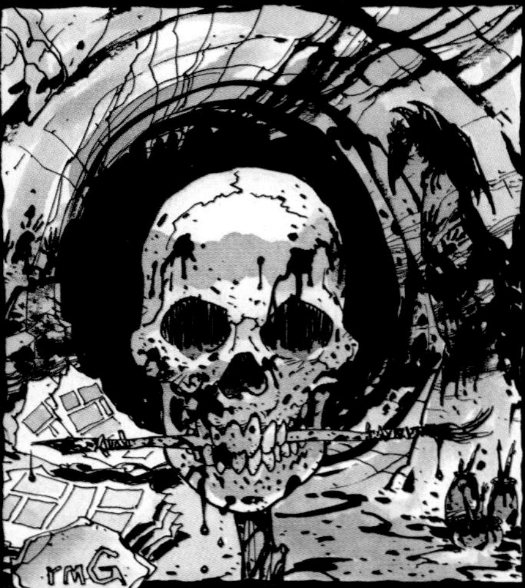
rmG

Rajko Milosevic, known as **r.m.Guéra** is a Serbian artist, living in Spain. He reached early fame and academic awards during 80s in former Yugoslavia. After moving to Barcelona, and after a decade of working in publicity and animation through works for museums and theaters, he published his first comic albums in France, through publishers Glénat and Delcourt. His worldwide breakthrough came with the crime series SCALPED, also written by Jason Aaron and published by Vertigo, DC Comics which garnered worldwide critical acclaim.

Guéra has worked with Quentin Tarantino on a comic book version of *Django Unchained*; continues to publish in France for JOUR J, in the UK for JUDGE DREDD, as well as for all US mainstream editorials including Marvel, DC, Dark Horse, on many one-shots, promotional posters, and covers.

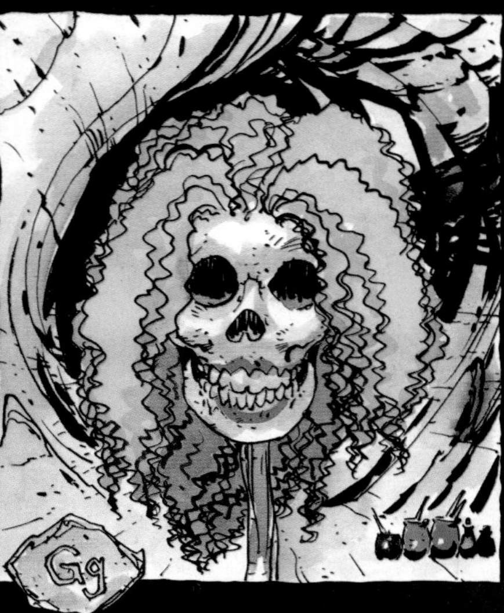
Gg

Giulia Brusco loves colours and ice cream, and she dreams of holidays that never materialise. She obtained a degree in Foreign Languages and Literature at the University of Bologna, writing her final dissertation on Kandinsky's poems *Klänge* (yes, he was a figurative artist, but he also wrote poems about sounds...) and the synesthesia approach to art. This contributes to her understanding of colours as evocative instruments in storytelling. Brusco has been colouring comic books since 2001, working on numerous titles and for various companies. She's best known for her years long collaboration with r.m.Guéra and for her heavy Italian accent while speaking English despite 23 years of life in London, England.

Cover Gallery
+
Sketchbook

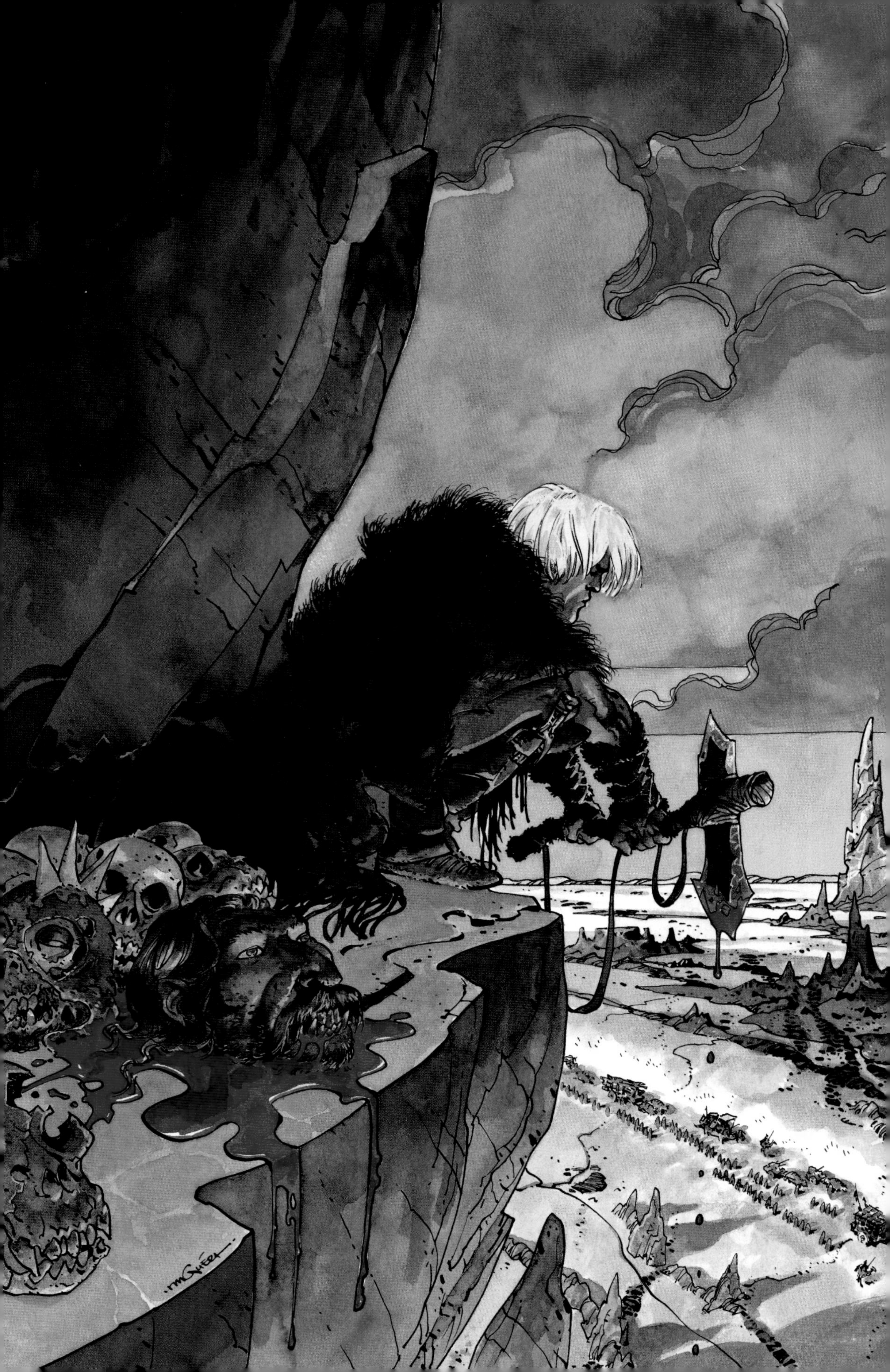

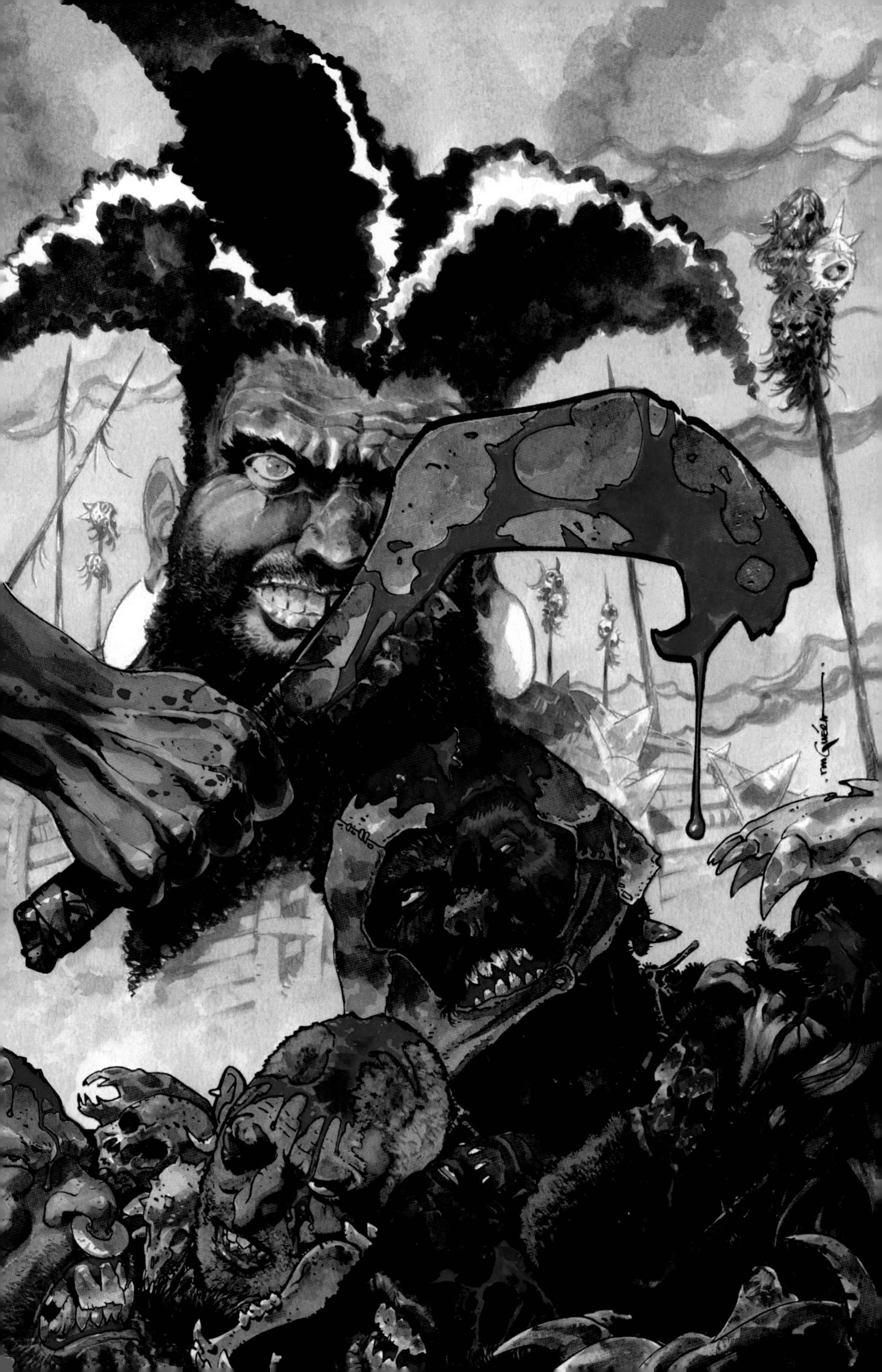

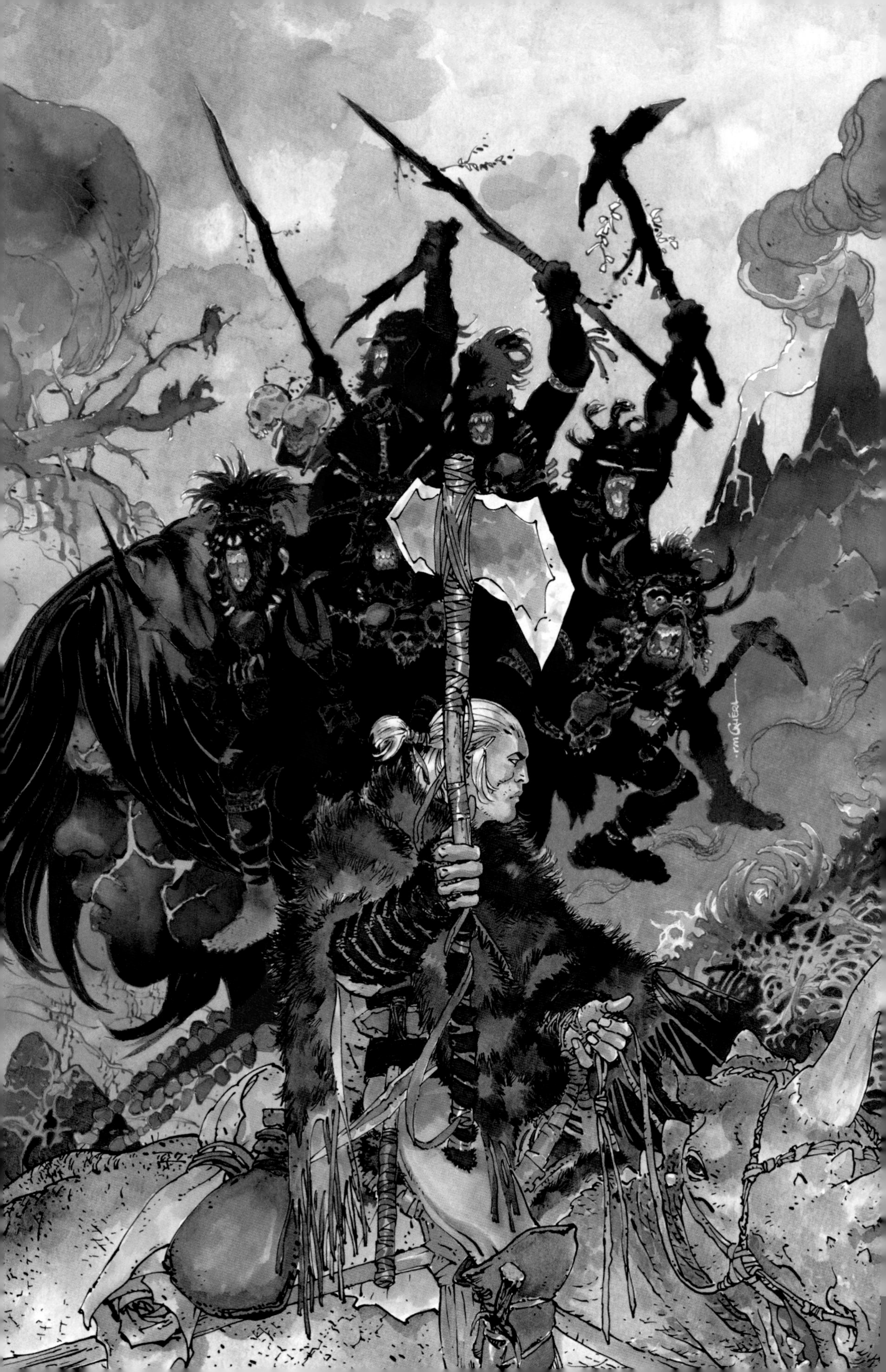

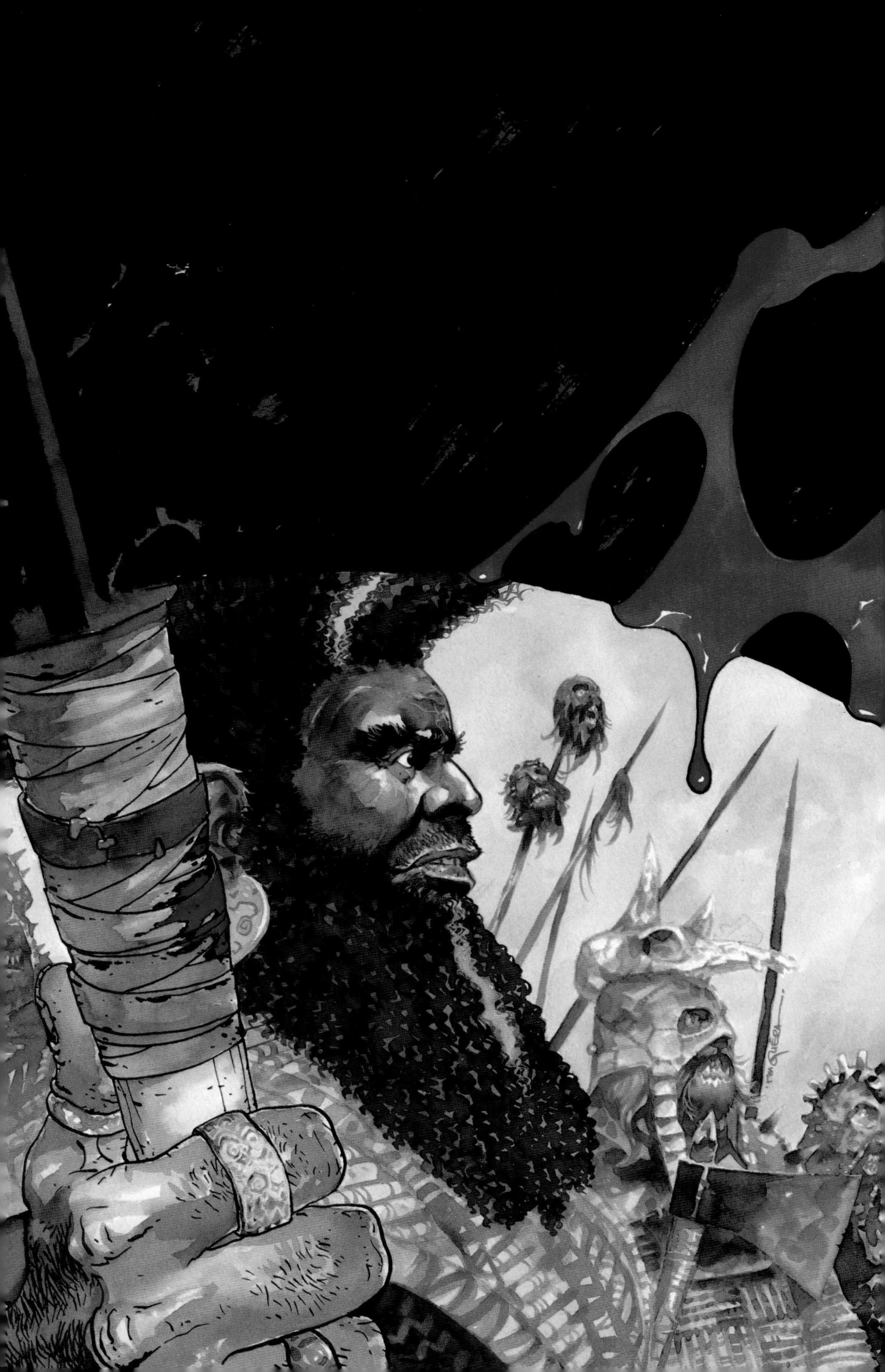

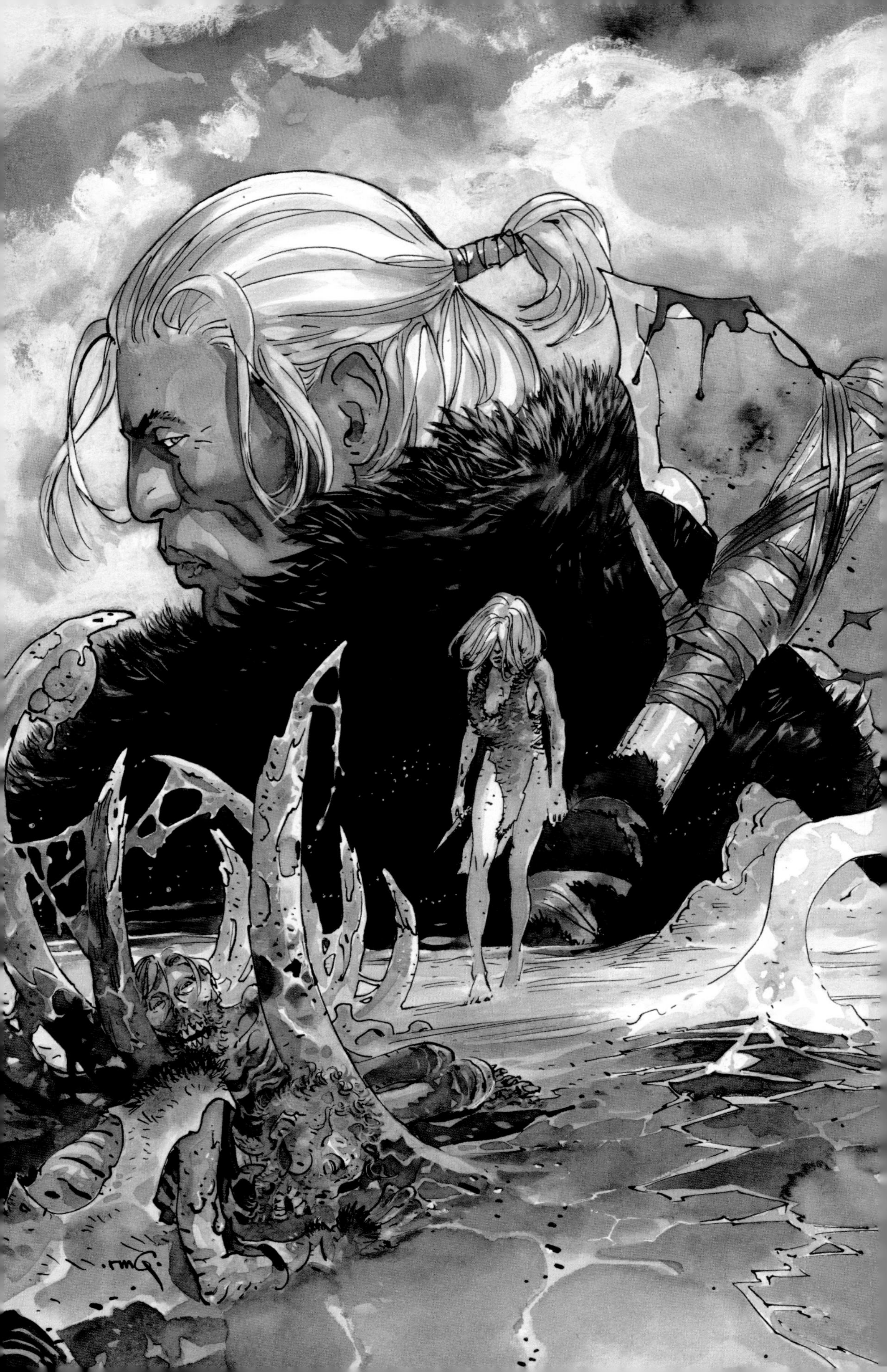

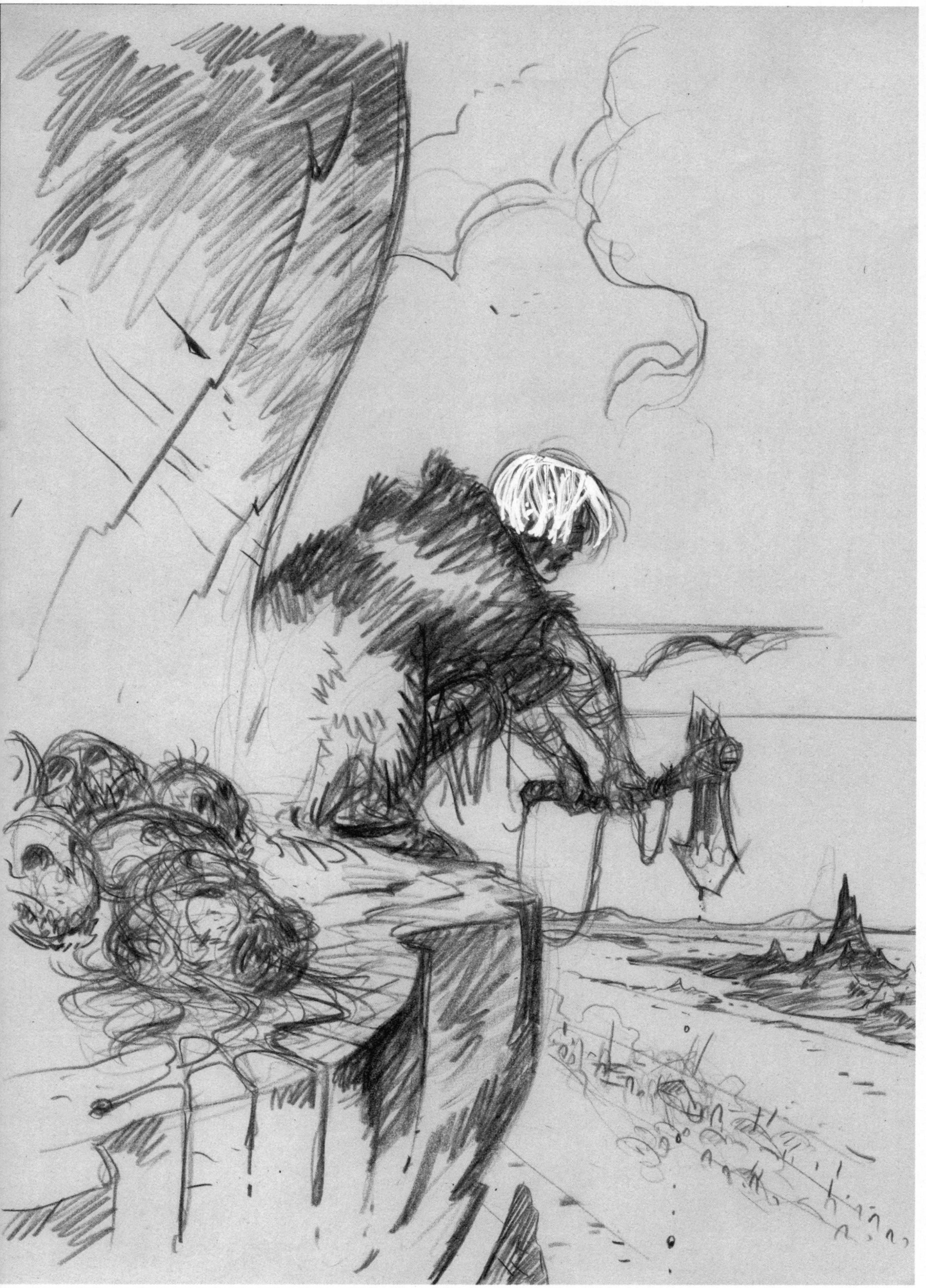

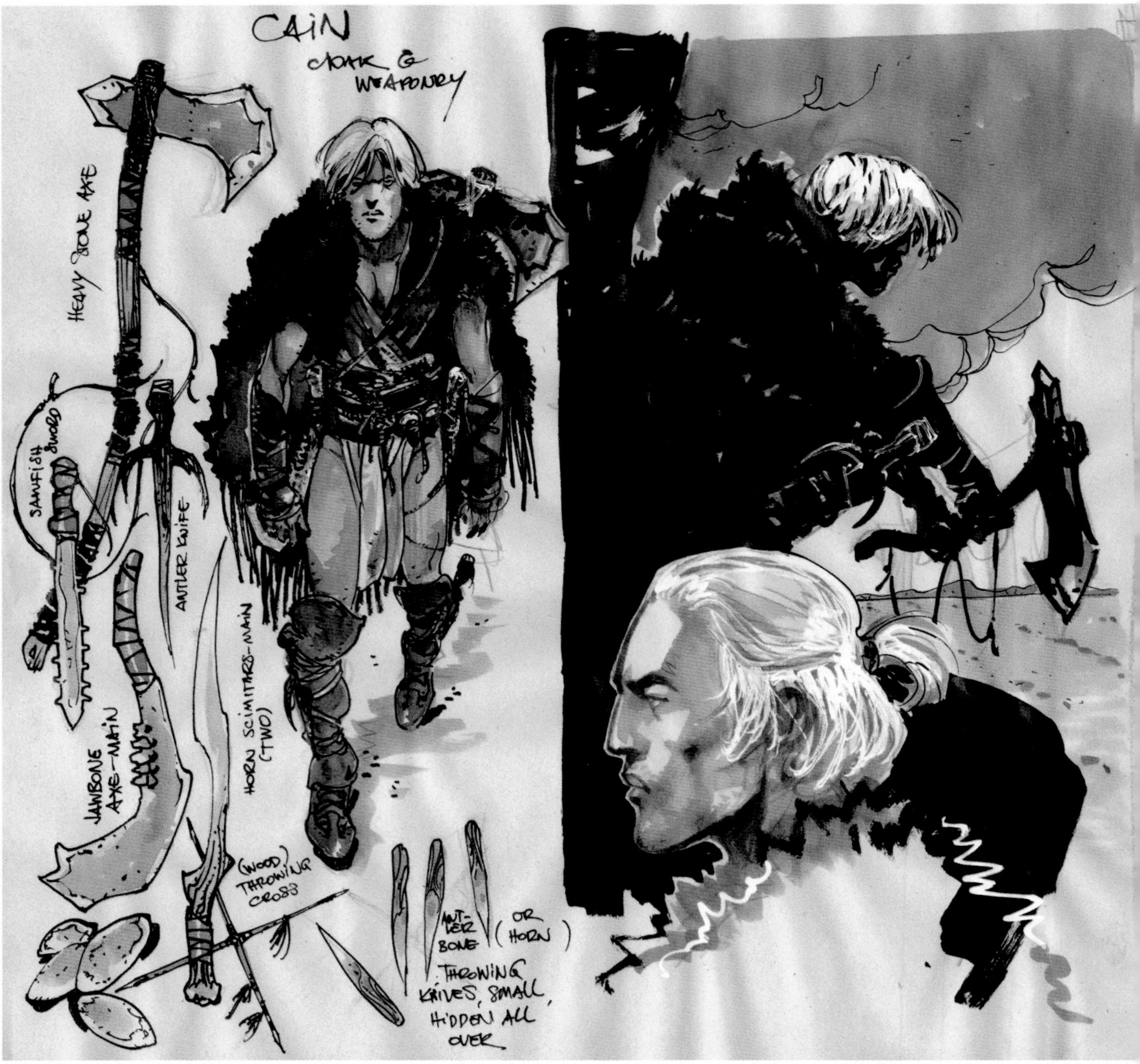
CAIN
CLOAK & WEAPONRY
HEAVY STONE AXE
SAWFISH SWORD
ANTLER KNIFE
JAWBONE AXE-MAIN
HORN SCIMITARS-MAIN (TWO)
(WOOD) THROWING CROSS
ANT-LER BONE
(OR HORN)
THROWING KNIVES, SMALL, HIDDEN ALL OVER

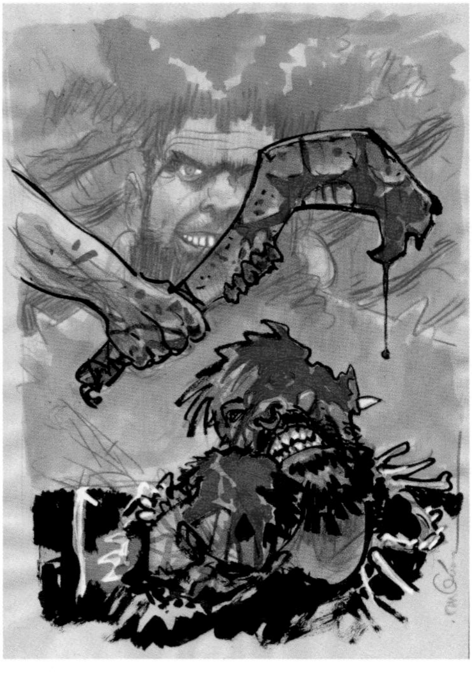

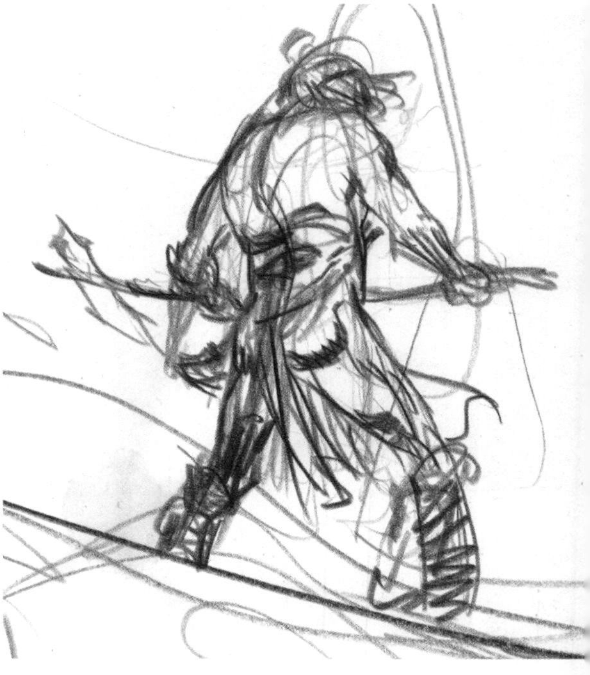

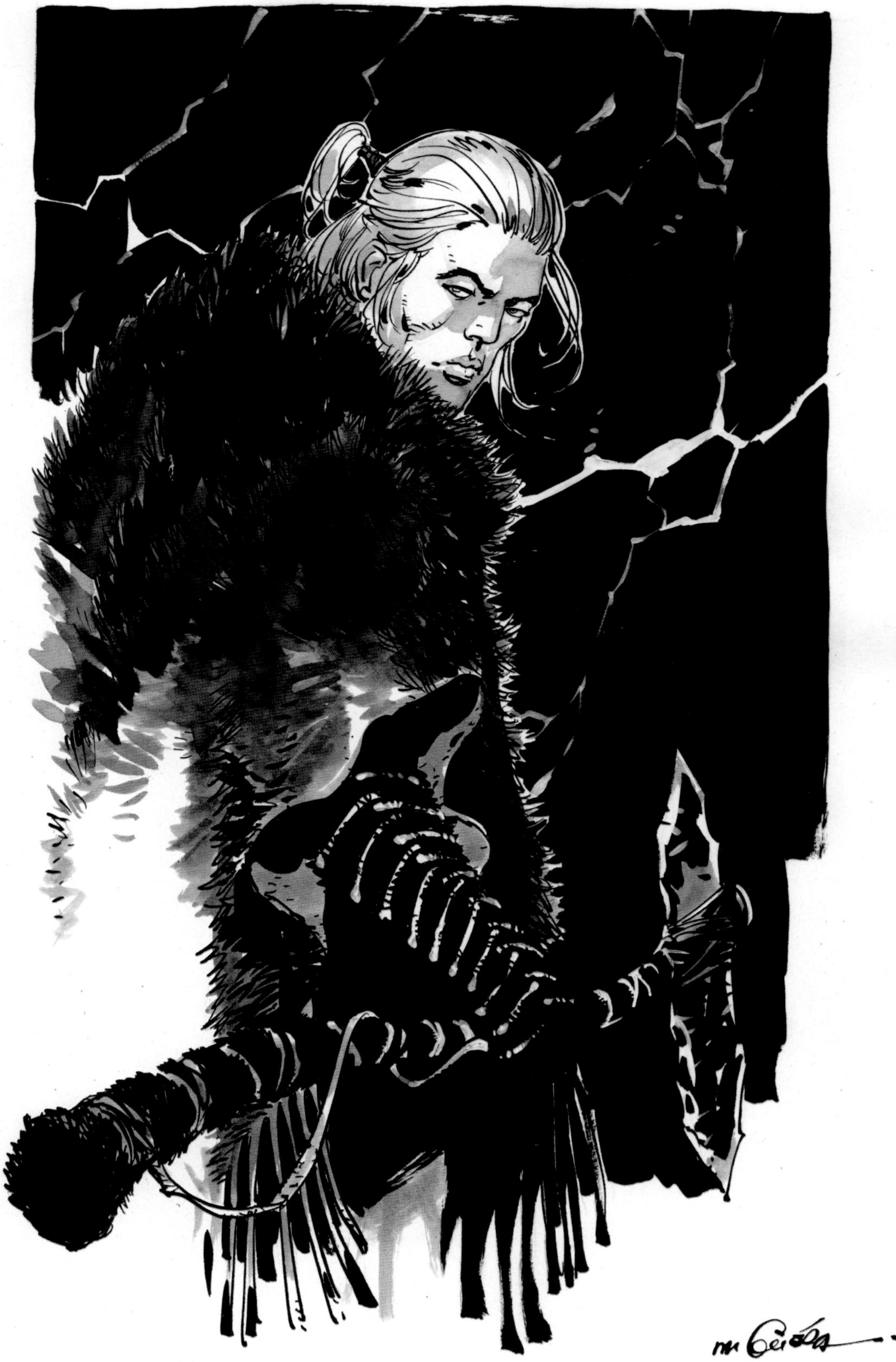

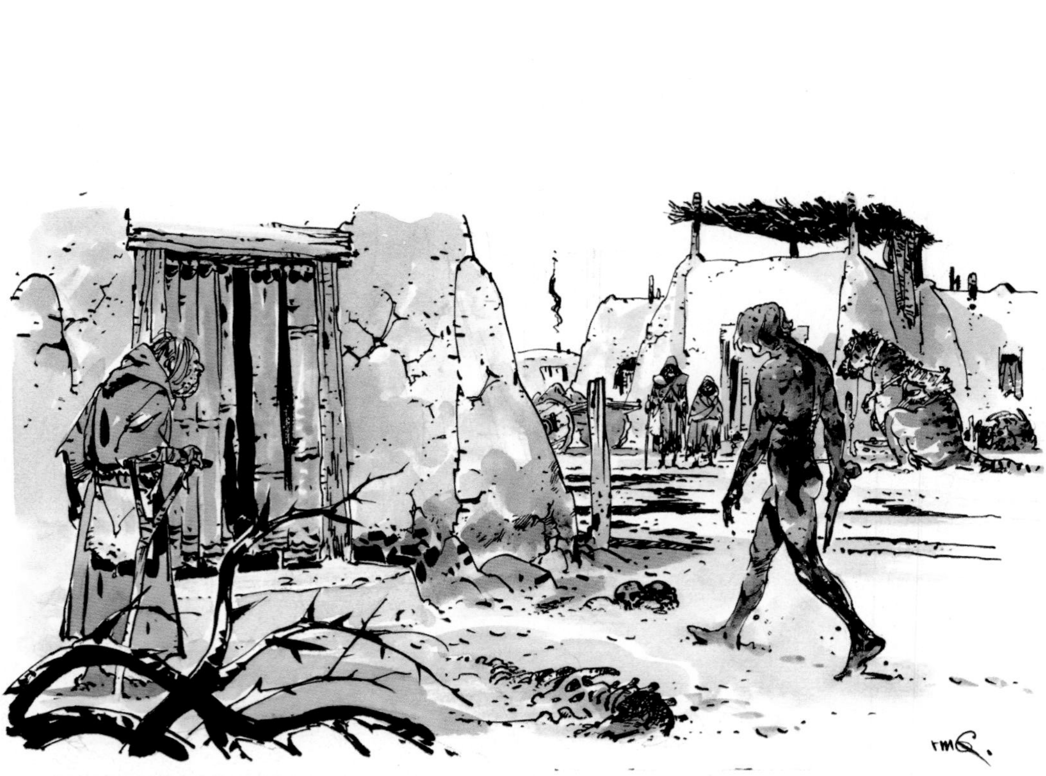

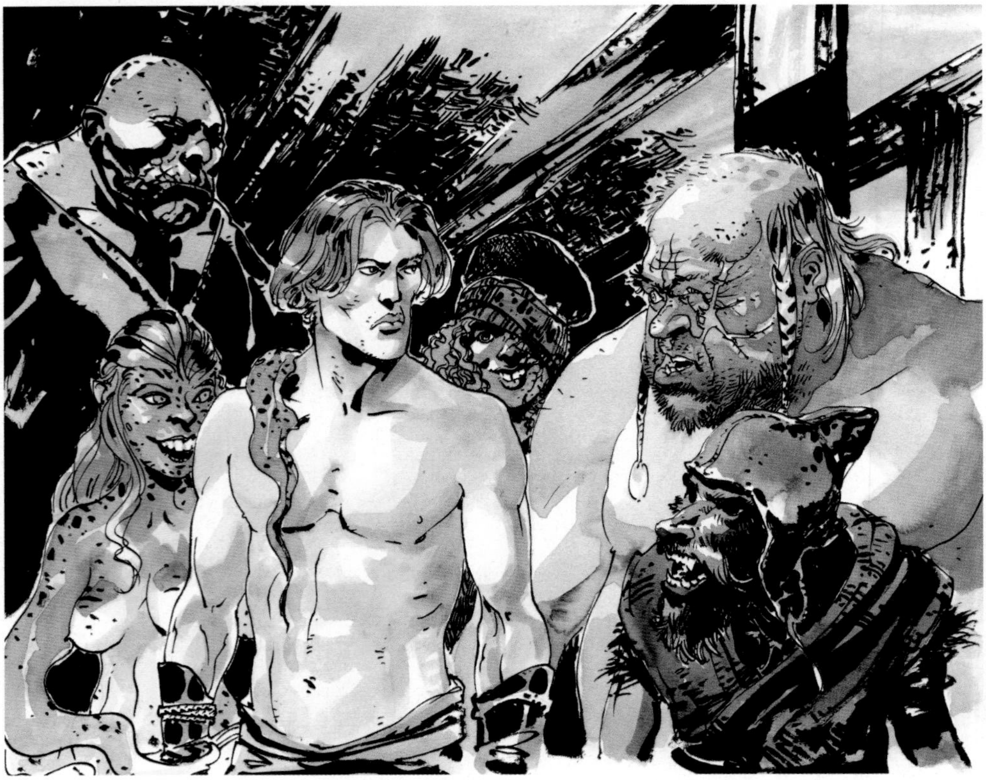

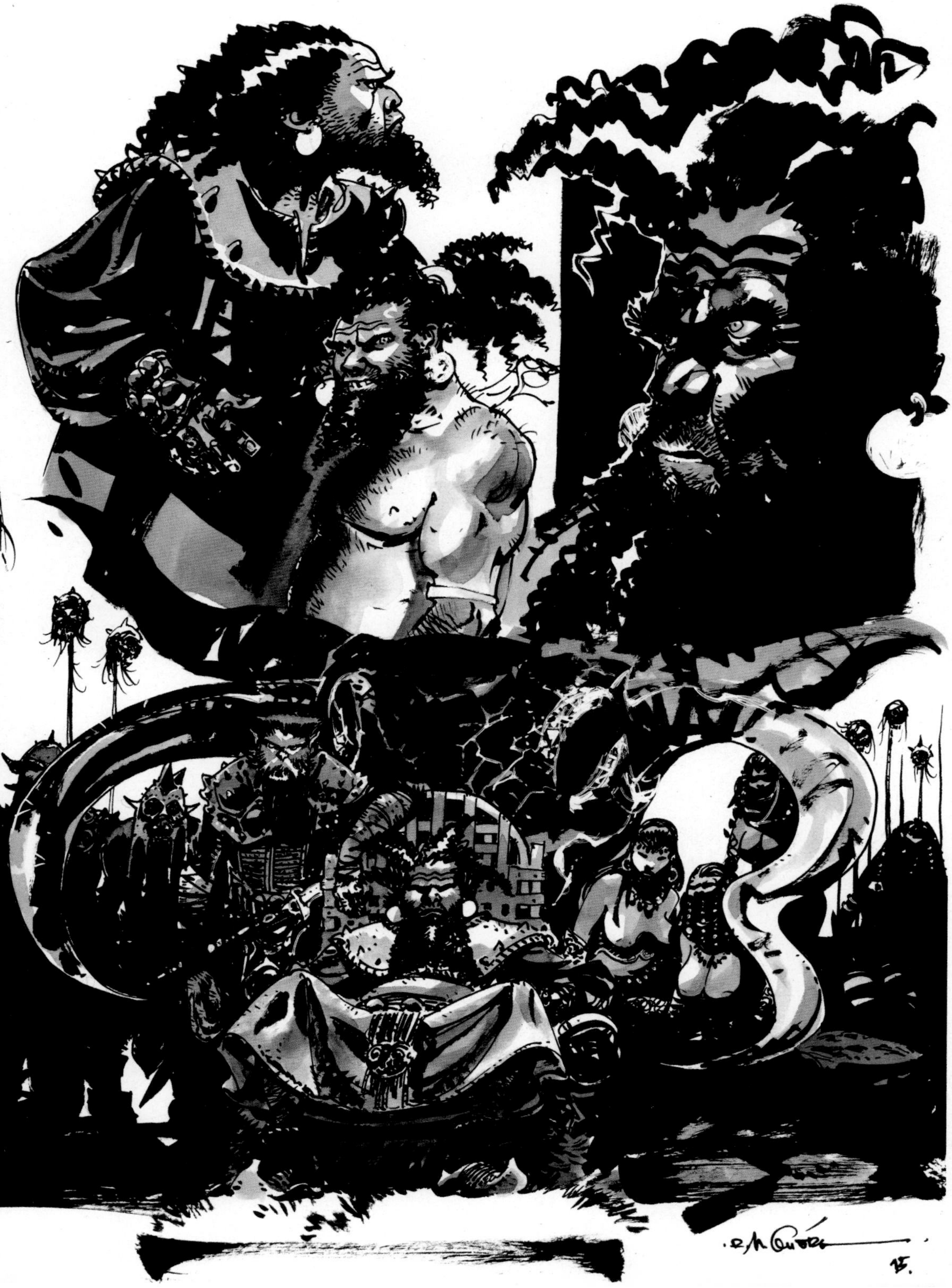

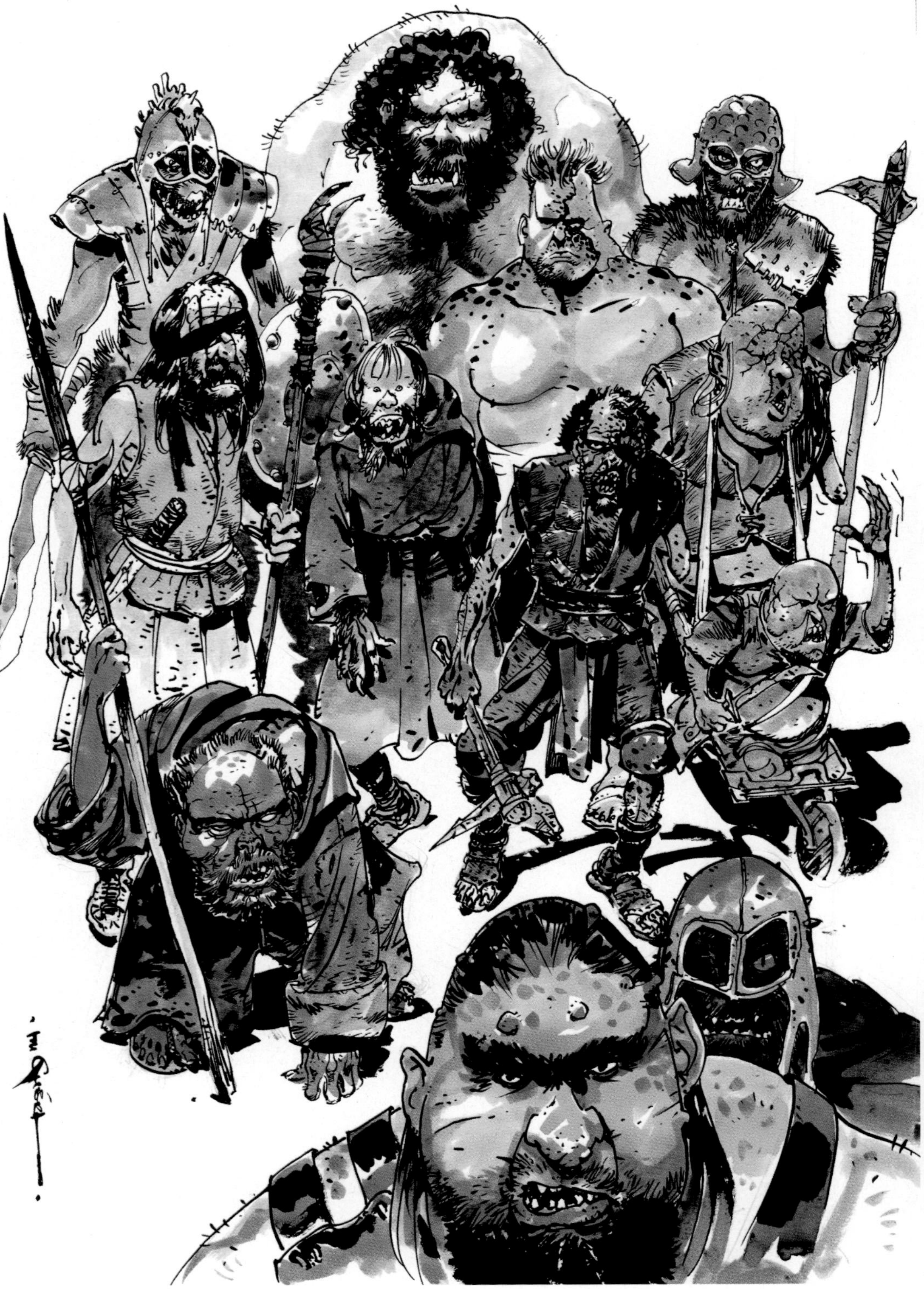

issue one variant cover by

Jock

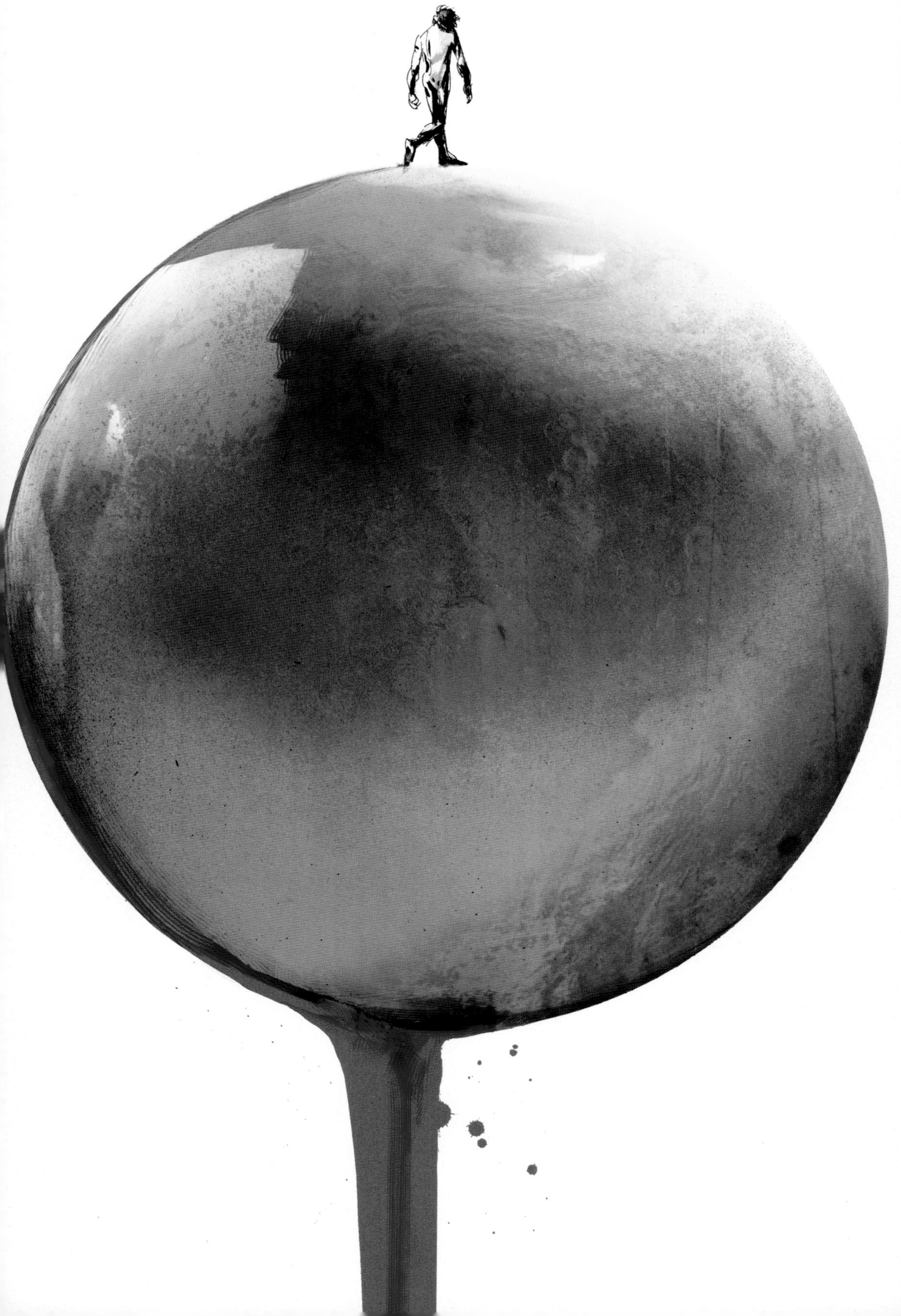

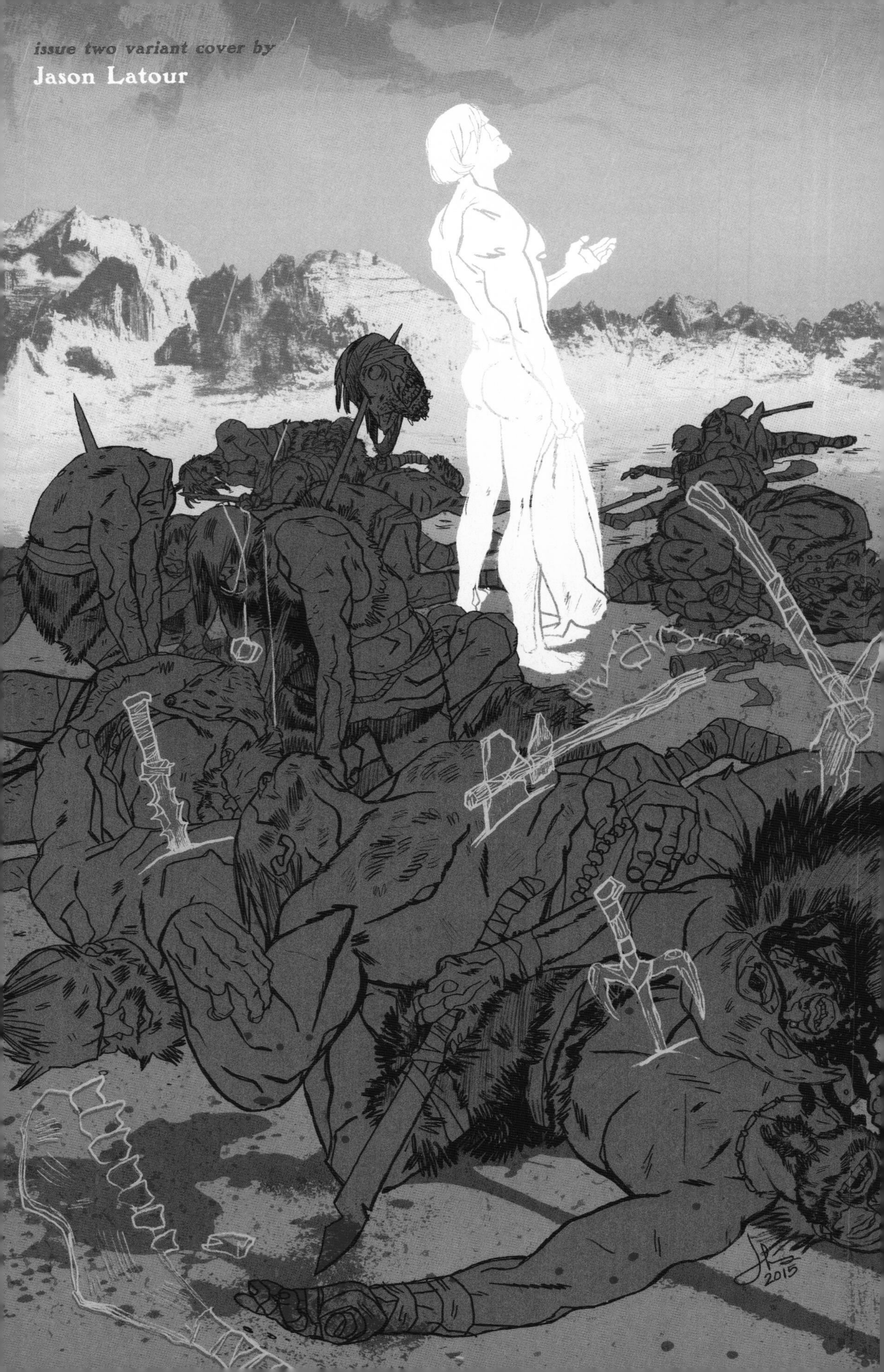
2015

issue two variant cover by
Jason Latour

issue three variant cover by

Esad Ribic

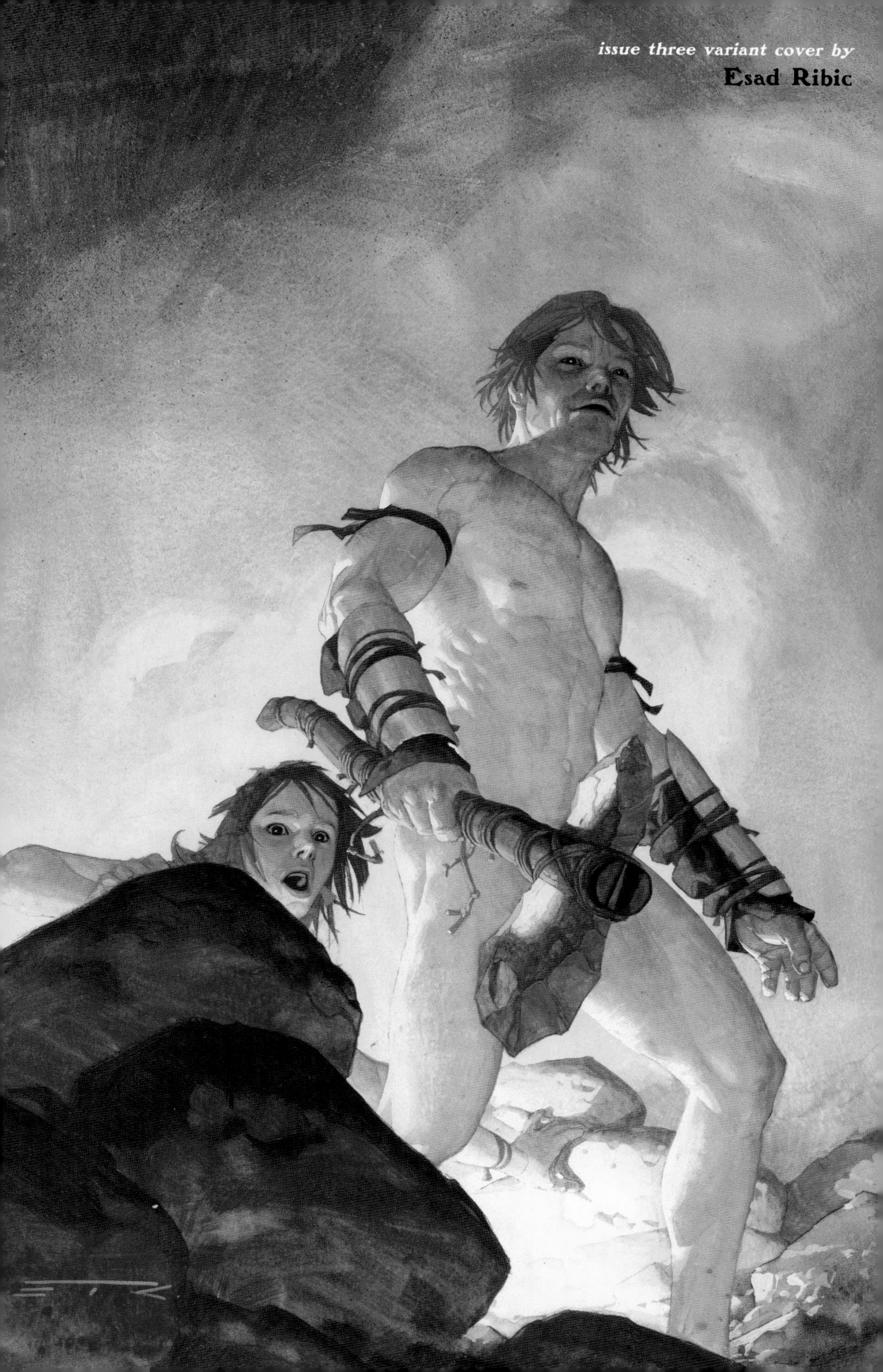

issue four variant cover by

Skottie Young

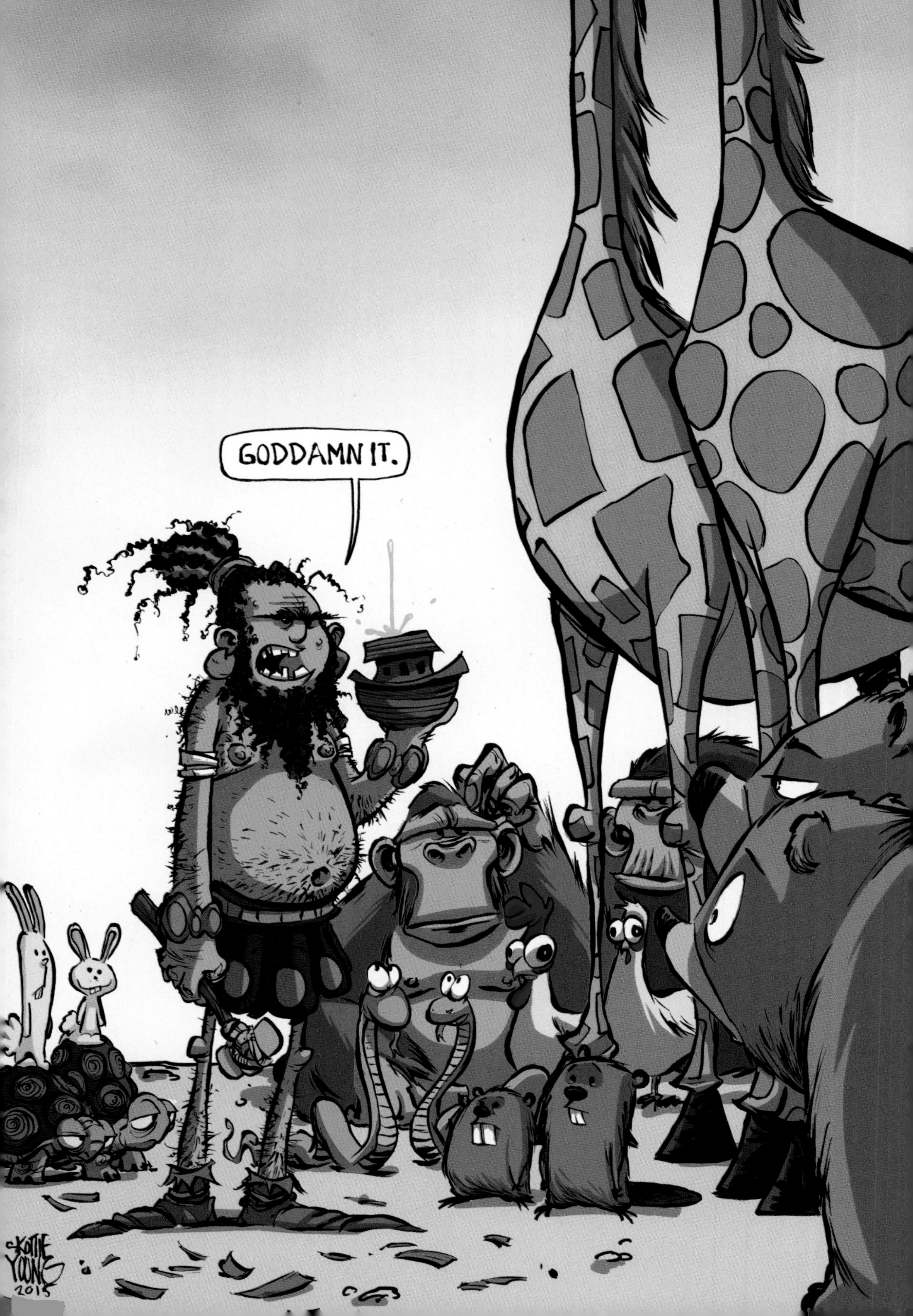
GODDAMN IT.
SKOTTIE YOUNG 2015

issue five variant cover by

Chris Brunner & Rico Renzi

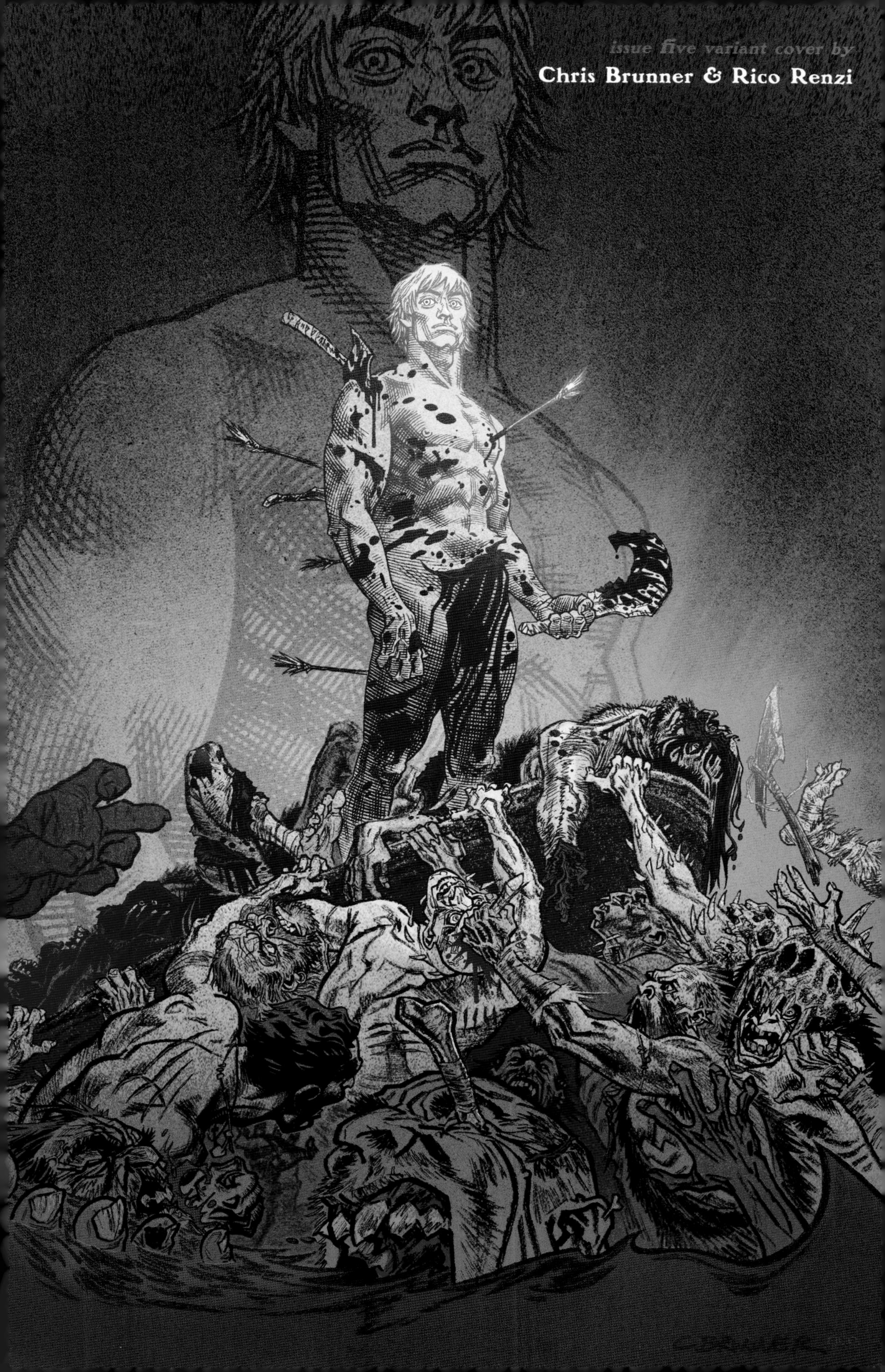

THE GODDAMNED™

next book
The Virgin Brides

Jason Aaron
r.m. Guéra
Giulia Brusco

THERE WERE GIANTS IN THE EARTH IN THOSE DAYS.

GENESIS 6:4